Routledge Revivals

Introductory Sketch of the Bantu Languages

Introductory Sketch of the Bantu Languages

Alice Werner

First published in 1919 by Kegan Paul, Trench, Trübner & Co., Ltd.

This edition first published in 2018 by Routledge
2 Park Square, Milton Park, Abingdon, Oxon, OX14 4RN
and by Routledge
711 Third Avenue, New York, NY 10017

Routledge is an imprint of the Taylor & Francis Group, an informa business

© 1919 by Taylor & Francis

All rights reserved. No part of this book may be reprinted or reproduced or utilised in any form or by any electronic, mechanical, or other means, now known or hereafter invented, including photocopying and recording, or in any information storage or retrieval system, without permission in writing from the publishers.

Publisher's Note
The publisher has gone to great lengths to ensure the quality of this reprint but points out that some imperfections in the original copies may be apparent.

Disclaimer
The publisher has made every effort to trace copyright holders and welcomes correspondence from those they have been unable to contact.

A Library of Congress record exists under ISBN: 20007678

ISBN 13: 978-1-138-61636-3 (hbk)
ISBN 13: 978-1-138-61639-4 (pbk)
ISBN 13: 978-0-429-46216-0 (ebk)

INTRODUCTORY SKETCH OF THE BANTU LANGUAGES

BY

ALICE WERNER

Reader in Swahili, etc., School of Oriental Studies, London Institution.

Author of *Language-Families of Africa*, *Native Races of British Central Africa*, etc.

LONDON:
KEGAN PAUL, TRENCH, TRUBNER & CO., Ltd.
NEW YORK: E. P. DUTTON & CO.

1919

MAGISTRO ET AMICO

C.M.

*Inter arma silent artes et amicitiæ :
ne sileant in æternum !*

IX. Kal. Sept. MCMXVIII

CONTENTS.

		PAGE
PREFACE	... ...	iv

CHAPTER		
I.	INTRODUCTORY	1
II.	THE ALLITERATIVE CONCORD	20
III.	THE NOUN-CLASSES	31
IV.	THE NOUN-CLASSES (*continued*)	54
V.	CASES: THE LOCATIVE	70
VI.	THE PRONOUN	86
VII.	THE COPULA AND THE VERB 'TO BE' ...	109
VIII.	THE ADJECTIVE	118
IX.	THE NUMERALS	133
X.	THE VERB	143
XI.	THE VERB (*continued*)—MOODS AND TENSES	156
XII.	ADVERBS AND PARTICLES	182
XIII.	WORD BUILDING	199
XIV.	SOME PHONETIC LAWS	218
APPENDIX I.	TEXTS—1. ZULU	232
,, ,,	,, 2. HERERO	248
,, ,,	,, 3. ILA	264
,, ,,	,, 4. NYANJA	272
,, ,,	,, 5. SWAHILI	276
,, ,,	,, 6. GANDA	295
APPENDIX II.	BIBLIOGRAPHY—I. GENERAL ...	307
,, ,,	,, II. SPECIAL LANGUAGES	309
INDEX	... ...	343

PREFACE.

It is well to state at the outset that this little book makes no pretensions to originality. It has not, in all cases, been possible to give detailed references for statements which may be recognised as derived from one or other of the standard authorities (they are not numerous) on the subject. Sometimes, in the course of studies covering, intermittently, a period of some thirty years, one assimilates an idea so thoroughly as to forget where one first picked it up; sometimes, too, doing first-hand work at a language, one may, unknowingly, arrive at facts or deductions already recorded. In all such cases, the original owners are requested to believe that no misappropriation was intended.

It may be as well to state that the languages at which I have worked *in situ*, that is to say, in the countries where they are spoken, are Nyanja, Swahili, Zulu, and, in a lesser degree, Giryama and Pokomo. Some others I have, to a certain extent, studied from the inside, with the help of books.

It will, I hope, be sufficiently clear from the title that the present work is *only* an " Introduction " and does not in any respect seek to enter into competition with those of Bleek, Professor Meinhof, Father Torrend and Sir Harry Johnston. I am under great obligations, more or less, to all four, though compelled to differ, occasionally, with all respect, from each; but I venture to think I have occupied some ground not completely covered by any of them, yet important from the beginner's point of view.

If I might venture to appeal to my own experience, I should say that my feeling on first introduction to Bleek's *Comparative Grammar* was one of mere bewilderment, caused, I think, partly by the highly technical character of the first part, which presupposes a considerable acquaintance with phonetics, and partly by the use of Lepsius's alphabet, which, though not very difficult, involves a little preliminary training if one is to use the book profitably. Moreover, this alphabet has been considerably modified (and, in my view, improved) by Meinhof, so that there is a slight additional difficulty involved for those who have already made the acquaintance of the latter.

It is superfluous to say anything in commendation of the *Lautlehre* and the *Grundzüge einer vergleichenden Grammatik der Bantusprachen;* they are as yet practically the only works of their kind,[1] with the exception of Mlle. L. Homburger's highly specialised study, which is of comparatively limited scope. But experience has taught me that they are of very little use to at least three-quarters of the students, whom it has been my lot to induct into one or other of the Bantu languages. For one thing, there is as yet no English edition of either, and—in spite of recent improvements in this respect—the number of English people who can study a subject by means of a French, German or Italian book (which is a different thing from gathering the drift of a novel or a newspaper article) is still deplorably small. For another, like Bleek, they presuppose a kind and degree of philological knowledge which few of the people who take up some Bantu language at short notice have had time or opportunity to acquire.

Here, parenthetically, at the risk of seeming to attempt the impossible feat ascribed to "Old Man Hyena," who split in two with the effort—I want to say a word about two opposite errors.

I have repeatedly insisted, in the following pages, on

[1] Father Torrend's book, valuable enough in some ways, has to be used with caution, not only because of the *errata* unavoidable in a pioneer work, but because the learned author has not been proof against that temptation to unbalanced theorising which is apt to beset the African philologist. De Gregorio's *Cenni di Glottologia Bantu,* so far as I have examined it, does not seem to go beyond the material furnished by Bleek and Torrend.

the danger of being misled by preconceived notions of grammar into erroneous treatment of Bantu speech. Therefore it would seem as if a knowledge of Latin and Greek were no help towards the acquisition of African languages, and indeed, as we shall see, such knowledge has in some cases given rise to positive stumbling-blocks. But the fact remains that those who have enjoyed a sound classical training are best fitted to cope with the unfamiliar prefixes, affixes and infixes of the " Lingua Bantu."

The truth is that—at any rate till quite recently—the classics have been the only subject taught in our schools and universities which provided a thorough grounding in the principles of comparative philology. Neither Latin nor Greek will by itself throw any light on the structure of, say, Zulu or Ganda—nor, for that matter (except for its greater approximation, in some points, to primitive characteristics) will Hebrew. No very great amount of classical scholarship is needed to discriminate between roots and formative elements, to distinguish and compare the functions of the latter and to ascertain and apply the laws of sound-shifting. But it is the method and the principle which make all the difference, and those who follow them will never go astray over fruitless comparisons with Akkadian, Tibetan or what not. So that, if some parts of my book should seem to be needlessly elementary, I may be allowed to point out that I have found them by no means superfluo to in practice.

I have not dealt with theories of origins or conjectures as to the successive Bantu migrations. Neither have I attempted a classification of the Bantu languages into " branches " (Bleek) or " clusters " (Torrend). I cannot help thinking that it would be premature at present and will be for some time to come. Father Torrend perceived that new facts had (to some extent) disturbed Bleek's arrangement; and there are still so many languages of which little or nothing is known, that we can scarcely regard his own as other than provisional. The queerest isolated links of affinity are continually cropping up in unexpected places and upsetting one's most cherished prepossessions; and, for my part, I am perfectly content, to take the languages as we find them, leaving the questions of how they came to be where they are, and whether they have a right to be there, to more competent heads and a future stage of inquiry.

Neither have I attempted to treat of Bantu phonetics from the strictly scientific point of view. This branch of the science, which is still more or less in the pioneer stage, is safe in the hands of Mr. Daniel Jones and Professors Meinhof and Westermann—I would only take this opportunity of emphasising its importance. The time has passed when the practical linguist or the research student could afford to rely on his ear and a certain amount of theoretic knowledge gained from the older works on the subject. It is one which can never be satisfactorily studied from books alone, and everyone intending to proceed to Africa ought to avail him or herself of the excellent practical courses now open.

I have tried to explain in the text the various shifts and compromises I have been forced to adopt in order to arrive at a working orthography for my own immediate purpose. Both Meinhof's diacritic marks and the alphabet of the I.A.P. have raised endless typographical difficulties, and I have found it best in the end to fall back on Steere's rule-of-thumb, explaining, where they occur, such symbols as he failed to provide for. It may be necessary to repeat that *kh, th, ph,* stand for the aspirated consonant and not (except where specially pointed out, as in the case of Herero *th*) for the sounds which we associate with those symbols.

The aim of the book is not to furnish all details with regard to any particular language, but to depict the broad principles underlying the structure of all belonging to the Bantu family, in such a form as to facilitate the subsequent study of the one specially chosen. Their grammar is of so homogeneous a character that it is unusually easy to construct such a general outline. Nor need the student be afraid with any amazement when he finds that his own chosen idiom fails to conform in one or more particulars to the outline here sketched.

PREFACE

By the time he has advanced so far as to discover this, he will know enough to fit the differences as well as the resemblances into the framework.

It has, of course, been impossible to provide for every contingency, for instance, I have just become aware that Chaga possesses an infixed adverbial (intensive) particle for which I know no parallel elsewhere. I shall be grateful to anyone who can give me any information throwing light on the distribution of this particle, if it is not an isolated phenomenon—but no doubt we shall be able to read all about it in Sir Harry Johnston's great book, when the present distress permits of its publication. Very likely it contains the answers to many other puzzles here suggested; but, all the same, I venture to repeat that there are some who will read it to better purpose, when it comes, after making use of the humble stepping-stone here offered them.

It only remains to thank those who, by word or letter, have contributed information, advice and encouragement, both in former years and recently. Chief among these I would mention Professor Meinhof; Sir H. H. Johnston; Dr. Cook, Miss Allen (of Gayaza), and the Rev. H. K. and Mrs. Banks (of Mbale), all of Uganda; the missionaries of the C.M.S. at Mombasa; the Rev. Dr. Hetherwick, Blantyre; Mrs. Lloyd of St. Faith's, Rusape, and the Rev. H. Buck (Rhodesia), the Rev. H. B. Barnes (Penhalonga, Rhodesia); Miss Nixon-Smith, U.M.C.A., Likoma; the Ven. Archdeacon Woodward and Miss Woodward; the Rev. W. A. Crabtree (late of Uganda) and others. I hope anyone accidentally omitted will not think me ungrateful.

Any criticisms or comments—especially coming direct from Africa, will be heartily welcomed.

Wasalaam !

A. WERNER.

School of Oriental Studies,
   Finsbury Circus,
      London, E.C. 2.

INTRODUCTORY SKETCH OF THE BANTU LANGUAGES

CHAPTER I

INTRODUCTORY

THE Bantu family of languages is spoken throughout Southern and Central Africa, as far as the Gulf of Cameroons on the north-west, and the Tana river on the north-east. This area is interrupted by the following islands or 'enclaves' of speech belonging to other families:

The Galla: between the Sabaki and Tana.

The Masai: to the east and south-east of Lake Victoria.

The Jaluo ('*Nilotic Kavirondo*'): at the north-eastern corner of Lake Victoria.

The Hottentots and Bushmen: in South Africa.

Also several small and little known tribes (Mbugu, Sandawi, etc.), in the depression south-east of Kilimanjaro, whom we need not specify more particularly.

In the Cameroons and along the southern edge of the Congo basin, the line of demarcation between Bantu and non-Bantu (in this case Sudan or 'Nigritian') languages is not very easy to draw. In the former territory we find several languages classed as 'Semi-Bantu,' or 'Bantoid,' which share certain characteristics with the family, though not apparently belonging to it. But these, and the exact delimitation of the frontier, need not concern us for the purposes of this book.

The number of known Bantu languages is well over 200; but as there are probably others yet to be recorded, and as some names may have to be omitted (being synonyms, or denoting mere dialects—if not altogether erroneous), this figure must be regarded as merely provisional.

The principal features of the Bantu languages are so clearly marked in all, that, as far as grammar goes, a knowledge of one materially facilitates the acquisition of the rest. Most of them differ from each other no further than do French, Spanish and Italian; in some, the resemblance is even closer. Natives of one tribe cannot, in general, understand the language of another, without learning it (though they pick it up very easily), nor can the European expect to do so; but the second language should cost him far less labour than the first. And an acquaintance with the framework of Bantu grammar, comprising, at least, those features which all the languages have in common (and which, to those who know only the idioms of Europe, are so striking and novel as to impress themselves readily on the memory) is a useful preparation for taking up the study of any particular language in Africa.

The name Bantu was first introduced by Bleek (1827-1875), who may be called the father of African philology. It is simply one form of the word for 'people,' which is used throughout the languages of this family. Various objections have been raised to this name, but no better one has been proposed, and it has now so far gained currency that it would be extremely difficult to displace. As its meaning is perfectly clear, and as it is easily pronounced, there seems to be no sufficient reason for rejecting it. We shall therefore continue to speak of the Bantu family.

Though the name was not introduced till

the middle of the nineteenth century, the existence of this language-family was at any rate conjectured as early as 1808, when the German naturalist, Lichtenstein (who had spent four years travelling in South Africa), published a paper entitled *Remarks on the Languages of the savage tribes of South Africa, with a short vocabulary of the most usual dialects of the Hottentots and Kafirs.* The two Bantu languages of which he collected specimens were 'Kafir' (Xosa) and Chwana. Many of his words are recognisable, in spite of a curious orthography; but he does not seem to have grasped the system of prefixes, and sometimes confuses the singular and the plural of a word. However, he had no doubt as to the relationship of these languages to each other and the fundamental difference between them and that of the Hottentots. He says: 'All the idioms of the South African savages must be regarded as dialects of one or the other of these two principal forms'; and the information he was able to obtain respecting the more northerly tribes led him to the conclusion that 'we are justified in considering all the inhabitants of the East Coast of Africa, from 10° or 12° S. to the frontiers of the Dutch Colony, as *one* nation . . . . . to which further research may perhaps compel us to add the inhabitants of the South-west Coast.'

A similar conclusion was reached independently, a few years later, by our own orientalist, William Marsden (1754-1836). In 1816, he drew up a paper of instructions for collecting words and sentences, to be used by the members of Captain Tuckey's ill-fated expedition to the Congo, in which he remarks on the similarity between the vocabularies previously obtained in Angola and Loango and the specimens of the Mozambique language dictated by a native of that country who had been Marsden's servant in India. But the study of the Bantu languages singly, and without reference to their place in a system, goes back to the middle of the seventeenth century. In the library of the British Museum is a curious little book—with Southey's autograph, dated 'Keswick, 1810,' on the title-page—printed in 1642 and containing a short exposition of elementary Christian doctrine, under the form of a dialogue, in the language of Angola, with a Portuguese version on the opposite page, and a few introductory hints (in Portuguese) on pronunciation and grammar. It was the work of a Jesuit missionary, P. Francisco Pacconio, but was revised and edited after his death by P. Antonio Do Couto, to whom it is generally attributed. The language is that now called Mbundu, and, though somewhat disguised by the Portuguese spelling, appears not to differ appreciably from that spoken to-day. Some years later, in 1659, an Italian friar, Giacinto Brusciotto, published in Latin a grammar of the Congo language to which we shall have occasion to refer more than once in subsequent pages. Cust remarks: 'The book is very small, and the author was not a linguist'; which seems to me unduly severe. He certainly grasped the characteristic features of the language in a way some later writers failed to do: Cust himself says, 'he remarks the use of prefixes, and he classes the nouns.' We have just seen that Lichtenstein did not understand the system of prefixes;—it is, of course, not surprising that a passing traveller, picking up, in the short time at his disposal, what linguistic information he can, should be unable to do more than record words and phrases without penetrating very far into their grammatical relations. But it does seem strange that Dr. Van der Kemp, whose help he acknowledges with regard to the Xosa language, should not have called his attention to peculiarities so striking and so unlike anything that could previously have come in his way.

But the great advance in the knowledge of African languages followed the remarkable development of missionary activity which characterized the end of the 18th and the beginning of the 19th century. Moffat's translation of the Bible into Sechwana was begun in 1831; Archbell's grammar of the same language appeared in 1837, Boyce's Xosa grammar in 1844; while at the same time Casalis, Arbousset and the other French missionaries were active among the Basuto and marking their progress by valuable linguistic work. About the same time, Krapf, on the eastern coast of Africa, was practically the first to make the Swahili language known to European scholars:—for, though two or three vocabularies had been collected (chiefly by the praiseworthy exertions of British naval officers) they do not seem to have attracted much attention. It was the material sent home by Krapf which first made possible anything like a scientific study of the subject, and the beginnings of this may be seen in three remarkable essays contributed by Ewald, Pott, and Von der Gabelentz to the first and second volume of the *Zeitschrift der Deutschen Morgenländischen Gesellschaft*—work produced in the golden age of German scholarship, before it had begun to lose itself in over-specialisation. These essays were the precursors of Bleek's *Comparative Grammar*, the first part of which appeared in 1862.

Bleek's book, though of course it has been supplemented by later research, and, as might be expected, requires some correction in detail, remains the foundation of everything that has been done since. I shall not attempt to give any account of this more recent work, though I shall frequently have occasion to refer to the outstanding names of the last thirty or forty years—men who have not merely given us grammars and dictionaries of separate languages, but examined their structure from a scientific point of view and done something towards determining their relationship to each other and to the other speech-groups of the world. Such have been Müller, Lepsius, Meinhof, De Gregorio, and others. In this country, Sir Harry Johnston is, sad to say, almost the only writer who has occupied himself with the Bantu languages not merely in detail but also from the comparative point of view.

Bleek confirmed Lichtenstein's view (which, considering the data he had to go upon, almost deserves the name of a brilliant intuition) that all the languages of South Africa fall into two groups,[1] and he was able, as Lichtenstein was not, to account for the differences on philological grounds. The one crucial distinction between them, he considered, lay in the fact that the one group—the Hottentot—has grammatical gender; the other—the Bantu—has not.

This difference, Bleek thought, was based on a fundamental difference of organization, and from it he deduced an ingenious argument, proving that people whose speech has no grammatical gender were not merely at present

[1] Bleek was uncertain whether to reckon two groups or three. He felt that not enough was known about the Bushman language to pronounce definitely as to its classification, but was inclined to think it of a distinct type from the Hottentot. Recent research goes to show that he was probably right and that it is allied to the Sudan family.

incapable of personifying nature, but that they could never in the future advance beyond a certain limited range of ideas. However, as fuller knowledge has shown many of his premises to be untenable (he thought, for instance, that the kind of animal-stories so well known to us through *Uncle Remus* was confined to the Hottentots and unknown to the Bantu), we need not occupy ourselves with his conclusion.

It is certainly remarkable that the three great inflected families of language—the Aryan, Semitic and Hamitic—corresponding to the three divisions of the ancient world and the civilizations (broadly speaking) of Europe, Assyria and Egypt, should possess grammatical gender and the rest be without it. But we need not think that the possession of this characteristic draws a hard and fast line on one side of which no progress is possible, for (setting aside the case of Japan and China), recent research has thrown a good deal of light on the way in which gender arose, and we find that some languages, classed with the Hamitic 'sex-denoting' family, only have it in a rudimentary form ; some Bantu languages show signs of a tendency to acquire it; and languages at a very advanced stage, as English, tend to lose it.

'Absence of grammatical gender,' it may hardly be necessary to say, means, not that no account is taken of sex-distinctions, but that they are not in any way shown by the *form* of words. All languages have words for 'man' and 'woman,' 'male' and 'female'; but those of which we are speaking have nothing corresponding to 'he,' 'she,' 'his,' 'her'; nor can they indicate a feminine noun by any change in the word: if it is absolutely necessary to distinguish the sex a word is added, as in our 'he-goat,' 'she-goat,' 'buck-rabbit,' 'doe-rabbit,' etc. Still less do they attribute sex, by a grammatical convention, to inanimate objects, as is done in Latin, French, German, etc.

The Sudan languages (which include Twi, Gã, Ewe and others, spoken in Western and Central Africa) have no grammatical gender; but neither have they, properly speaking, any grammatical inflections at all. The Bantu languages, however, *do* indicate number, person, and, in a limited sense, case; and, for verbs, in addition, voice, mood and tense.

They are usually reckoned as belonging to

the class of *Agglutinative* languages. These are distinguished from the *Isolating* languages on the one hand and the *Inflected* on the other by the fact that, while they indicate grammatical relations by particles prefixed or suffixed to the root, these particles are recognizable as independent words and can be used as such. This, as we shall see, does not quite apply to the Bantu languages, where some of the 'formative elements' (prefixes and suffixes) can no longer be used separately, and sometimes we even find internal changes in a word, comparable to those by which in English we form the plural of a noun like *foot* or the past of a verb like *run*.

So that it would be nearer the truth to call them 'partially inflected languages,' or 'languages in course of acquiring inflection.' For we must remember that the three classes just mentioned are not hard and fast divisions, like water-tight compartments; but a live language is continually growing and changing and will sooner or later pass from one class to another.

The first point which strikes one on beginning to examine these languages is the employment of prefixes where we should expect to find suffixes—*e.g.*, to indicate the plural of nouns, the agreement of adjectives, etc. We shall find that suffixes are also used in certain cases; but the system of prefixes is so characteristic and peculiar that Bleek rightly regarded it as a distinguishing feature of this family, which—before finally adopting the designation ' Bantu '—he called the ' prefix-pronominal languages.'

It was also noticed by Brusciotto who, at the very outset of his Grammar, says: ' In the first place it must be observed, in general, that in this language we have to attend, not to Declensions (*i.e.*, terminations), but rather to Principiations (*i.e.*, Prefixes).'

For want of acquaintance with this principle we sometimes give a double plural to an African word, as when we speak of ' the Basutos,' ' the Mashonas,' or use a plural for a singular, as ' a Basuto,' ' a Bechwana '—the singular in these cases being *Mo-suto*, *Mo-chwana*. Besides these prefixes indicating singular and plural, there are others indicating *the language* (as *Ki-swahili*, *Lu-ganda*, *Se-chwana*, *Chi-nyanja*) and *the country* (as *U-kami*, *Bu-ganda*, etc.)—varying, of course, with different tribes. It may be well to note in this place that we shall uniformly throughout this book use the names of languages without prefix, as Chwana, Ganda, Swahili, etc.

Though Bantu nouns have no gender and so cannot be classified as masculine, feminine and neuter, they are divided into several classes—usually eight or nine, distinguished by their prefixes. These prefixes are repeated, in one form or another, before every word in agreement with the noun; and this method of indicating agreement (which will be fully explained and illustrated in the next chapter) is called the *Alliterative Concord*.

These three points: the absence of grammatical gender, the system of prefixes, and the Alliterative Concord, may be called the principal characteristic features of the Bantu family.

We may mention a few others, put on record long ago by Lepsius, as distinguishing the Bantu family from the Sudan languages on the one hand and the Hamitic (Berber, Galla, Somali, etc.) on the other.

(1) Personal Pronouns are always prefixed to verbs, never suffixed—as they are in Hebrew, Arabic and the Semitic languages.

(2) The Genitive always follows its governing

word. That is, they always say 'the house of the man,' never (as in the Sudan languages) 'the man's house.'

(3) The usual (but not invariable) order of words in the sentence is: Subject + Verb + (Noun) Object.

(4) The object-pronoun is inserted ('infixed') between the subject pronoun and the verb-root. Thus, in Zulu, *ngi-ya-m-bona*, ' I see him,' is made up of *ngi* = ' I,' *ya* (tense particle), *m* = ' he,' *bona* = ' see.'

(5) Syllables always end in a vowel.

Here it is well to say a word about *stress* (accent) and *intonation*.

In many Bantu languages it is an invariable rule that the accent—at any rate the accent most readily noticed—falls on the penultimate syllable, and, if a syllable is added, the accent moves forward. Thus, in Zulu, we have *bóna*, ' see,' which becomes, in the causative, *bonísa*, ' make to see.' In Swahili, *nyúmba* is ' house,' but, the locative, ' in the house,' is *nyumbáni*. This is called the 'rhythmic stress,' but there is also an 'etymological stress,'—*viz.*, one on the root syllable. In words like *bona, nyumba*, these coincide; but otherwise, in Zulu and Swahili, the rhythmic stress seems to be much more strongly marked. In Ganda, it is the stress on the root-syllable which is noticed. There are a few languages which have the rhythmic stress on the antepenultimate.

Intonation, or *pitch*, is a very important feature in some languages, as in Chwana, where it serves to distinguish many words otherwise similar. It exists in Zulu, Xosa, Nyanja, etc.,—probably to a much larger extent than has hitherto been observed. All learners are advised to attend to this point very carefully.[1]

This book being devoted to the *grammatical structure* of the Bantu languages, it does not enter into my plan to discuss their *sounds* from a scientific point of view. Indeed many of them have not been examined at all in this respect, and others very imperfectly. Almost the only comprehensive work on Bantu phonetics at present in existence, Professor Meinhof's *Lautlehre der Bantu-Sprachen*, is not yet published in an English edition,

---

[1] It is possible that in some cases, pitch and stress have been confused. This, also, requires particular attention.

though a translation is being prepared. Some of the Bantu languages are being phonetically analysed by Mr. Daniel Jones, Reader in Phonetics in the University of London, who has published some provisional results of his studies in *Le Maître Phonétique*, in his pamphlet *The Pronunciation and Orthography of the Chindau Language (Rhodesia)*, and more recently in the *Sechuana Reader* (see Bibliography in Appendix).

The *sounds* of the Bantu languages are, superficially, not very difficult, except in a few cases which at once strike the newcomer by their strangeness, such as the clicks in Zulu (which, however, do not properly belong to Bantu), the 'laterals' in this and some other South African languages; the Thonga and Venda 'labio-dental,' the very common 'bilabial' f and v, etc. But there are subtler gradations, both of vowels and consonants, which are at once perceived by a trained phonetician, and which an untrained linguist with a good ear will consciously or unconsciously adopt without being able to define them, but which frequently escape the notice of the average person. Thus, perhaps, in Nyanja, the learner will be in doubt whether the word for 'five (people)' is *asanu* or *asano*; and an old resident who knows the language fairly well will tell him that 'these endings are very uncertain, and the people themselves sometimes say one and sometimes the other.' The truth is that the sound is intermediate between u and o, the mouth-opening being wider than for the first and narrower than for the second. As this is not a treatise on phonetics, I shall make no attempt to spell the words quoted as examples according to the system of the International Phonetic Association, more especially since the sounds of so few Bantu languages have been sufficiently analysed to make this possible. For my purpose, the spelling introduced by Bishop Steere for Swahili and generally used in Swahili books is, in general, sufficient. Its principle may be stated thus: the vowels are pronounced with the sound they have in Italian, the consonants (including the compound symbols ch, sh, th) as in English—each symbol standing for one sound and no more, and no sound having more than one symbol. On this system, c, q, and x are superfluous, so are sometimes used to denote sounds not provided for in the Roman alphabet, as the clicks in Zulu.[1] (C is often used for the sound of *ch* in " church " but may also stand for the somewhat different " palatal plosive."

As, however, some languages have sounds not found in Zanzibar Swahili, on which Steere's *Handbook* is based, a few extra symbols will be needed in our examples, and these will be explained where they occur. But it must be repeated that this can give only a very general idea of the sounds, and that anyone who has to acquire a Bantu language for practical use cannot do better than take a course of general phonetics, which will enable him to accomplish very useful work in recording correctly the sounds of unwritten, or, as is sometimes the case, hitherto atrociously mis-spelt, languages.[2]

[1] Dinuzulu (late Chief of the Zulus) used to say that the English alphabet needed 'several more letters' in order to write Zulu satisfactorily. The Europeans who first recorded the language have in some cases expressed two entirely distinct sounds by the same symbol.

[2] See D. Jones, *The Pronunciation of English* and Noël-Armfield, *General Phonetics*. A table of the International' Phonetic Association's Alphabet, and also of a script largely used on the Continent (Meinhof's modernization of Lepsius's *Standard Alphabet*) will be found in *Language-Families of Africa*.

CHAPTER II

THE ALLITERATIVE CONCORD

IN Latin we say, '*Equus albus currit*'—'the white horse runs'; in the plural, '*Equi albi currunt.*' The termination of the noun indicates the declension, case, and number; of the adjective, the gender, case, and number in agreement with the noun; of the verb, the tense, number, and person. The terminations of the noun and adjective are the same; that of the verb is different and has no relation to them.

This arrangement is somewhat different from that of the Alliterative Concord in the Bantu languages, but will help us to understand it, if we try to imagine the endings all alike[1] and transferred to the beginning of the word. Let us take a specimen sentence in Zulu.

---

[1] They are not really as much alike as the word 'alliterative' might imply, but they are all recognizable as derived from the prefix.

Umfana omubi uyatshaya inkomo yomfundisi wami, ngiyakumlungisa. 'The bad boy is beating the ox of my teacher: I will punish him.'

This sentence contains nouns of two different classes and words agreeing with them. *Umfana* is a noun of the first or 'person'-class: the root is *fana*, the prefix *um-*, shortened from *umu-* (as seen in *umu-ntu*, 'person'). *Omu-bi*, 'bad,' is an adjective agreeing with *umfana* the prefix assumes the form *omu* because it was formerly preceded by a demonstrative particle *a*, and *a+u* coalesce into *o* (*i.e.*, the broad *o*, pronounced like *ou* in 'ought').[1] This means that, when the adjective is used *attributively* (that is, as in 'the bad boy'—not predicatively, as in 'the boy is bad'), it is really a *relative construction* that is employed: —'the boy who is bad.' We shall be able to make this clearer in the chapter on relative pronouns. In the same way 'good' is *omu-hle* (*a+umu-hle*).

The equivalent for an adjective can never be given in its complete form, unless the noun

---

[1] When it is necessary, in this book, to distinguish this o from the narrow o (as in 'stone'), it is printed with a line under it, as in Meinhof's notation.

with which it agrees is known. 'A good' (or 'handsome') 'person,' is *umu-ntu omu-hle;* 'a fine ox,' *inkabi en-hle;* 'a beautiful country' *ili-zwe eli-hle;* 'a fine cattle-kraal,' *isi-baya esi-hle;* 'a beautiful face,' *ubu-so obu-hle;* 'beautiful language,' *uku-kuluma oku-hle.* For this reason, adjectives must be given in the dictionary *under their root only:* -hle, -bi, -kulu (large), etc. But these roots are never found standing by themselves in any Bantu language. They are always used with the prefix of the class to which they belong—*viz.*, that of the noun with which they are in agreement.

U-ya-tshaya. Tshaya is a verb meaning 'beat.' The bare root in this form is never found alone, except in the second person singular of the imperative. Everywhere else it has some addition. Even the second person plural of the imperative takes a suffix, *-ni: tshaya-ni =* 'beat ye.' The other moods and tenses all take prefixes.

U- is the personal pronoun of the first (or 'person') class. It will be recognised at once as part of the prefix *umu.* (The prefix, except in some languages which have departed considerably from the original type, is not in all cases identical with the pronoun.) This is the *subject-pronoun*: the second part of the prefix, *-mu* (usually contracted to *-m*) is used as the object-pronoun, as we shall see presently. It should be noted that this subject-pronoun, *u*, can never be used apart from a verb or its equivalent. There is a separable, or independent, pronoun, of quite a different form, which will be considered in the chapter on Pronouns.

-ya- is a tense-particle: originally the auxiliary verb *ya*, 'to go.' It imparts a kind of habitual continuative force: *uyatshaya* is rather 'he is beating,' or 'he is in the habit of beating,' than simply 'he beats.' In Zulu, the *-ya-* tense is the present most commonly used, though it cannot always be translated as above.

In-komo, 'a cow,' is of the class which has the prefix *i*, or *in-* originally *ini-*. Nouns have no indication of case (except that they suffix *-ni* for the locative), so that they have no distinct form for the objective, though some pronouns do.

Yomfundisi is for *ya umfundisi*. *Ya* is the particle corresponding to 'of,' which expresses the genitive case and varies its initial according to the noun with which it agrees—which is always the thing possessed, not the possessor. *I*, the initial vowel of *inkabi*, becomes *y* before a vowel: $i+a=ya$. In Zulu, *a* before *u* amalgamates with it to form *o*, which is an intermediate position of the mouth between the two. In many other languages this amalgamation does not take place, because the initial vowel has been lost; thus, in Nyanja, we say *ya muntu*, not *yomuntu—ya+umuntu*.

Um-fundisi, a noun of the person-class meaning 'teacher,' derived from the verb *fundisa*, 'teach.'

W-ami—'my.' The roots of the possessive pronouns are: *-ami*, 'my'; *-ako*, 'thy'; *-ake*, 'his, her'; *-etu*, 'our'; *-enu*, 'your'; *-abo*, 'their.' They take as prefixes the pronoun of the class with which they are in agreement: in this case the thing possessed is of the person class (*umfundisi*), and the pronoun will be *u*. But *u* before a vowel becomes *w*, $u+ami=wami$. Similarly, 'thy teacher' is *umfundisi wako* ($u+ako$), and so on.

Ngi-ya-ku-m-lungisa. *Lungisa* (causative of *lunga*) is properly 'make right,' 'straighten,' and so 'correct,' 'punish.' *Ngi-* is the inseparable subject-pronoun of the first person singular. *Ya-* is the tense-particle already mentioned, but, in combination with the following particle—*ku*—it indicates the *future*. *-m-* is the object-pronoun of the third person singular='him.'

All these prefixes change for the plural. Supposing we take as our English sentence:

'The bad boys are beating the cows of our teachers; we will punish them."

The Zulu will be:

Aba-fana aba-bi ba-ya-tshaya izin-komo zaba-fundisi betu, si-ya-ku-ba-lungisa.

This needs no further analysis; but we may call attention to two points: the plural pronoun (inseparable) of the first person, *si-*, and the double plurality, if one may say so, of the possessive *betu*. It must be 'our,' plural of 'my,' in order to agree with the *possessors*, ('we,' understood), but the initial must be *b-*, not *w-* in order to agree with the things (or persons) possessed (*abafundisi*). This double concord of the possessive is an important point, to which we must recur later on.

The same sentence would read in Ganda as follows:

Omu-lenzi omu-bi a-kuba en-te yomu-igiriza wa-nge; n-na-mu-kangavula.

Aba-lenzi aba-bi ba-kuba en-te zaba-igiriza ba-nge tu-na-ba-kangavula.

Here, though the roots are mostly different, the identity of the formative elements will be evident on examination. The chief differences are: *a* instead of *u* for the pronoun of the third person singular (which will be noticed in the chapter on the pronouns), and *e* instead of *i* as the initial vowel for the *in-* class. The possessive of the first person is *-nge* instead of *-mi*, but this is evidently connected with the Zulu subject-pronoun of the first person, *ngi-*, which, in Ganda, has been reduced to *n-*.

This sentence affords a very good illustration of the fact that, in comparing languages, one should take into account the grammatical structure rather than the vocabulary. All the noun-roots are entirely different from the Zulu ones; so are the two verbs, *kuba* and *kangavula*. If we looked to these alone, disregarding the prefixes, we might come to the conclusion that there was no sort of relationship between the two languages. But we should not be justified in doing so, for a comparison of single words may very easily lead us astray.

Take the case of four European languages, which we know to be closely related: English, German, Dutch, and Danish. Here are four words which cannot possibly be derived from the same root:

Boy; *Knabe; jonge; Dreng.*

Yet the Dutch word exists in English as the adjective 'young,' and is used in German (*junge*) side by side with *Knabe*, which is our 'knave'—an instance of the way in which the same root may assume different meanings. *Dreng* is found in Anglo-Saxon in the sense of 'warrior,' and the old Icelandic use of it to mean 'a valiant youth,' supplies the connection between the two.

'Queen' is the same word as the Danish *Kvinde*, 'a woman,' and therefore has nothing to do with the German *Königin*, which is the regularly-formed feminine from *König*, or the Danish *Drottning*, which, though used as the feminine of *Konge* ('king') is really that of an obsolete word *Drott*, meaning 'lord.'

Or take the French word *cheval*: it has nothing in common with the Latin *equus*, but is derived from a different word, *caballus*, not used by the classical writers, but existing in the language of the people. Again, the

Spanish *comer*, 'eat,' cannot possibly come from the same root as the French *manger*; and the classical Latin is *edere*, which, at first sight, does not seem to be connected with either. But *comer* is derived from *comedere*, properly 'to eat up'—a more colloquial and popular word than *edere*—and *manger* comes from *manducare*, properly 'to chew'; whence also the Italian *mangiare*.

Why one language should choose the first of these two words, and another the second, is a question which, in the present state of our knowledge, cannot be answered—or only in the same way as Molière's doctor explained why opium sends people to sleep by saying that 'it has a dormitive virtue.'

So the roots, *lenzi, kuba, iga* ('learn,' from which are derived *igiriza*, 'teach, and *omuigiriza*, 'teacher') and *kanga* (frown,' of which *kangavula*, 'rebuke' or 'punish' is a derivative) are probably to be found in other Bantu languages, though I have as yet been unable to trace them. *Ente*, I believe, is not Bantu, though I cannot say whence it has been adopted. *-bi*, 'bad,' will be recognised as identical: it is found in most Bantu languages.

Let us now take, from Swahili, an example

of the concord in another class, which has the prefix *ki-*, in the plural *vi-*.

Ki-ti cha-ngu cha m-ti ki-me-vundika, ni-me-ki-ona ki-ki-anguka.

' My wooden chair is broken; I saw it when it fell.'

Ki-ti, 'chair,' is originally 'a wooden thing' —*ti* being a root which, with the prefix *m-*, means 'tree.' (The most primitive form of seat, after the mere stump or fallen log, is the stool cut out of a solid block, the cross-section of a tree.) 'Of' in this class is *cha*, because *ki* becomes *ch* before a vowel. The possessive pronoun consists of *chā* prefixed to the pronoun-root, which is for the first person *-ngu* (cf. Ganda, *-nge:* the subject-pronoun for the first person is *ni*). *Cha mti*, 'wooden,'— literally ' of wood,' or ' of tree.' *Ki-me-vundika*, ' it is broken ': *ki-*, subject-pronoun of the *ki-*class, agreeing with *kiti; -me-*, a particle denoting the perfect tense of the verb; *vundika* is the neuter-passive of the verb *vunda*, ' break.' *Nimekiona:* *ni-* subject-pronoun of the first person singular; *-me-*, tense-particle; *-ki-*, object-pronoun agreeing with *kiti; ona*, verb, meaning ' see ' (in Zulu, *bona*); *anguka* is a verb, meaning ' fall '; the first *ki* is the subject-pronoun agreeing with *kiti;* the second a tense-particle equivalent to 'if' or 'when,' often giving the verb a kind of participial force.

The plural of the above is:

Vi-ti vy-etu vya mti vi-me-vundika, tu-me-vi-ona vi-ki-anguka.

This needs no further explanation.

We thus see that the prefix of the noun is repeated, in a form more or less recognizable before every word in grammatical agreement with it. The way in which it enters into the composition of pronouns other than the simple subject and object prefixes, will be explained later.

CHAPTER III

The Noun-Classes

We have already referred to Giacinto Brusciotto as the author of the first attempt at a Bantu Grammar. He was an Italian Capuchin, Prefect of the Apostolic Mission to the Kingdom of Congo, about the middle of the seventeenth century. Judging from his book (published at Rome in 1659), his linguistic aptitudes were of no mean order, and no doubt he had profited by many years' residence in the country. It is remarkable, at least, that he succeeded in grasping the principle of the noun-classes, which eluded more than one of his successors. We have seen that Lichtenstein missed it; and—even more unaccountably—Burton, writing about 1860, with the work of Krapf and Rebmann before him, could speak of 'the artful and intricated system of irregular plurals' in

Swahili.[1] In Cavazzi's *History of the Kingdom of Congo*,[2] first published in 1671, it is stated that a missionary, after six years spent in trying to learn the rules of the language, only found out that there were none! It is strange that this book takes no notice whatever of Brusciotto or his grammar.

The first section of Brusciotto's manual[3] has the following heading: 'Of the Declen-
'sion of Nouns, or, as it is better expressed,
'their Principiation, and their Rules; wherein
'it is shown what articles are to be attributed
'to each noun, both in direct and oblique
'cases, for their correct construction in them-
'selves, or when they are joined to other
'words; and generally this is first to be noted
'that in the present tongue we must not look
'for declensions but rather principiations, for
'which we have the following Rules.' . . .

---

[1] Zanzibar, I, 443.

[2] *Istorica Descrizione de' tre Regni, Congo, Matamba et Angola, situati nell 'Etiopia Inferiore Occidentale e delle Missioni Apostoliche esercitatevi da Religiosi Capuccini*, accuratamente compilata del P. Gio. Antonio Cavazzi da Montecuccolo. (Milan, 1671.)

[3] *Regulae quaedam pro difficillimi Congensium idiomatis faciliori captu, ad Grammaticae normam redactae.* (Rome, 1659.)

THE NOUN-CLASSES

Later on, having reached the end of the 'Principiations,' he says, once more:

'As has been said above, the language of the Congos and others of Negro lands is not founded, nor forms its rules upon the declension of words, but on their principiation; therefore the rules which are distinguished and marked in this idiom are chiefly taken from the various principiations of the substantives and varied accordingly.' From this it appears that he duly appreciated the importance of the noun-classes as a feature of the language.

The first thing we have to do in studying Latin is to master the declensions—the classes into which nouns are divided according to their terminations and genders. Such classes exist, though to a less extent, in German; they have almost disappeared in Dutch, and entirely so in English. When we think of declensions, we also think of cases, each having its own case-endings.

It was quite natural that anyone educated, like Brusciotto, mainly on the classics, and more especially on the Latin grammar, should, in trying to discover the laws of an entirely strange language, look first for the declensions.

He soon recognized that the plural of nouns was formed in different ways, according to distinct rules, but that the inflection came at the beginning of the word instead of at the end, so that he invented, as we have seen, the name of 'principiations' for the different classes so distinguished. Of these he enumerates eight, which can be identified without difficulty in present-day Kongo,[1] allowing for differences of dialect and for some mistakes and confusions. It is curious that he does not notice the person-class, but makes 'gentile nouns' exceptions to his first and second principiations. At the end of his chapter, he quaintly adds:

'Note, with regard to the preceding, that
'there is no rule so strictly observed as to be
'without many exceptions, all which by
'practice and the Spirit of God inspiring, will
'be easily understood and by continuous and
'unwearied labour overcome.'

Exceptions are the refuge of the imperfect grammarian, and a knowledge of the Bantu

---

[1] This spelling is preferred in modern books when referring to the particular language treated by Brusciotto, while 'Congo' is retained as the name of the river or its adjacent territories.

languages, unattainable by our pioneer (though not, in his case, for want of 'continuous and unwearied labour') would have shown that they usually exemplify rules not immediately obvious.

Brusciotto may have been led astray partly by his belief in the existence of an article—a part of speech which, as we understand it in English, is not found in Bantu. He is not alone in giving this name to the initial vowel of the prefix—a point as to which we shall have more to say presently;—but it is less easy to see why he should have extended it to the possessive particle (*wa*, *ba*, *ya*, etc.). We shall return to this point in the fifth chapter.

The number of noun-classes, as the 'principiations' are now generally called, varies in different languages, but is mostly eight or ten. There is some uncertainty about the original number, and Meinhof's theoretical table is, as he points out, not complete, since some languages have anomalous forms only to be interpreted as survivals of lost classes, and more of these may yet be discovered.

Meinhof, following Bleek, counts singular and plural classes separately, thus arriving at a total of twenty-one. Some singular prefixes have no corresponding plural, while some plural prefixes are attached to two or more classes having different prefixes in the singular.

As the order in which these classes are arranged is hardly the same in the grammars of any two Bantu languages, it seems most convenient in this book to follow Meinhof's arrangement and refer to the prefixes by his numbers. Some advantages are secured by placing singular and plural in the same class, and in drawing up a practical grammar it might be better to follow that arrangement; but the want of uniformity makes reference very difficult in a comprehensive survey. When we find, *e.g.*, most Zulu grammars giving as the second class what Steere, in Swahili, calls the fifth, the French Fathers in Ganda the sixth, and Madan in Lala-Lamba the ninth, one is ready to ask why we cannot adopt some uniform system. But, when we remember how many classes have been dropped by one language and another (Duala, *e.g.*, having only seven in all) we see that it is impossible to number them always in the same way, though we may keep in every case the same relative order. Some writers, conscious of the difficulty, have frankly given up the numbers and simply designate the classes by their prefixes ('the *mu-ba* class,' 'the *mu-mi* class,' and so on). But as the prefixes assume different forms, and are sometimes lost, this arrangement is useless for comparative purposes unless some standard form is agreed upon. The following table contains the forms which Meinhof has arrived at as probably the original ones. Even if this view should be erroneous in some cases, it is at least possible to see how all the forms actually in use could have been derived from them; and, in any case, this does not affect their use as a means of reference.

The prefixes are given in Prof. Meinhof's orthography, as to which the following points should be noted: *v* is the sound called 'bilabial v' which is very common in present-day Bantu, though in some languages it has become *b* or *w*.[1] *î* may here be disregarded, merely remembering that in Meinhof's opinion the vowel of the *vî*-prefix originally differed from that of the *ki*-prefix, also the *li* of the tenth class from that of the fifth. The etymological importance of

---

[1] See Noël-Armfield, *General Phonetics*, p. 71.

this 'heavy i' is shown in his book on Bantu phonetics. γ stands for the 'voiced sound' (which does not occur in English) of Scots ch in 'loch.'[1]

It may be as well to state here that the orthography used in this book for specimens of Bantu languages is that adopted in the printed texts available for each particular language. Where it has been found necessary to depart from this orthography, or where any symbol needs special explanation, the fact is mentioned in a note. No attempt has been made to unify the various systems: the only satisfactory uniformity would be that obtained by transcription into I.A.P. characters, and for this the study of Bantu is not sufficiently advanced. The reader not already familiar with this script, is referred to Mr. Noël-Armfield's *General Phonetics* (1915).

He will also find a table of it facing page 30 of the author's *Language-Families of Africa*.

    1. mu-
    2. va-   Plural of 1.
    3. mu-
    4. mi-   Plural of 3.
    5. li-

---

[1] For which, in this book, we use the Greek character χ.

THE NOUN-CLASSES

6. ma-   Plural of 5 and 14.
7. ki-
8. vî-   Plural of 7.
9. ni
10. lî-ni Plural of 9 and 11.
11. lu
12. tu-   Plural of 11, 13 and 19.
13. ka
14. vu
15. ku   No plural.
16. pa ⎫
17. ku ⎬ Locatives. No plurals.
18. mu ⎭
19. pî
20. γu
20*a*. γa   Plural of 20.
21. γî

Other classes and prefixes of which occasional traces survive, will be discussed later on.

It will make matters clearer if we subjoin to the above skeleton table of prefixes, which are mere abstractions and, as such, difficult to grasp and remember, specimen nouns from eight fairly typical languages, showing the forms in actual use for each class, with their concords as exhibited in the adjective and the possessive particle. As far as possible, words have been chosen which are found in all the eight languages, so as to facilitate a comparison of roots.

THE NOUN-CLASSES

No. 1 NOUN-

Class		Zulu	Chwana	Herero
1	Human Being	umu-ntu	mo-tho	omu-ndu
2	Do. pl.	aba-ntu	va-tho	ova-ndu
3	Tree	umu-ti	mo-re	omu-ti
4	Do. pl.	imi-ti	me-re	omi-ti
5	Tooth	i(li) zinyo	le-ino	e-yo
6	Do. pl.	ama-zinyo	ma-ino	oma-yo
7	Chest (thorax)	isi-fuba	se-huba	[otyi-na = thing]
8	Do. pl.	izi-fuba	li-huba	[ovi-na]
9	Elephant	in-dhlovu	tlou	on-dyou
10	Do. pl.	izin-dhlovu	li-tlou	ozon-dyou
11	Wand	u(lu)-ti	lo-re	oru-ti
12	Do. pl.	—	—	otu-ti
13	Little stick	—	—	oka-ti
14	Human nature	ubu-ntu	vo-tho	o-undu
15	Death	uku-fa	χo shwa	oku-ta
16	Place, at	—	—	opona
17	— to	—	—	okona
18	— in	—	—	omona
19	[Diminutive]	[Found in Duala, *e.g.*, i-seru "dwarf antelope"		
20	Clumsy person	—	—	—
20A	Do. pl.	—	—	—
21	Giant	—	—	—
21A	Do. pl.	—	—	—

NOTE.—Words in square brackets are inserted when

THE NOUN-CLASSES

CLASSES.

Nyanja	Swahili	Ganda	Gisu	Kongo
mu-ntu	m-tu	omu-ntu	umu-ndu	mu-ntu
a-ntu	wa-tu	aba-ntu	baba-ndu	a-ntu
m-tengo	m-ti	omu-ti	[kumu-ba= sugar-cane]	[mu-nse= sugar-cane]
mi-tengo	mi-ti	emi-ti	[kimyuba]	[mi-nse]
dz-ino	j-ino	eri-nyo	li-sino	d-inu
ma-no	m-eno	ama-nyo	kama-sino	m-enu
chi-fua	ki-fua	eki-fuba	[kiki-ndu= thing]	[ki-nzu=pipe]
zi-fua	vi-fua	ebi-fuba	[bibi-ndu]	[i-nzu]
njobvu	ndovu	en-jovu	i-tsofu	nzau
njobvu	ndovu	en-jovu	tsi-tsofu	nzau
[u-konde=net]	u-ti	[olu-ga=cane]	[lu-hingo= bow]	[lumbu= fence]
—	—	[otu-dzi= drop of water]	—	[tumbu]
[ka-ntu= little thing]	—	aka-ti	[ka-busi, little goat]	—
u-untu	u-tu	obu-ntu	bubu-ndu[1]	uwu-ntu
ku-fa	ku-fa	oku-fa	ku-fwa	(ku)fwa
pa malo	[nyumbani (pa)]	wa-ntu	ha-ndu	v-uma
ku malo	[nyumbani (kwa)]	[ku-mpi, near]	ku-ndu	k-uma
m'malo	[nyumbani (mwa)]	[munda= the inside]	mu-ndu	m-uma
—pl. lo-seru 12, and Ny-wema fi-ulu "bird," pl. tufulu 12]				[fi-mbele= little knife]
—	—	ogu-ntu	—	—
—	—	aga-ntu	—	—
—	ki-ji-tu	—	gugu-ndu	—
—	mi-ji-tu	—	gimi-ndu	—

that with the same meaning has a different root.

Zulu and Ganda—both too well-known for further comment—indicate, approximately, the two extremities of the Bantu area. Herero—called by South African colonists Damara—is spoken in the south-western territory which till recently was German. It is a language, in many respects, of the highest interest; but its speakers are now sadly reduced in numbers. Nyanja extends, more or less, from the north end of Lake Nyasa to the Zambezi and is closely cognate—if not virtually identical—with the main speech of Southern Rhodesia—usually, though not very correctly, called 'Mashona' or 'Chiswina.' The range of Swahili is roughly from Warsheikh on the Somali coast to Cape Delgado (though the people themselves limit the name 'Swahilini' to the coast north-east of the Tana mouth), but it has been carried as a trade language far into the interior, and even to the Congo. Gisu, sometimes called 'Masaba,' is a very remarkable tongue, whose principal speakers live round Mount Elgon in the north of the Uganda Protectorate: it has, perhaps, preserved more ancient forms than any other. Kongo (sometimes called Fiote) is spoken by large numbers of people on both sides of the

Lower Congo, as far up as Stanley Pool, and in the old 'Kingdom of Congo' south-east of the river, where the Portuguese missionaries laboured.

Originally, we may suppose that some definite meaning attached to each class, just as, in languages possessing grammatical gender, the masculine and feminine terminations corresponded to a real distinction of sex. It would be difficult now to give any reason why *hortus* should be masculine, or *mensa* feminine; but no doubt, when it had once become an accepted fact that nouns in -*us* were mostly masculine and nouns in *a* mostly feminine, words which happened to end in these ways were ranged under one category or the other, without regard to their meaning.

Sometimes it is still possible to say that a class consists of nouns denoting a certain kind of objects, such as the first (or 'personal') class, the fifteenth, which contains verbal nouns (infinitives), and the diminutive class found in some languages. Again, certain sets of nouns may be found in one class—*e.g.*, trees in the third, though it contains others as well. Much ingenuity has been expended—and, I cannot but think, wasted—in drawing up definitions of the classes: the attempt seems to be hopeless at the present day, because prefixes originally distinct may have become identical in form, through elision or contraction, and so two or more classes have been merged into one. We know this to have happened in Swahili, where 11 (*lu*) and 14 (*vu*) have alike been contracted into *u* and are now treated as one and the same class.

Class 3-4 (*mu-mi*) contains, besides trees, a number of the parts and organs of the body, which may, at one time, have formed a distinct class.[1]

It should also be noted that the same word is found in two or more languages with different prefixes, *e.g.*, 'year'; Zulu, *umnyaka*, 2; Nyanja, *chaka*, 7, etc.

The Fulfulde language of West Africa has a most remarkable system of noun-classes, much fuller and more clearly defined than anything now to be found in Bantu. Professor

---

[1] It is quite possible that they were originally locatives with the prefix *mu* (*mu-kono*, really 'in the hand'), which became confounded with this class owing to the similarity of the prefix. To understand how this might have happened, we may refer to Nyanja, where the noun *kamwa*, 'mouth,' is never used by itself—only *pa-kamwa* and *m-kamwa*, 'at' and 'in the mouth.'

Meinhof's theory as to this language and its possible connection with the Bantu family is set forth in his *Introduction to the Study of African Languages*.[1]

In some cases, the distinction of meaning implied by the prefix is quite clear. There is no doubt about the diminutives, nor the infinitive used as a noun (15); 1 indicates persons; 7, (sometimes) collectivity; 14, either abstractions, or some substance taken in the mass, such as grass, wool, flour, etc. And we find, over and over again, that the same root may take different prefixes and have its meaning modified accordingly. In Zulu *umu-ntu*, 1, is 'a person'; *isi-ntu* 7, 'the collectivity of beings'—'the world'; *ubu-ntu*, 'human nature.' *Umu-ti* 3, is 'a tree'; *u(lu)-ti* 11, 'switch' or 'wand' (this has suggested to some writers that Class 11 consists mainly of long, thin objects—which is scarcely borne out by the facts);[2] *ubu-ti* 14,

---

[1] Pp. 99, 100. See also *Language-Families of Africa*, Chapter VI.

[2] It is true that some words in Herero suggest this idea; thus *omu-ndu*, 1, is 'a person,' *oru-ndu*, 11, 'a tall, thin person'; *otji-tenda*, 7, 'iron,' *oru-tenda*, 'a long, thin piece of iron.'

'poison'; and in Swahili, we have *ki-ti* 7, 'chair'—*i.e.*, 'the thing made of a tree,' or perhaps 'the little tree (thing)'[1]—(see ante p. 29).

Though, as we have seen, Bantu knows no linguistic distinction of sex, a very definite line is drawn between the living and the lifeless—or rather, perhaps, between the human and the non-human. The first (*mu*) and second (*ba*) classes, in every Bantu language, consist pre-eminently, if not exclusively, of names denoting human beings.

As a rule, even ghosts and other preternatural beings are not placed in the same class. In Zulu *i-zimu* (usually translated 'cannibal,' but in reality a kind of ogre or goblin), *ama-tongo* and *ama-dhlozi* (ancestral spirits) are of 5 and 6; in Nyanja, *mzimu*, the most usual word for spirit, is 2, and so is *Mulungu*, which sometimes designates an ancestral ghost, though at others it seems to be used in a sense almost implying a 'High God.' Some languages include animals in the first class, but this is evidently an afterthought.

The African mind, in general, inclines to treat

[1] *Ki-* may here be the diminutive prefix—see next Chapter.

animals as persons;—we see in their folk-tales
that the distinction is kept up with difficulty.
(Uncle Remus is sophisticated enough to be
conscious of the confusion, and reminds his
hearer that, once upon a time, 'creatures had
sense same like folks.') While most of them are
usually of the 9th (*ni*) class (cf. in Zulu, *imbuzi*,
'goat,' *inkomo*, ' cow,' *ingwe*, 'leopard,' *indhlovu*
'elephant,' etc.), it seems to have been felt that
this was quite illogical, so some languages (as
Swahili) removed them into the first class without changing their form—*i.e.*, treated them, in
respect of all their agreements, as first-class
nouns; others gave them a special plural, by
placing the second prefix before their own
plural one. The few names of animals which
in Zulu and Chwana are included in the first
class are treated in a special way, suggesting
that they did not always belong to it. Their
plural prefix is *o-*, not *aba-*, which is also
taken by certain nouns denoting degrees of
relationship (as *u-yise* 'father,' pl. *o-yise*,
u-nina 'mother,' pl. *o-nina*) and all proper
names.[1] Perhaps there was once a separate

[1] Proper Nouns are often used in the plural, to mean
'a person and those with him.' See Colenso, *First Steps
in Zulu-Kafir*, § 29.

class for names of relationship (which in most Bantu languages are treated exceptionally in some way or other) and it is worth noting that most (not all) Zulu names of animals coming under this heading are compounded with *uno-* (= *unina*). The corresponding nouns in Chwana take the prefix *bo-* (*vo-*).

This first class has the prefix *mu-* —sometimes heard as *mo-*, sometimes worn down to *m*, and sometimes changing to *un-*, especially before t or d. In Zulu it is *umu-* or *um-*, sometimes contracted to *u-*. One might be tempted to think that the longer form is the more primitive one, and that languages like Chwana and Nyanja have lost the initial vowel. There seems reason, however, to think that this initial vowel is not really part of the prefix, but the remnant of a demonstrative which has become amalgamated with it. Gisu—a language in a very archaic stage—supplies the clue: not in this class indeed, but in the second, third, and fourth, where we have *baba-ndu* 'people,' *kumu-kono* (elsewhere *umkono*, *mukono*, *mkono*), 'hand,' plural *kimi-kono*.

Meinhof thinks that this demonstrative originally had the form γ*a* and assimilated its vowel to that of the syllable which followed it, while the γ passed, sometimes into *ng*, sometimes into *k*. Thus γ*a umuntu* would become *ngumuntu*, Gisu *kumundu*, and, the consonant being dropped, the prefix would remain as *umu-*. This pronoun survives as the 'copula' (to be treated in a later chapter), and in Zulu we have *ng'umuntu*, 'it is the man,' *ng'umuti*, 'it is a tree.' This is pointed out by Bleek in his *Comparative Grammar*.[1] On this theory of its origin, it is quite intelligible that he should call the initial vowel an article, especially as it is chiefly absent in cases where the employment of an article would be inadmissible—always in the vocative, and in certain negative sentences. However, as it is impossible by its means to make any distinction corresponding to that indicated by the use of 'a' and 'the,' the initial vowel can hardly be called an article in our sense.

This original γ*a* probably accounts for the fact that in some languages (*e.g.*, Swahili, Nyanja, etc.) the pronoun of the third person

---

[1] Pp. 150, 151. Of course he knew nothing of the Gisu language, which has so fully justified his deductions.

(see Ch. VI.) is *a*- instead of *u*[1]. Forms like *omuntu, omuti,* perhaps show that sometimes, instead of the *u* assimilating the vowel which followed it, contraction took place:

$$(\gamma) + aumuntu = omuntu.$$

Names of tribes may be either of the second or the sixth class: *Abasutu, Bechwana, Barolong, Amazulu, Makaranga, Waswahili, Agiryama, Abaganda.* Those of the second have corresponding singulars of the first: *Umsutu, Mochwana, Morolong.* But sixth class nouns do not always have a singular of the fifth: *I-zulu* does not seem to be used for an individual of the Zulu nation—perhaps because it is the same as the word for the 'sky'—but we have *i-Bunu*, 'a Boer,' *i-Lawu*, 'a Hottentot,' *i-Xosa*, 'a Cape Kafir.'

The concords of Class 3 are almost identical with those of Class 1. There are, however, two differences in the pronouns, which we shall notice in a later chapter. Class 4 has the same pronouns as Class 10, though its prefix (and consequently its agreement with the adjective) is different. Besides the names of

---

[1] Also for *gu, gi* and *ga* being occasionally found as pronouns in the third, fourth and sixth classes, instead of the more usual *u, i* and *a*.

trees and parts of the body (usually: 'arm,' 'finger,' 'leg,' 'foot,' 'heart,'—sometimes 'head,' etc.) this class contains some words not easily placed under any special heading, such as 'village' (*i.e.*, a 'kraal' or collection of huts of any size, up to what can be fairly described as a town)—*umu-zi, mo-tse, mu-dzi, m-ji, mu-nzhi, mu-ndi*.[1] (Herero, curiously enough, places it in 11: *oru-dhe*.) Words denoting streams or rivers (though differing in form) very often belong to this class. So do, many proper names of rivers: Zulu *Umgeni, Umzimkulu*, etc.; others are found in Class 11.

The fifth prefix is *li-*, in Zulu *ili-*, usually contracted into *i-*, as *i-tshe* (for *ili-tshe*), 'stone,' *i-zwi*, 'word,' etc. In some languages this prefix has assumed the form *di-*; in some it is lost altogether, except before roots beginning with a vowel, where it is sometimes represented by *dz* or *j*: Nyanja *dz-ina*, 'name,' which is in Swahili *j-ina*, (Yao *l-ina*). In Swahili, the pronoun *li* and the possessive particle *la*, used with nouns like *neno*, 'word,' *ziwa*, 'pool,' would be something of a puzzle if it were not

---

[1] Bleek thinks these may have originated as locatives in *mu-*. See his *Comparative Grammar*, p. 130.

known from other languages that these words must originally have begun with *li*.

Names of fruits are found in this class, differing only by prefix from the name of the tree which produces them: Swahili *m-buyu*, 'baobab,' *buyu*, 'calabash' (which grows on it), *m-kuyu*, 'fig-tree,' *kuyu*, 'a fig,' *m-chungwa*, 'orange-tree,' *chungwa*, 'orange';[1] Zulu *um-kiwane*, 'wild fig-tree,' *i-kiwane*, etc.

Many words denoting liquids, or substances handled in bulk, which are not individualised and therefore have no singular, belong to the sixth class; *e.g.*, 'water': Zulu *ama-nzi*, Swahili *ma-ji* or *ma-i*, Nyanja (and other languages), *ma-dzi*, Kongo *ma-za*, Duala *ma-diba*, etc.; 'milk': Swahili *ma-ziwa*, Ganda *ama-ta*, Chwana *ma-shi;* 'sour milk': Zulu *ama-si*, Herero *oma-ere;* 'millet': Zulu *ama-bele*, Nyanja *ma-ere*, *ma-pira*, etc., etc.

Here we may mention a feature which at first sight seems puzzling in Chwana and some other languages. Nouns of Class 9, besides their own plural sometimes take a second in

---

[1] *Nazi*, 'coco-nut,' *tende*, 'date,' *ndizi*, 'banana,' are exceptions, being of the ninth class. But none of these three seem to be original Bantu roots. The names of the trees are quite regular: *m-nazi*, *m-tende*; but the banana-tree is *m-gomba*, not *m-dizi*.

ma-, indicating that there are *very many* of the thing in question; *e.g.*, *nku*, 'a sheep,'—plural *li-nku*, but 'many sheep' = *ma-nku*. These may be regarded as collectives with no singular, and they are possibly connected with the lost augmentative class, to which we shall recur at the end of the next chapter.

It will be seen by reference to the Table that the form assumed by the sixth prefix in Gisu is *kama-*, in accordance with the principle already explained. I have not met with any other example of this form; but the original γa prefixed to the *ma* explains why the pronoun in some languages (Giryama, Ganda, etc.) should be *ga*. It is usually *a* or *ya*.

It is less easy to see why the prefix should appear in Herero as *oma-*. But that language, as the Table shows, has a tendency to make *all* the initial vowels *o*: the only exception is the fifth prefix, which has assumed the form *e-*.

CHAPTER IV

THE NOUN-CLASSES (*continued*)

THE forms of the seventh and eighth prefixes vary considerably. Besides those shown in the Table, we have:—

    Duala . . . *e-, be-: e-koto,* 'cap,' pl. *be-koto.*
    Ila (Middle Zambezi) . . . *chi- shi-: chi-bia,* 'pot,' pl. *shi-bia.*
    Kikuyu (British East Africa) . . . *ki-, i-: ki-hato,* 'broom,' pl. *i-hato.*
    Konde (north end of Lake Nyasa) . . . *iki- ifi-: iki-tala,* 'bedstead,' pl. *ifi-tala.*

In Ronga (Delagoa Bay), and in some dialects of the language spoken in Rhodesia the eighth prefix has a very peculiar sound, written in the International Phonetic Alphabet σ and by Meinhof *s*. It is produced by getting ready to say *th* (as in 'thin') and then rounding the lips, as if for *w*, and somewhat resembles the whistle which results from blowing into a key. Venda (North Transvaal) gives this prefix the voiced sound, which is written ρ and by Meinhof *z*.

This class, like some others, consists of two or three originally distinct ones, which may account for the prefix conveying several different senses. Sometimes it has a kind of instrumental force and is then used to make a noun out of a verb, implying the thing by means of which the action is accomplished, as *isi-hlalo* (Zulu) 'a seat,' from *hlala*, 'to sit'; Nyanja *chi-psero*, 'a broom,' from *psera*, 'to sweep'; *chi-peta*, 'a winnowing-basket,' from *peta*. Sometimes it seems to convey a collective sense, as in Zulu, *isi-ntu* (already remarked on), *isi-Zulu*, 'the whole of the Zulus, the Zulu nation,' *isi-zwe*, 'tribe, nation,' from *i-zwe*, 'country.' This is distinct from the use of the prefix to express *language* (which does not occur in Zulu): Chi-Nyanja, Ki-Swahili, Se-Sutu; or, more accurately, 'likeness, fashion, manner,' as its application is not confined to language. Again, it forms a kind of abstract noun, expressing, not a quality, but the action of a verb, as Swahili *ki-lio*, 'weeping,' from *lia;* Nyanja *chi-funo*, 'wish,' from *funa*.

In Swahili, a great many nouns in *ki-* are

diminutives, *ki-* having taken the place of the thirteenth prefix *ka-*, as it has also done in Kongo.[1] In Nyanja, curiously enough, the old augmentative class (20) has become merged in the seventh, exchanging its prefix *γu* for *chi-*.

On the other hand, nouns which have dropped their prefixes, and whose stems begin with *chi, ki, shi,* etc., are liable to be mistaken for nouns of the seventh class. These are fairly numerous in Nyanja, as *chinga,* 'fence,' pl. *ma-chinga, chindu,* 'roof,' pl. *ma-chindu.*

This class also contains some nouns meaning persons. In Zulu these are derived from verbs as *isi-hambi,* 'a traveller,' from *hamba,* 'go,' *isi-gijimi,* 'runner,' from *gijima,* 'run.' In Swahili we find in this class personal nouns implying some defect, as *ki-pofu,* 'a blind person,' *ki-ziwi,* 'a dumb person,' etc. Probably these originally belonged to a 'depreciative class,' which will be mentioned later on.

The ninth prefix is usually found as *in-* or *n-* : in Ronga *yin-*, Ganda, *en-*, Herero *on-*, Makua usually *i-* without the *n*, as *i-kuo,* 'cloth,' which

---

[1] In Kongo, however, diminutives are distinguished from the nouns in *ki-* by reduplication of the root, as *ki-mwanamwana,* 'a little child.'

is equivalent to the Swahili or Yao *nguo*.[1] *n* becomes *m* before stems beginning with a labial, as *im-buzi* (Zulu), 'goat,' for *in+buzi*.

The tenth class properly has the plural prefix in addition to the singular (Zulu *izi-n-dhlu*, *izi-m-buzi*), but the former often disappears through contraction, so that singular and plural are alike, as Kongo *nzo*, Swahili and Nyanja, *nyumba*, 'house. Some dialects of Nyanja, however, have *zi-nyumba* 10, and Herero, *ondyuo* 9, *odho-ndyuo*[2] 10, Ronga *yin-dlu* 9, *tiyin-dlu* 10. Ronga sometimes contracts both prefixes, as *ndlebe*, 'ear' (Zulu *in-dhlebe*), plural *tin-dlebe*, and may drop even the *n*, as in *huku*, 'fowl,' plural *tihuku*. Chwana Sutu and Venda have the tenth prefix *li* : *puli*, 'goat,' pl. *li-puli*; *kχomo* 'cow,' *li-kχomo*. This suggests that the primitive form may have been *li-ni-*.

---

[1] Both in Chwana and Makua there is a tendency to substitute the voiceless stop for the voiced stop and nasal (*i.e.*, *p* for *mb*, *t* for *nd*, *k* for *ng*). Cf. *puli*, 'goat,' Nyanja, *mbuzi*; *itotwa* (Makua) 'star,' Yao, *ndondwa*.

[2] *Dy* is probably the nearest equivalent to this sound in ordinary English spelling, but it may be that represented in the International Phonetic Alphabet by inverted f. Instead of *z*, Herero has the sound of *th* in 'there'—here represented by *dh*.

So far as any rule can be laid down for them, most names of animals belong to the ninth class. Many of these are the same throughout the greater number of the Bantu languages. We give a few of the most striking examples:

Cow or ox: Zulu, *inkomo*, Chwana, *kxomo*, Ronga, *homu*, Herero, *ongombe*, Nyanja (and many other languages), *ng'ombe*,[1] Bobangi (Middle Congo), *ngombo*. Even where the root is different, as Ganda *ente*, the word still belongs to the same class.

Goat: Zulu, *imbuzi*, Ronga, *mbuti*, Chwana, *puli*, Nyanja (and many others), *mbuzi*, Bobangi, *mboli*, Duala, *mbodi*, Herero, *ongombo* (a different root), Kongo, *nkombo*, and in some dialects, *ntaba*.

Sheep: Zulu, *imvu*, Chwana, *nku*, Nyanja, *nkosa*, Swahili, *kondoo*, Giryama, *ng'ondzi*, Ganda, *endiga*.

The dog is usually *mbwa* or *imbwa*—quite recognisable as representing his bark,—but in

---

[1] *Ng'* thus written has the same sound as in 'ring,' 'sing,' etc. Meinhof writes it ṅ. Where no apostrophe follows, the sound is that heard in 'finger.' The former does not seem to occur in Herero or Pokomo. In the latter language 'cow' is *ngombe*, which would be ridiculed as a mispronunciation by Swahilis or Anyanja.

Zulu this has become *inja*, because *w* cannot in that language follow another nasal.

The eleventh prefix is found in most present-day Bantu languages, though its presence is frequently disguised by the fact that it has been contracted into *u-*; as Zulu *u-ti* for *ulu-ti*. Here it is still easily distinguishable by its concord—when we hear *uti olude lwa leyo 'nkosi*, 'the long staff of that chief,'—we know that *uti* cannot be one of the first-class nouns which have *u-* for their prefix (*u-baba*, etc.). Moreover, when used as proper names, (as any noun may be in Zulu, keeping its own prefix, and changing only the initial vowel), they appear in the uncontracted form; thus we have *uLuzipo*, a man's name, from *u-zipo*, 'a claw,' *uLutuli*, from *u-tuli*, 'dust.'

In Swahili, the distinctive concord is no longer seen, the pronouns, etc. being identical with those of 3: *uti m-refu u-me-anguka*, 'the long stick has fallen.' Moreover, 14 has undergone a like contraction, so that these two classes are merged in one. The *lu*-class still exist separately in Yao and Ila: in Nyanja there are a good many nouns beginning with this prefix, but they are treated as belonging to the fifth. In Ronga, though still distinct, it has modified its prefix to *li-*, while the fifth prefix is *ri-*. As will have been noticed in Herero, some languages sound this prefix with *r* rather than *l*. Sometimes it is used (instead of 7) to express language: *Lu-ganda*, *Lu-nyoro*, *Lu-gisu*: this seems to be confined to the northern region of the great lakes.

There is considerable divergence in the plural prefix appropriated to this class. The most usual appears to be the tenth, but sometimes we have the sixth. In Herero, Ndonga, Kongo, it has retained its original one, the twelfth (*tu-*), which also belongs to the diminutive class. Sometimes we find that, as in 10, the plural prefix is added without rejecting the singular; thus in Swahili, *uti* makes *nyuti* = *ni* + *uti*; in Mbundu (Angola), we have *lubango*, 'stick,'—pl. *ma-lu-bango*[1].

The twelfth and thirteenth classes have dropped out in a good many languages. *Ka-* is properly the sign of the diminutive, and is still so used in Herero, Nyanja, Yao, Ila, Ganda, Pokomo, Giryama, Zigula, etc.

As we have seen, Swahili and some others have substituted the seventh prefix for it.

---

[1] Meinhof thinks this was at first the rule with all the classes and that the second prefix gradually dropped out.

Zulu, Ronga, Chwana, and their cognate dialects have got rid of it altogether, and express their diminutive by a *suffix*—perhaps under the influence of the Hottentot language. E. g., Zulu, *indhlwana* (*indhlu-ana*), 'a little house'; Chwana *pitsa*, 'pot,' *pits-ana*, 'little pot.'

Though *tu-* seems to be the original plural prefix attached to the thirteenth class, a variety of others have taken its place, and the learner should be prepared to meet with *pi-* (a form of 8), *u-*, *bu-*, (14, as in Herero), *ma-*, *vi-*, and *tin-* (10).

In Ganda, where the plural of *aka-ntu*, 'a little thing,' is *obu-ntu*, the twelfth prefix has a distinct and very curious use—*otu-dzi*, 'a single drop of water,' from *ama-dzi*, *tu-nyu* 'a little salt,' from *mu-nyu*.[1] That is, it is used to individualise a single particle of something which has to be looked at or handled in the mass, like liquids, flour, grain, etc. These, as we have seen, when belonging to Class 6, have no singular; when of Class 14, they have no plural—or, it would be more correct to say, they have neither singular nor plural. This formation is also found in

[1] Conversely, *lu-nyu* 'a lot of salt.'

Pogoro, a language spoken east of the northern end of Lake Nyasa.

In Nyanja, the diminutive plural prefix is *ti-* (which, Meinhof thinks, may have been a distinct class) : *ka-mbalame*, 'little bird,' plural, *ti-mbalame*.

Duala has a different diminutive class, traces of which occur elsewhere, but only in the western part of the continent: it is the one numbered 19. Its prefix *i-* is supposed to have been originally *pi-*, and its plural prefix is the twelfth, which has here assumed the form *lo-*: *i-seru*, a small kind of antelope—pl. *lo-seru*. In Kongo the prefix has assumed the form *fi-* and constitutes an additional diminutive class, which, however, has no plural of its own. This class is also found in Nywema and some other languages of the central regions between the Great Lakes and the Upper Congo.

The fourteenth class, as already stated, includes abstract nouns. (*e.g.*, Zulu *ubu-ntu*, Swahili *u-tu*, etc., 'human nature'), and names of materials which are not properly speaking either singular or plural: *ubu-si* (Zulu), *u-chi* (Nyanja), 'honey,' *utshwala* for *ubwala* = *ubu-ala* (Z.), 'beer,' *utshane* for *ubu-ane* (Z.), 'grass,' *ub-oya* (Z.), *ubwea* (Ny.), 'hair of an animal.' If nouns of this class are ever put into the plural, they usually take the sixth prefix (*ma*): thus 'night,' *ubu-suku*, has no plural in Zulu, but the Chwana *bo-siχo* has the plural *ma-siχo*.

But there seems reason to suspect that most fourteenth class nouns which take a plural do not originally belong to the class at all, as they denote concrete objects which there seems no reason for including here. Probably the same thing has happened as with the *ki-* and *u-* classes in Swahili. *Uta*, 'bow'—originally *bu-ta* or *vu-ta*—is found in nearly every Bantu language. In Nyanja it has the concord *bu*, which stands almost alone: *uta bu-funa kutyoka*, 'the bow is likely to break' (lit. 'wants to break'). The same is the case with *boa*, 'mushrooms,' said in Scott's *Dictionary* to be of Class I (no explanation is offered of the anomalous concord, but the existence of the *bu-* class in other languages makes it quite clear): *boa bwanga bu-li apa* (*li* is here the verb 'to be')—'my mushrooms are here.'

Then we have *bwato*, 'canoe,' stated to be of the fifth class, with plural *ma-bwato*; but forms like Pokomo *waho* (*u-aho*), pl. *m-aho*, seem to show that *bw-* is the prefix (*bu-ato*). Nyamwezi has *vato* 14 and Konde *ubwato* (*ubu-ato*). This last has its plural of Class 4: *imyato* (*imi-ato*), which may point to a still further confusion. The little group of north-western Bantu languages, of which Duala is the chief (Benga, Dikele, Isubu), make the plural of the fourteenth class in *mi-*: the same word is in Benga *bwalu*, *mi-alu*, in Duala *b-olo*, *mi-olo*. Duala has *bw-ele*, 'tree,' pl. *mi-ele*: a curious exception, as regards the singular.

These last can scarcely be explained as collectives, or nouns of material, though 'mushrooms' might: being considered in the first instance as food they would be thought of by the basketful. Even as to *uta* I am not quite clear: *uta* in Swahili seems to mean a bow with quiver and arrows all complete (the 'artillery' that Jonathan carried), while *upindi* is a bow pure and simple. The plurals *nyuta* and *mata* are given in the dictionaries, but they may be later formations. In Nyanja the plural *mauta* apparently has the same collective sense—at least, as applied to the three stars in Orion's belt, I understand it to mean ' The

Bow and Arrows,' not 'The Bows.' *Ubu-so* (Zulu), 'face,' is found almost everywhere and has the same root as *i-so*, 'eye'—as though it were a sort of abstraction: the 'eyeness,' if one might coin the word. In fact one does sometimes hear 'eyes' used to mean 'face,' in Nyanja and probably elsewhere.

The fifteenth prefix, *ku-*, denoting infinitives of nouns, offers little difficulty and has the same form (except for the occasional presence of an initial vowel) almost everywhere. In Chwana it is modified to χo, and several western languages are without it, though it has left traces in Kongo.

There are a few nouns in *ku* with plurals in *ma-*, which are certainly not infinitives and are perhaps remnants of a lost class. They sometimes retain the *ku-* in the plural, after the *ma-* prefix: Nyanja *kutu*, 'ear,' pl. *ma-ku-tu;* but Herero *oku-twi*, *oma-twi*, Kongo *ku-tu*, *ma-tu*. Several of the western Bantu languages have the words for 'arm' and 'leg' similarly formed, and Herero has a few more besides. Meinhof thinks these are locatives, a theory which will be more fully explained in the next chapter.

Classes 16, 17, 18 are not found in Zulu or

Chwana, though slight traces of them exist. They can better be discussed in the next chapter, in connection with the locative; here it may be sufficient to say that they differ from most other classes by having a movable prefix: a preposition is added before the usual prefix and entirely changes the concord. The preposition and its noun are treated as a single word. It is somewhat as though, instead of saying 'The house is near a field,' we said 'Near-the-house *n*-is a field,' or 'By-the-house *b*-is,' etc.

The locative prefixes have entirely disappeared in Swahili, but the concord remains, as we shall see.

The nineteenth class, already referred to, was not recognized by Bleek.

The remaining two classes—more properly four—were also unknown to Bleek and only survive in a rudimentary condition. Ganda has a prefix *ogu-*, which seems to convey a notion (1) of size, (2) of depreciation: *ogu-ntu*, 'a clumsy thing,' pl. *aga-ntu*, *ogu-nyo*, 'a large quantity of salt' (*omu-nyo*), as opposed to 'a small quantity' of the same, *otu-nyo*. In Gisu there is a class denoting large things, with the prefix *gu-* in the singular, *gi-mi-* in the plural:

gu-koko, 'a giant fowl,' pl. *gimi-koko*, with a prefix now virtually equivalent to the fourth. It might be preferable therefore to enumerate them thus: 20 γu 21 γa 22 γu 23 γî (γîmi).

But as a matter of fact, no language to-day seems to have kept both 20 and 22 independently. Both classes survive in Swahili, though one is completely merged in the fifth and sixth, and the other would be but for its anomalous plural. To express unusual size, a noun loses its original prefix in the singular and takes *ma* in the plural, as *dege*, 'a large bird,' (from *n-dege*), pl. *ma-dege*. If the stem begins with a vowel it prefixes *j*, as *joka*, 'large serpent,' from *nyoka*. But if it is implied that a thing is not only large but monstrous, or ill-conditioned, the form is the same for the singular, but the plural has the prefix *mi-:* as *jombo* (from *ch-ombo*), 'a big ugly vessel,' pl. *mi-jombo*, *vua*, 'heavy rain' (implying something abnormal), pl. *mi-vua*. (Some of these forms in *mi-* have no singular corresponding to them). But these distinctions are becoming blurred, and a further source of confusion is the insertion of *-ji-* between the prefix and stem of monosyllabic diminutives. We may add that *ki-* sometimes has a depreciatory sense.[1]

It has already been pointed out that some seventh class nouns in Nyanja (beginning with *chi-*) are really relics of an old augmentative class. In Kinga (spoken among the mountains E. of the north end of Lake Nyasa) there is a class with the prefix *ugu-* which does not seem to have a plural and conveys either an augmentative or a depreciative sense: it is no doubt an amalgamation of 20 and 22. Traces of the same are also found in Venda. Ganda uses both the *ki-* and *lu-* prefixes with augmentative force. There is no need to follow out the matter any further, but the student should keep it in mind as a possible explanation of seemingly exceptional forms.

Hints of several other classes are found:

(1) We have already said that Meinhof considers the Nyanja diminutive plural *ti-* as a distinct prefix, parallel with *tu-*, as *li-* is with *lu-*

(2) There are in Nyanja one or two words,

---

[1] Steere's *Handbook of Swahili*, p. 19, '*ki-buzi*, a poor little goat.' We have already referred to the depreciatory sense of *ki-* when applied to persons, as *kipofu*, *kiziwi*, etc.

tulo, 'sleep,' *tubsi*, 'dung,' which seem to stand in a class by themselves. The concords (*tulo t-ambiri*, 'much sleep,' *tulo t-ache*, 'his sleep,') indicate that *tu-* is the prefix. We find *otu-lo*, 'sleep,' in Ganda, but it does not seem possible to place it, as the French Fathers[1] do, in the *tu-* class which denotes 'small quantities.' However, they may have been originally thought of as plurals and, as such, would belong to Cl. 12, like *tuvia* 'fire' (Kongo) which, though generally used in the plural, seems to have a singular *luvia*.

(3) Some languages have personal nouns in *ka-* which are not diminutive—this is especially marked in Herero—and we might compare Ganda *ka-baka*, 'king,' *ka-tikiro*, 'prime minister.' And we might suggest the large number of animal names in Nyanja, which begin with *na* and *nanka* (*nadzikambe*, 'chameleon,' *nakodzwe*, 'water-buck,' *nankabai*, 'hawk'). But enough has been said to show that the number of classes was once probably far greater than it is now, and to show that in languages not yet fully studied we are quite likely to come upon traces of extra classes.

[1] *Manuel de Langue Luganda.* Einsiedeln, 1894, p. 31.

CHAPTER V

CASES: THE LOCATIVE

IF I begin by saying that Bantu nouns have nothing which can, properly speaking, be described as *case*, it will appear as if this chapter, being of the same kind as the famous one on 'Snakes in Iceland,' had better be left unwritten.

However, as we have already seen, there is a Possessive—if of a somewhat peculiar character. There is no difference in form between the noun-subject and the noun-object, but some pronouns have distinct forms for the accusative, as we shall see in the next chapter. There is something like a vocative. Perhaps the dropping of the initial vowel in Zulu, as '*Zatshuke*,' when addressing a man (instead of '*u Zatshuke*') is too slight to be mentioned in this connection; but Chwana (at least in some dialects) has a different terminal vowel for a noun, according as the person referred to is spoken *to* or spoken *of*. And Duala prefixes *a* to nouns in the Vocative. Finally, the Locative in *-ni*, though confined to a comparatively small number of languages, is a feature which must be taken into account, and it can hardly, for the purposes of this sketch, be classed under any other heading than that of Case.

If we limit the term 'case' to those relations which are expressed by inflexions of the noun-stem (declensional endings), we shall have to admit that English nouns are entirely without it, except when the possessive is indicated by '*s*. Case-endings are becoming obsolete in Dutch, though they still exist in German; they are better exemplified in Latin and Greek, and still more so in Sanscrit, which has seven cases.

The Latin declension, for instance (*mensae*, 'of the table,' *rei*, 'to the thing,' *horto*, 'from the garden'), indicates by means of the termination what we express by a preposition, or by the order of words in the sentence, which is our only way of distinguishing subject from object. The same relations are expressed in the Bantu languages by means of prepositions.[1]

Indo-European prepositions are invariable. 'From,' 'to,' 'by,' 'with,' never change their shapes, whatever nouns they may precede or follow; and neither do the Latin *ab*,[2] *de*, *ex*, *pro*, *super*, etc.

This is not the case with Bantu prepositions, though the difference is perhaps more apparent than real. We have already seen, in the second chapter, that the equivalent for 'of' assumes different forms according to the noun it follows. It is as though we said in English: 'the house *h*of the man,' 'the child *ch*of the house,' 'the door *d*of the room.' This is because the initial of the noun-prefix is combined with the root -*a*, which, whatever its original force may be—we can for practical purposes assume to mean 'of.'

We can now see why Brusciotto called this *wa, ya*, etc., *an article*. He saw that one part

---

[1] This word is used for convenience. Meinhof points out that there are, strictly speaking, no prepositions in Bantu, the words serving as such being really pronouns or possessive particles—except *na* 'with,' which might equally well be rendered 'and,' and called a conjunction.

[2] The alternative forms *a, ab, e, ex* are not variations in the sense here intended.

CASES: THE LOCATIVE 73

of it meant 'of,' and—reminded of the way in which *di* ('of') combines with the article in Italian (*del, dello, della, dei, degli, delle*)[1] concluded that the other part of the word might be an article. The combination seemed to carry out that reversal of European rules which had struck him so forcibly in connection with the prefixes, and the conclusion he came to was a very natural one under the circumstances and does credit to his linguistic insight. He might have represented the whole thing in a diagram, thus:

$$D-EL$$

$$W-A$$

—the Italian article *il* having originally been the Latin demonstrative pronoun *ille*, while *u* (which becomes *w* before *a*) is the prefix-pronoun of its class. With nouns of other classes, we should have *ya, la, za*, etc., just as in Italian with a feminine singular noun we

[1] This combination (the 'partitive article') is better seen in Italian than in either French or Spanish, where it is not carried through consistently (*du, de la, des; del, de la, de los*). In Italian too, not only *di* and *a*, but the other prepositions *con, in, per*, are combined with the article and constitute something like a declension.

have *della*, with a masculine plural *dei-* or *degli*, and so on. But *wa* fulfils no function of the article as we understand it, the pronoun in it being purely representative and not demonstrative.

This *possessive particle* is closely connected with the *possessive pronoun*, to be considered in a later chapter. But I mention it here, because the next point can only be illustrated by the help of possessive pronouns in European languages. In English, as we know, possessive pronouns are among the few parts of speech which have grammatical gender—which show by their form the sex of the nouns they represent—or the absence of it. Possessive pronouns agree in this respect with the noun which stands for the *possessor :* ' his mother,' ' her father,'—while the reverse is the case in French : *son père, sa mère*, leave the sex of the possessor quite uncertain, though beginners insist on translating ' her father ' by *sa père*.

Bantu nouns follow, with a difference, the French principle ; ' the man's child ' is in Zulu : *um-ntwana wendoda* (for *wa-indoda*) and not, as it would be if the concord followed the class of the possessor : *um-ntwana yendoda* (*ya-indoda*).

I say 'nouns' advisedly, for we shall see, when we come to treat of them in the proper place, that possessive *pronouns* agree both ways: that is, the first part follows the class of the thing possessed, the last that of the possessor.

It is scarcely necessary to say, after giving the above examples, that the thing possessed always precedes the possessor, as in French (*l'enfant de l'homme*). In English, we have it both ways, according as we use the inflected possessive or not—'the man's child,' and 'the child of the man.' The Sudan languages[1] put the possessor first and say 'man child'— having nothing corresponding to article or inflection, though sometimes a particle indicating ownership is suffixed to the first word.

There is no way of showing whether a noun is subject or object except by its position in the sentence, the subject coming before the verb and the object after,[2] just as in English.

---

[1] See *Language Families of Africa*, p. 40.

[2] Arabic, which uses case-inflections, usually puts the verb first, the subject next, and then the object; but as the two latter are sufficiently distinguished by their endings, it really does not matter in what order they are put.

Sometimes, where there can be no possibility of mistake, inversion is used for the sake of emphasis—as by us in rhetoric or poetry; but the outsider had better not meddle with figures of speech such as this, and it is scarcely necessary to mention them in a general outline.

We now come to the Locative; and this has to be treated under two different headings: the locative formed by prefixed prepositions and the suffixed locative in -*ni*, which seems to be a later development. There are not many Bantu prepositions, as we shall see in the chapter on Particles: the principal ones, which (or, at any rate, traces of them), are found in every Bantu language, are *pa*, *ku*, *mu*.

Pa, roughly speaking, conveys the notion of 'at' or 'upon'; *mu*, of 'in,' and *ku*, of 'motion to and from,' though it sometimes has the meaning of 'outside.' It also serves as the sign of the infinitive; but here its function, if not its origin, is different, so that we are quite right in treating 15 and 16 as separate classes.[1]

---

[1] Meinhof thinks that the use of *ku* as infinitive prefix was a later development from its locative function.

CASES: THE LOCATIVE

Pa, ku, mu are the prefixes of Classes 16, 17, 18 respectively; but they differ in one important respect from the other prefixes. These, as a rule (with the exception, in some cases, of augmentatives and diminutives), are attached to the bare root, which cannot be used without them, while *pa, ku, mu* are prefixed to the whole noun, root and all, as in Nyanja *pa-chilindo*, 'at the look-out,'[1] *ku-chilindo, mu chilindo;* not *pa-lindo, ku-lindo, mu-lindo*. But in all other respects they are true prefixes and take their own concord, entirely superseding the one properly belonging to their noun when used by itself. For instance, *chilindo*, being a noun of the seventh class, would take the possessive particle, *cha* and pronoun *chi*:

Chi-lindo ch-a Pembereka chi-ri cha-bwino: (The) watch-hut of Pembereka it is good.

But *Pa-chilindo pa Pembsreka pa-li pa-bwino* would mean, 'At Pembereka's watch-hut it is (a) good (place).'

So we may have also:

[1] *Chilindo*, also called *nsanja* ('staging' or 'platform') is a small temporary structure raised on poles, open or roofed, erected in the fields so that watchers can overlook the ripening crops and scare away birds, monkeys or other depredators.

Ku-chilindo kwa Pembereka ku-li kwa-bwino, with much the same meaning as the last sentence, except that the place is thought of from the standpoint of one who is at a distance from it and going, or thinking of going, towards it; while *m'chilindo* (for *mu-chilindo*) *mwa Pembereka mu-li mwa-bwino*, means: 'the inside of Pembereka's watch-hut is good.'

Some nouns, as *kamwa*, 'mouth,' are never found without the locative prefix—we have *pa-kamwa*, *ku-kamwa* and *m-kamwa*, but never *kamwa* alone. The word is evidently connected with *mwa* 'drink,'—perhaps *ka* is the prefix of a lost class distinct from the diminutive.

Here are some further illustrations, also from Nyanja:

A-li-ku-nka ku munda kwa Champiti: he is
  going to (the) garden of Champiti.
Ku-mudzi kwanu ku-li kwa-bwino: at our
  village it is good.
*Ku-Mlanje ku-li mpunga, koma ku-Kabula
  kuno ku-libe:* at Mlanje there is rice but
  at Kabula here there is none.

Kuno, 'here,' is really a demonstrative, agreeing not with '*Kabula*,' but with '*ku-Kabula*,' as though, instead of 'here at Kabula,' one had said 'at this at-Kabula.'

A mistake to be found in some of the older grammars is illustrated in Steere's *Handbook of Swahili* (p. 22) by the statement that a class (the seventh, in his arrangement) contains 'the 'one word *mahali*, place or places, which re- 'quires special forms in all adjectives and pro- 'nouns.' *Mahali* is really a borrowed Arabic word, which is sometimes Bantuized (oftener, I think, at Zanzibar than at Mombasa) by substituting *pa* for the first syllable, as if the latter were a removable prefix, and so making it into a noun of the sixteenth class. Steere mentions the locative concord a little later on, but does not call it a class (though including it in his 'Table of Concords'). The change undergone by the Swahili locative (which we shall discuss presently) has so obscured the relation between it and *mahali* or *pahali* that without a fuller comparative study than was possible when Steere wrote, it was not likely to be perceived.

Several languages have a word for 'place' which is either *pa-ntu* or some cognate form and may have the same root as *mu-ntu*. In Ganda, where primitive Bantu *p* becomes *w*, we have the nearly obsolete *wantu*, which was at first thought to constitute a class by itself.[1] But *wa*, as well as *mu* and *ku*, is prefixed to other nouns, which are also used as adverbs: *wa-nsi*, 'the ground' or 'below'; *mu-nda*, 'the inside,' 'or within.' There is also a prefix *e*, not generally found among the locatives, but which may possibly have some connection with the peculiar Zulu form.

In Pokomo we have *fantu* (bilabial *f*, for *p*), in Giryama *hatu*, elsewhere *hantu*, *handu*, etc. (A great many East African languages substitute *h* for *p*, except in certain particular cases: *e.g.*, Giryama has *hendza*, 'love,' for Swahili *penda*.)

Some languages have this word also with the prefix *ku*: *kuntu*, *kundu*; but *mu-ntu*, *mu-ndu*, if used at all is less common, perhaps because it would have the same form as the word for 'person.'[2]

---

[1] 'The tenth class contains the single word *wantu*, "place"; this word is obsolete except in the single expression *buliwantu*, "everywhere." But its influence in the language is great, because adjectives, pronouns, verbs and adverbs are all formed with the prefix *wa-*, referring to this disused word, *e.g.*, *wano wa-lungu*, "this is a pretty spot." '—Pilkington. *Wano walungu* exactly corresponds with Nyanja *pano* (*pa li*) *pabwino*.

[2] In Zigula 'the prefix appropriate to the word *hantu* "place" is *ha*, and as it belongs exclusively to this word, its mere presence is sufficient to indicate that *place* is the

Kongo has *vuma* (v for p), *kuma*, *muma*, as three different forms of the word for 'place.' These take the locative concords as we find them elsewhere, but other nouns preceded by the corresponding prepositions keep their concords instead of taking a locative concord. *Muma* seems sometimes to be treated as the plural of *vuma* : this may arise from a confusion of the *m*- with the sixth prefix (as though it were contracted from *ma-uma*) and possibly indicates that the whole system is dying out in some of the western Bantu languages. Bentley remarks concerning *vuma:* 'In most Bantu 'languages a corresponding word for place 'will be found standing in a separate class of 'its own, and wearing a prefix *va, pa,* or 'something similar.' This is the same mistake adverted to just now, and no doubt one reason for it is that the prefixes of these words are not, as a rule, removable; but they really come under the same heading as the locatives

substantive referred to, so that the word *hantu* is often omitted. The same rule refers to the more indefinite *ku-ntu* and its appropriate syllable *ku-*, and also to *mu-ntu, mu-*.'—Kisbey.

Archdeacon Woodward, though mentioning the *mu*-concord, does not refer to the word *mu-ntu,* 'in a place,' which, however, certainly occurs in the Likoma dialect of Nyanja.

which are made up as wanted and simply put the preposition before the ordinary noun-prefix. We draw a distinction between the two—but the Bantu speaker feels none.

We now come to the suffixed locative in *-ni*, which seems to be confined to Bleek's South-Eastern Branch of the Bantu family and to a few languages in East Africa, of which Swahili, Bondei, Hehe, and Makua are the chief, if not the only ones—and in Makua it is combined with the prefixed locative—*mashi* = water; *va-mashi-ni* = at the water; *m-mashi-ni* = in the water.

But the prefix has quite disappeared in Swahili, and the locative is simply formed by suffixing *-ni*, which may mean 'in,' 'at,' 'on,' 'from,' 'to,' etc.

nyumba-ni = in the house. The accent is always
mji-ni   ' = to the town. shifted forward by the
kiti-ni   = on the chair.   locative suffix, see p. 15.
etc.

But the concord differs according to what is implied in the suffix. '*In* my house,' is *nyumbani mwangu*, '*to* my house' *nyumbani kwangu;* 'he is sitting on my chair,' *anakaa kitini pangu*, and so on.

CASES: THE LOCATIVE

A-li-anguka mlangoni pangu.
He fell down at my door.
Atakwenda shambani kwake.
He will go to his plantation.
Amelala nyumbani mwako.
He is lying down in your house.

This concord is not found in Zulu, where, however, the rules for applying the suffix are not quite so simple as in Swahili. We may suppose that it originally had the form *-ini*: this is rendered probable by the effect it has on the final vowel of the noun. *A* becomes *e*, *e* and *i* remain unchanged; *o* becomes *we*, and *u*, *wi* (or sometimes *i*, eliding the final vowel instead of changing it into *w*). The initial vowel is changed into *e* (in a few cases, in 11 and 14, into *o*), for which I can suggest no reason, though it may possibly have some connection with the locative prefix which appears in Ganda as *e-*.

intaba	= mountain	makes	*entabeni*.
izwe	= country	,,	*ezweni*.
isi-hlalo	= seat	,,	*esihlalweni*.
in-dhlu	= house	,,	*endhlwini* or *endhlini*.

In Chwana this locative is found in the form *ng*, as in the well-known place-names Mafeking and Shoshong. The same termination is used to form a kind of participle, to which we shall refer later on, in connection with the relative pronoun and the verb. In Ronga and other languages of the Delagoa Bay district, the locative suffix is *-ni*, though the final *i* is frequently dropped: *tikwen*, 'in the country,' from *tiko*.

The preposition *ku* still exists in all these languages (in Chwana under the form χo), but *pa* and *mu* are no longer found independently. That they did exist in Zulu is shown by the adverbs *pansi*[1], *pezulu* (= *pa* + *izulu* = 'on the sky' = 'above'), *pa-kati*, 'in the midst,' *pa-ndhle*, 'outside,' etc. When used as prepositions these are followed by *kwa*, as *pakati kwendhlu* (*kwa-indhlu*), 'inside the house,'—which properly, should only go with *ku-* but has quite usurped the place of *pa-* and *mu-*. The latter, however, survives in Chwana, in combination with the suffix, as *mo motseng*, 'in the village' (*motse*).

Some nouns whose presence in the *ku-* class

---

[1] *-nsi* is no longer used in Zulu as a noun, but it is found in Swahili as *nti*, *nchi*, meaning 'land,' 'earth.' Instead of the adverb *pa-nsi*, 'down,' 'below,' *ti-ni* or *chi-ni* is used. In Chwana the root and prefix (*ha-tse*) have become so closely welded together that they are looked on as inseparable and have been given a fresh prefix, *le-hatse* 5.

CASES: THE LOCATIVE

is difficult to understand and is rendered still more perplexing by the fact that they have a plural in *ma-*, are to be accounted for as Locatives. The Nyanja *kutu*, 'ear,' pl. *ma-kutu*, might be taken if it stood alone as a fifth-class noun which has dropped its prefix *li-*; but it cannot be dissociated from the Herero *oku-twi*, pl. *oma-twi*, and Ndonga *oko-tshwi*, pl. *oma-kotshwi*. Properly, the word means 'to the ear,' 'the place of the ear,' and then, the word being generally used with the locative prefix, the separate nature of the latter was forgotten, as was the case with the Chwana *hatse*. The same applies to the Herero *oku-oko*, 'arm,' pl. *oma-oko;* Kongo *k-oko*, pl. *m-oko*. Other examples in Herero are *oku-rama*, 'leg'; *oku-ti*, 'veld, open country,' *oku-ruo*, 'hearth,' *oku-apa*, 'armpit.' It is evident that all these may have a locative sense, and that, wherever similar words are found, they should be placed in Class 17. The uncertainty about the prefixes shows that their original meaning is almost, if not quite forgotten, and that they tend more and more to be regarded as part of the stem.

CHAPTER VI

THE PRONOUN

The Pronoun is one of the most important features of the Bantu Languages. I do not even add 'next to the Prefixes,' because the two are so intimately associated that it is difficult to say which should have the priority.

It used to be thought that the Pronouns and Prefixes were, in the last resort, identical, whatever their origin—whether they were nouns which had lost their distinctive character and become mere formative elements (like the suffixes of 'king-dom,' 'man-hood,' 'lord-ship,' which have long ceased to have any independent value)—or whether they already, even as separate words, had the force of pronouns. (Bleek's discussion of this subject—*Comparative Grammar*, pp. 123-131—should be carefully read, though time has shown that it requires some modification.)

Meinhof (*Grundzüge*, p. 35) points out that

the prefix and pronoun are not identical, but that the latter is really the demonstrative particle, discussed in Chapter III., which became incorporated with the prefix and was then, in many cases, lost, but survives, *e.g.* in Zulu, as the 'initial vowel.' It was, as we have seen, originally γ*a*, but assimilated its vowel to that of the prefix which followed it.

Thus we have:

3 γ*a*+*mu*=γ*umu*=*umu*, and the pronoun γ*u*=*gu, u*
4 γ*a*+*mi*=γ*imi*, =*imi* ,, ,, ,, γ*i*=*gi, i*
6 γ*a*+*ma*=γ*ama*=*ama* ,, ,, ,, γ*a*=*ga, ya, a*
9 γ*a*+*ni*=γ*ini*=*in-* ,, ,, ,, γγ*i*=*yi, i*

Where the prefix does not begin with a nasal, *e.g.*, in 2, 5, 7, 8, the demonstrative (or 'article') disappears without leaving a trace, and the noun-prefix only remains, to serve as pronoun—so we get the pronouns *ba, ki, li*, etc.[1]

---

[1] Class 1 has been omitted here because, as Meinhof says, 'it contains all sorts of irregularities, as is not surprising in a class so much used.' One would expect its pronoun to be γ*u*, like that of Class 3, and in fact *u* and *o*, which are found in Zulu and Chwana, evidently come from that form. But the Swahili *yu* cannot have come from it, so Meinhof thinks there must have been a second pronoun γγ*u*, of which he explains the formation on p. 36 of the work cited in the text, whence the substance of this note, and of the paragraphs imme-

THE PRONOUN

This simplest form of the pronoun is never —or, if at all, very seldom—used by itself, but is always attached to a verb, or to an adjective with the verb 'to be' understood. We shall refer to it, henceforward, as the 'Inseparable Pronoun.' Its use as the 'copula'—where, in some cases, it assumes a different form—will be discussed in the next chapter.

The following Table shows the 'Inseparable Pronoun' in our eight typical languages, as compared with the noun-prefixes. Some languages—especially Duala and Kongo—tend to use the unaltered prefixes of all classes before verbs by a merely mechanical repetition, having lost their feeling for the pronoun as such. This explains the occurrence of such forms as *mi-* and *ma-*, where we should expect *i-* and *a-*.

The pronouns of the first and second

---

diately preceding it in the text, is taken. As for the alternative pronoun *a*, which has almost displaced *yu* in Swahili, it is no doubt a remnant of the unaltered *γa*; but it is not clear why it did not assimilate its vowel to the first prefix, or why, in Herero and Chwana, for instance, *a* is sometimes used in dependent sentences, while in principal sentences we have *u* or its equivalent. This last fact may possibly be connected with the function of *a* as relative particle.

persons have, of course, no noun-prefixes corresponding to them and stand outside the framework of the classes. They are therefore placed by themselves at the head of each column in the Table.

The use of these pronouns is illustrated in Chapter II. They are used both as subject and object; the first class and the second person, singular and plural, are in almost all cases the only ones with separate objective forms. And, even of these, the second person plural is not common. (Swahili has *-wa-*, Zigula, *-mi-*, Ganda, *-ba-*). Whatever other particles are prefixed to the verb-root, the object-pronoun must always come next it.

E.g., *u-ya-ngi-bona* (Zulu), 'he sees me'; *wa-ku-tshaya* (Zulu), 'he beat thee'; *a-li-m-fundisha* (Swahili), 'he taught him.'

Duala and Kongo have no object-pronoun before the verb—though it exists in some cognate dialects such as Isubu. The object is expressed by a separable pronoun following the verb.

The reflexive pronoun, which is alike for all persons and numbers, is placed in the same position as the object-pronoun. In Zulu it is *zi*, as in *uku-zi-tanda*, 'to love one's self'; in

	Zulu		Chwana		Herero		Nyanja		Swahili		Ganda		Gisu		Kongo	
1st Pers. 2nd „	Si. ngi- „ u- Pref.	Pl. si- „ ni- Pron.	Si. ke- „ o- Pref.	Pl. re- „ le- Pron.	Si. mbi- „ u- Pref.	Pl. tu- „ mu- Pron.	Si. ndi- „ u- Pref.	Pl. ti- „ mu- Pron.	Si. ni- „ u- Pref.	Pl. tu- „ m- Pron.	Si. n- „ o- Pref.	Pl. n- „ mu- Pron.	Si. n- „ u- Pref.	Pl. ku- „ mu- Pron.	Si. n- „ o-, u- Pref.	Pl. tu- „ nu- Pron.
Class																
1	umu-	u-	mo-	o-	omu-	u-	m-	a-	m-	a-	omu-	a-	umu-	a-, u-	m-	o-
2	aba-	ba-	va-	va-	ova-	ve-	a-	a-	wa-	wa-	aba-	ba-	baba-	ba-	a-	ba-, be-
3	umu-	u-	mo-	o-	omu-	u-	m-	u-	n-	u-	omu-	gu-	kumu-	ku-	mu-	mu-
4	imi-	i-	me-	e-	omi-	vi-	mi-	i-	mi-	i-	emi-	gi-	kimi-	ki-	mi-	mi-
5	i(li)-	li-	le-	le-	e-	ri-	li-	li-	—	li-	eri-	li-	li-	li-	di-	di-
6	ama-	a-	ma-	a-	oma-	ye-	ma-	ya-	ma-	ya-	ama-	ga-	kama-	ka-	ma-	ma-, me-
7	isi-	si-	se-	se-	otyi-	tyi-	chi-	chi-	ki-	ki-	eki-	ki-	ki-	ki-	ki-	ki-
8	izi-	zi-	di-	di-	ovi-	vi-	zi-	zi-	vi-	vi-	ebi-	bi-	bi-	bi-	yi-, i-	yi-, yi-
9	in-	i-	—	e-	o-	i-	n-	i-	n-	i-	en-	e-	in-	i-	n-	i-, yi-
10	izin-	zi-	di-	di-	odho-	dhe-	zi-	zi-	n-	zi-	en-	zi-	tsin-	tsi-	n-	ji-, za-
11	u(lu)-	lu-	lo-	lo-	oru-	ru-	u-	u-	u-	—	olu-	lu-	lu-	lu-	lu-	lu-
12	—	—	—	—	otu-	tu-	—	—	—	—	otu-	tu-	—	—	tu-	tu-
13	—	—	—	—	oka-	ke-	ka-	ka-	—	—	aka-	ka-	ka-	ka-	—	—
14	ubu-	bu-	vo-	vo-	ou-	u-	bu-	bu-	u-	u-	obu-	bu-	ku-	bu-	u-	u-
15	uku-	ku-	χo-	χo-	oku-	ku-	ku-	ku-	ku-	ku-	oku-	ku-	ku-	ku-	kw-	ku-
16	—	—	ha-	ha-	opo-	pe-	pa-	pa-	—	pa-	wa-	wa-	ha-	ha-	—	—
17	—	—	χo-	χo-	oko-	ku-	ku-	ku-	—	ku-	ku-	ku-	ku-	ku-	—	—
18	—	—	mo-	mo-	omu-	mu-	mu-	mu-	—	mu-	mu-	mu-	—	—	—	—

Nyanja, *dzi*; in Swahili *ji*; in Herero *ri*; elsewhere *i*, *yi*, etc. Meinhof thinks the original form was γî.

There are longer forms of the pronouns, which can stand by themselves and need not be used with the verb except for emphasis. The different languages form these in various ways, and in some of them it is difficult to trace any resemblance to the Inseparable Pronoun. In fact they are built up rather on what is called the 'prepositional form' of the pronouns (though some of them depart considerably even from this), which, accordingly, it will be better to take first.

This is a form which is *suffixed* to prepositions: expressions like 'with me'; 'to him,' etc., being treated as one word. There is a form for every class—just as there is of the Inseparable Pronoun—as well as for the First and Second Persons. Thus we have (in several languages) *nami* ($= na + mi$), 'with me,' 'and I,' *kumi*, 'to me,' etc. These forms are also used in connection with Relative Pronouns, as we shall see presently.

Like the Inseparable Pronoun they are never found alone—if not attached to prepositions, they are suffixed to the possessive particle, in a way which will be explained presently.

The separable, or independent, pronouns are usually—if not always—built up out of these forms. They exist in most languages for the three persons singular and plural, and, in some, for all the classes. But some, like Swahili and Nyanja, have none for any classes after the first and second, using the demonstrative pronouns instead.

The Possessive Pronoun consists of two parts and has to be considered under two aspects.

It is made up of:

(1) The possessive particle of *the class to which the thing possessed belongs* (*wa, ba, ya,* etc.), and
(2) Either (*a*) a special pronoun-root for the first and second persons, or (*b*) the 'prepositional form' of pronoun indicating *the class of the possessor*. The first class is usually exceptional in this respect, having a different suffix for the Possessive.

We will now take the six possessive pronouns of the three persons singular and plural in the same eight languages as before. Chwana seems to be exceptional in having some of the

	Zulu	Chwana	Herero	Nyanja	Swahili	Ganda	Gisu
1stPers. 2nd ,,	Si. Pl. -mi, -ti -we, -ni	Si. Pl. -no, -ro -o, -lo	Si. Pl. -ami,-ete -ove,-ene	Si. Pl. -ne, -fe -we, -nu	Si. Pl. -mi, -swi -we,-nyi	Si. Pl. -nge, -fe -we,-mwe	Si. Pl. -se, -fe -wo,-nywe
Class 1	-ye	-e	-e	-ye	-ye	-ye	-ye
2	-bo	-vo	-awo	-o	-o	-bo	-we
3	-wo	-o	-awo	-wo	-wo, -o	-gwo	-kwo
4	-yo	-yo	-avyo	-yo	-yo	-gyo	-kyo
5	-lo	-lo	-aro	-lo	-lo	-lyo	-lyo
6	-wo	-o	-ao	-wo	-wo	-go	-ko
7	-so	-so, -sho	-atyo	-cho	-cho	-kyo	-kyo
8	-ze	-cho	-avyo	-zo	-vyo	-byo	-byo
9	-yo	-yo	-ayo	-yo	-yo	-yo	-yo
10	-zo	-cho	-adho	-zo	-zo	-zo	-tso
11	-lo	-lo	-arwo	-wo	-wo	-lwo	-lwo
12	—	—	-atwo	-to	—	-two	—
13	—	—	-ako	-ko	—	-ko	-ko
14	-bo	-vyo,-yo	-awo	-bo	-wo	-bwo	-bwo
15	-ko	-χo	-akwo	-ko	-ko	-kwo	-kwo
16	—	—	-apo	-po	-po	-wo	-ho
17	—	—	-akwo	-ko	-ko	-kwo	—
18	—	—	-amo	-mo	-mo	-mu	—

This form of pronoun does not appear to be used in Kongo.

SUBSTANTIVE PRONOUNS.

	Zulu		Chwana		Herero		Ganda		Kongo	
	Si.	Pl.	Si.	Pl.	Si.	Pl.	Si.	Pl.	Si.	Pl.
1stPers.	mina,	tina	nna	rona	owami, owete		nze	fwe	mono	yeto
2nd ,,	wena	nina	wona	lona	ove, owena		gwe	mwe	nge	yeno
Class 1	yena		ene		eye		ye		yandi	
2	bona		vone		owo		bo		yau	
3	wona		one		owo		gwe		wau	
4	yona		eone		ovio		gye		miau	
5	lona		yone		oro		lye		diau	
6	wona		one		owo		ge		mau	
7	sona		shone		otyo		kye		kiau	
8	zona		chone		ovio		bye		yau	
9	yona		eone		oyo		ye		yau	
10	zona		chone		odho		ze		zau	
11	l(w)ona		lone		oruo		lwe		luau	
12	—		—		otuo		twe		twau	
13	—		—		oko		ke		—	
14	bona		yone		owo		bwe		wau	
15	kona		χone		okuo		kwe		kwau	
16	—		—		opo		we		vau	
17	—		—		oko		kwe		kwau	
18	—		—		omo		mwe		mwau	
19	—		—		—		—		fiau	

Nyanja, Swahili and Gisu use the Demonstratives for all classes but the first.

Nyanja. 1st Pers. Si. ine 2nd iwe 3rd iye
Swahili. ,, ,, mimi ,, wewe ,, yeye
Gisu. ,, ,, ise ,, iwe ,, niye

Nyanja. 1st Pers. Pl. ife 2nd inu 3rd awo
Swahili. ,, ,, sisi ,, ninyi ,, wao
Gisu. ,, ,, ifwe ,, inywe ,, abo

forms reduplicated (-*aχaχo* instead of -*aχo*=*ako*). There are also forms in some dialects which are simply these separable pronouns with the possessive particle prefixed to them— -*a rona*, ' our ' (lit. ' of us ') ; -*a lona*, ' your ' ; -*a vona*, ' their.'

	Zulu	Chwana	Herero	Nyanja	Swahili	Ganda	Gisu	Kongo
MY	-ami	{-ame / -aka}	-andye	-anga	-angu	-ange	-ase	-ame
THY	-ako	-aχaχo	-oye	-ako	-ako	-o	-owo	-aku
HIS	-ake	-aχaχwe	-e	-ache	-ake	-e	-ewe	-andi
OUR	-etu	-eshu	-etu	-atu	-etu	-afwe	-efe	-eto
YOUR	-enu	-eno	-enu	-anu	-enu	-amwe	-enywe	-eno
THEIR	-abo	-avo	-awo	-ao	-ao	-awe	-awe	-au

These, if the thing possessed is of the first class, have the possessive particle *wa* prefixed to them : *wami, wame* (some Chwana books print *o ame*), *wandye, wanga, wangu*, etc.

In Zulu, ' my child' is *umntwana wami ;* in Nyanja, *mwana wanga*, and so on. ' My children,' would be *abantwana bami, ana anga ;* ' my village,' *umuzi wami, mudzi wanga,* ' my country,' *izwe lami, dziko langa.* There is no need to multiply examples.

In all these pronouns, the second part of the

word does not vary, but *if the possessor is of the third person and of any class except the first*, the suffix has often to change as well as the prefix.

In Zulu, *ihashi lake* is 'his horse,' supposing that 'his' represents a noun of the first class—say *umu-ntu*, *um-fana*, etc. But it might stand for a fifth-class noun: *i-Bunu*, 'a Boer,'—or a seventh: *isi-hambi*, 'a traveller,'—or a ninth: *in-doda*, 'a man'; *in-kosi*, 'a chief.' In these cases we must say:

>   His (the Boer's)   horse = *ihashi lalo*.
>   „ (the traveller's)   „   = *ihashi laso*.
>   „ (the chief's)   „   = *ihashi layo*.

That is, the first part of the word is the possessive particle agreeing with the thing possessed, and the second the pronoun agreeing with the possessor.

In this way, the number of classes multiplied by itself will give the number of possible possessives—or would, if some of the forms did not coincide, so as to make them less numerous. There is a neat diagram of Gisu forms on p. 34 of the Rev. J. B. Purvis's *Lumasaba Grammar*. We need not give a table, as, the principle being known, it is quite easy to combine any form wanted from the previous tables.

The double agreement seems to be confined to the more archaic Bantu languages. It is found, as we have just seen, in Zulu and Gisu; also in Chwana, Herero, Ganda, Kinga and others; but not in Swahili, Nyanja or Kongo.

Demonstrative Pronouns.—These are usually three in number; one, equivalent to 'this,' denoting what is near the speaker; a second, what is somewhat farther off (in some cases, what has been referred to before); and the third, what is at a distance. They are built up, in different ways, from the Inseparable Pronoun; a very common modification is that the first demonstrative ends in *u*, which is changed in the second to *o*, while the third is formed by suffixing another syllable to the first, or to its latter half. This process is most clearly seen in Swahili and Nyanja. Sometimes the first half appears to be taken, as in Kongo (*o-yu*, and *o-na*, *a-ya*, and *a-na*). *Li* (Ganda) and *la* (Gisu) may be the same element as *le*, which, Meinhof thinks, may be connected with the root *-le*, *-de*, 'long,' and so suggest distance. This and other points relating to the origin of the demonstrative, which it is no part of my plan to discuss, may be found in the second chapter of the *Grundzüge einer vergleichenden Grammatik der Bantu-sprachen.*

	Zulu	Chwana	Herero	Nyanja	Swahili	Ganda	Gisu	Kongo
THIS	lo	e n	ingui	uyu	hu-yu	ono	uno	oyu
THAT	lowo	eouo	ngo	uyo	hu-yo	oyo	uyo	oyo
THAT YONDER	lowaya	eole	nguini	udya	yu-le	oli	ula	ona
THESE	laba	vano	imba	awa	ha-wa	bano	bano	aya
THOSE	labo	vauo	mbo	awo	ha-wo	abo	abo	owo
THOSE YONDER	labaya	vale	mbeni	adya	wa-le	bali	bala	ana

There are other demonstrative forms built up from these—*e.g.*, the two 'emphatic demonstratives' in Kongo, which we need not notice here.

In Nyanja we have two other demonstrative roots which may be mentioned here, because they are used in a way which illustrates the transition from the demonstrative to the relative. They are -*mwe*, 'the same,' and -*mene*, 'this same,' 'that same,' 'that very one,' etc., with their compounds, formed by suffixes corresponding to the three degrees of the demonstrative already given. -*Mene*, when used without these suffixes, simply means 'who,' or 'which,'—as

> *mu-ntu a-mene a-na-gwira nchito.*
> The man who did work.
> *zi-ntu zi-mene zi-na-ni-sautsa.*
> The things which grieved me.

But

muntu ameneyu = this same man.
muntu ameneyo and *amene udya* = that same man.
chi-ntu chi-mene-chi = this same thing.
kasu li-mene-lo = that same hoe, etc., etc.

We shall return to these two pronouns in the course of the next section.

A special form of demonstrative—sometimes called 'adverbial demonstratives,' and meaning 'Here he is,' 'here they are,'—is especially noticeable in Zulu—*nangu, nanku, naba*, etc. They need not be further noticed here.

The Relative Pronoun.—This constitutes somewhat of a difficulty in many Bantu languages, though some cannot be said to have any relative at all. The relative, as we understand it, hardly belongs to the earlier stages of speech. It implies a co-ordination of ideas—a fitting of separate notions together, whereas children, and primitive people, think of one thing at a time and express it in a sentence by itself. The child will say, 'I saw a man. The man had a dog,'—putting the two ideas, as it were, side by side. The next step is—'I saw a man; *he* had a dog'; and then we come to—'I saw a man *who* had a dog." In the second case, we have two co-ordinate sentences, of equal importance; in the third, a principal and a subordinate sentence, which together make up a complex one. Many Bantu languages cannot form complex sentences at all, and those which can, only do so to a limited extent.

In Nyanja there is no true relative. The typical form of sentence runs thus :

> *muntu a-na-dwala dzulo wafa.*
> The man (who) was ill yesterday is dead:

—literally, 'The man, he was ill yesterday: he died.' But, to make the reference of the second clause more definite, a demonstrative is inserted. One could say, *uyo wafa*, or *udya wafa;* but more commonly either *-mwe* or *-mene* is employed.

> *muntu yemwe anadwala dzulo wafa.* Or
> *muntu amene anadwala dzulo wafa.*
> *mbalame zimene zinadia mbeu za-gwidwa.*
> 'The birds which ate the seeds have been caught.'

Pamene (Class 18), 'the place which,' is used for 'where'—and, by an extension of meaning, for 'when.'

In other languages the relative is rendered by a particle prefixed to the verb and the 'prepositional form' of a pronoun placed after it. The simplest form of this is found in Swahili: *a-sema-ye* (or, in Mombasa dialect, *a-sema-e*), 'he who speaks'; *li-anguka-lo*, 'that (fifth class) which falls'; *ki-waka-cho*, 'that (seventh class) which burns.' This, when analysed, is seen to be really equivalent to 'he speaks (that is) he'; 'it falls (that is) it.' This seems to be nearer the mark than to speak of a 'relative pronoun expressed by a syllable formed of the letter -o, preceded by the initial consonants proper to its antecedent' (Steere's *Exercises*, p. 22); but the construction is exceedingly difficult to make clear, except in the light of comparative grammar.

When the relative is the *object*, it may be expressed by using the same form, but inserting the proper object-pronoun before the verb and making the suffixed pronoun agree with the object, not the subject.

Thus '(the knife) which I want,' is (*kisu*) *ni-ki-taka-cho*—literally, 'I it want (that is) it.'

-Po, *-ko*, and *-mo*, as relatives, indicate the notion of 'where' or 'when'—*ni-lala-po*, 'where (or when) I sleep'; *a-taka-po*, 'when he wishes.' As we see, this relative is intimately combined with the verb—so it is in many other cases; and this once more illustrates the difficulty of applying our received grammatical classification and arrangement. In Steere's *Handbook of Swahili*, the treatment of the verb has in some degree to be anticipated in the chapter on pronouns, while that on the verb has to include the application of the relative pronoun to certain tenses.

While the use of the accepted nomenclature is, up to a certain point, convenient and even necessary; we must never allow ourselves to think of its definitions as rigid boundaries, as though words could be isolated in closed compartments, like specimens in a museum. This applies even in English: if children are taught, for instance, in parsing a sentence like 'Tell him that he must not do that,' to call the first 'that' a conjunction and the second a pronoun, they will be apt to lose sight of the connection between the two. But if we treat grammar as a kind of unchanging framework

THE PRONOUN

into which every language must be fitted, we get such absurdities as conjugating a verb 'to have' which does not exist, or 'declining' a Bantu noun, which, as we have already seen, cannot be done.

A more elaborate form of the Swahili relative combines the two pronouns with a tense-particle as well as the verb and thus forms three tenses; in the simpler form no tense-distinction is possible.

Present: *a-na-ye-piga, u-na-o-piga, li-na-lo-piga.*
'he (it) who (which) strikes.'

Past: *a-li-ye-piga, u-li-o-piga, li-li-lo-piga.*
'he (it) who (which) struck.'

Future: *a-taka-ye-piga, u-taka-o-piga, li-taka-lo-piga.*
'he (it) who (which) will strike.'

Na, li, and *taka* must be reserved for discussion in the chapter on verbs.

If the relative is the object, the pronouns are changed as before indicated, the only difference being displacement of the suffix (since the object-pronoun must always come next to the verb-root).

'The thing which I like.'
Kitu ni-na-cho-ki-penda (*penda* = like).

'The house which we bought.'
Nyumba tu-li-yo-i-nunua (*nunua* = buy).

In neither of these forms do we find anything like a special relative particle, different from the pronouns which, as has been said, may be met with in other connections. In Zulu, we have two such particles: *a-*, which is prefixed and usually combined with the Separable Pronoun as subject, and *-yo*, which is suffixed —in all cases, whatever the class of the antecedent. Perhaps we can trace a similar tendency at work elsewhere, for in Zanzibar Swahili 'there is a disposition to make *-o* 'the general relative' (Steere), as *alio-* for *aliye-*, *lilio-* for *lililo-*, etc.

Examples of the Zulu relative are:

umuntu o-bona-yo (for *a-u-bonayo*) = 'a man who sees.'

aba-ntu a-ba-kala-yo = 'people who cry out.'

indhlela e-lungile-yo (for *a-i-lungile-yo*) = 'the right path.'

(*Lungile* is the perfect of the verb *lunga*, 'to be straight' or 'right').

The object is inserted in the same way as already shown:

umuntu a-m-bonayo[1] = 'a man whom he sees.'

We shall again have to notice this relative particle *a* when we come to the Adjectives.

In Ganda, the principle of the Relative formation is that of prefixing *a-* to whatever other pronoun comes before the verb. Thus *abantu a-ba-laba*, 'people who see.' (The singular, *omu-ntu a-laba*, is indistinguishable from that which means 'a man sees,' because *a + a* coalesces with *a*.) This prefix appears as *o* or *e* according to the class of the subject: *omu-li o-gu-gwa*, 'the tree which falls'; *emi-ti e-gi-gwa*, 'the trees which fall.'

Chwana indicates the relative by suffixing the locative termination to the verb, without any change in the pronoun.

'He who has come'—*eo o tsileng*, (*tsile*, perf of *tsa*) this one he has-come.'

Perhaps the most literal rendering of *tsileng* would be 'is-at-having-come': the perfect indicating a state of completed action. In fact, this form of the verb is often called a

---

[1] When the object is in the relative, with a subject of Class 1, *a-* is used without the pronoun (*u-*)—*i.e.*, the relative prefix is *a-* and not *o-*.

participle, and is used as such : *mo χo yeng*—
'in eating'; and, looked at closely, it is easy
to see that the idea of the participle and that
of the locative may run into one another.

In Ronga the relative construction consists
of:

(1) the demonstrative, followed by the Inseparable Pronoun.
(2) *-ka* suffixed to the verb, if present, *-iki*, if past.

mhunu lweyi a-famba-ka = 'the man who walks.'
(man that he-walks.)

Tihomu leti ti-famba-ka = 'the cattle which walk.'

Tihomu leti hi-ti-shab-iki = 'the cattle which we bought.'

(*shaba* = 'buy'; *hi* = 'we.')

M. Junod thinks this *ka* is originally an auxiliary verb.

Herero seems to come nearest to our conception of the relative. There is a special form of pronoun, different from the demonstrative and used exactly as we use 'who' or 'which'—though, of course, it varies with the class of the antecedent.

(1) *omundu ngu muna* = 'the man who sees.'
(2) *ovandu mbe muna* = 'the people who see.'
(3) *omuti mbu ua* = 'the tree which falls.'
(4) *omiti mbi ua* = do. (plural).

(5) *eho ndi muna* = 'the eye which sees.'
(6) *omeho nge muna* = do. (plural).

The above is the 'participial present' tense, which is of simpler formation than the 'present.'

There are variations for other tenses, which need not be given here.

Finally, Kongo has no relative, properly speaking; 'the relative pronouns are identical in form and usage with the demonstrative.'

We might enumerate other varieties; but the above are sufficient to show that various stages of evolution from the simple to the complex sentence are illustrated in different parts of the Bantu language-field.

This is, perhaps, the best place to mention the Interrogatives, some of which, by function, are pronouns, some adjectives, and some adverbs. Some are invariable; others take the class-prefixes; and of the latter, some, which are used as adjectives (and also the words for 'all' and 'only'), are inflected like pronouns. (This point will be more easily made clear when speaking of adjectives.)

The following Table shows how the treatment of these words varies, even when the roots are cognate.

THE PRONOUN

	Zulu	Chwana	Herero	Nyanja	Swahili	Ganda	Gisu	Kongo
WHO?	ubani?	-mang?	-ani?	ndani?	nani?	-ani?	nanu?	nani?
WHICH?	-pi?	-he?	-ne?	-ti?	-pi?	-ki?	—	nkia?
WHAT?	-ni?	-ng?	tyike?	chi ani?	nini?	ki?	kina?	nki?
WHERE?	-pi?	kae?	pi?	kuti?	wapi?	-wa?	hena?	veyi? kweyi? mweyi?
WHEN?	nini?	leng?	rune?	liti?	lini?	di?	lina?	—
HOW MANY?	-ngaki?	-kae?	-ngapi?	-ngati?	-ngapi?	-meka?	-enga?	-kwa?
OF WHAT KIND?	-njani?	-ang?	-ke?	-tani?	gani?	-tya?	-rye	—

The forms without hyphens are invariable.

There is a set of pronouns sometimes called the 'Indicative Form,' meaning 'It is I,' 'It is he,' etc. But, as they are a combination of the Pronoun and the Copula, it will be better to reserve them for the next chapter.

CHAPTER VII

THE COPULA AND THE VERB 'TO BE'

In most European grammars, the first thing learned is the conjugation of the verbs 'to have' and 'to be.' In Bantu there is no verb 'to have,' and 'to be' is relegated, comparatively speaking, to the background. 'Have' is expressed by 'be with,' or simply by 'with,' with the 'be' understood. 'I have a house' is in Swahili *nina nyumba:* literally 'I with house'; in Zulu 'we have maize' is *sinombila* (*si-na-umbila*). This one fact shows how necessary it is for those who draw up grammars to take the language as they find it, instead of trying to fit it into the framework of any pre-conceived scheme. The late Dr. Henry began his *Chinyanja Grammar* —in many respects an excellent piece of work—by conjugating the non-existent verb 'to have.'

Most—if not all—Bantu languages have a verb 'to be,' but it is not often used in more than one or two tenses, and, in many cases, does not appear at all just where we should expect to find it. Thus its place may be supplied by the inseparable pronoun, as, in Zulu: *l'itanga* 'it is a pumpkin,' *l'ulwandhle* 'it is the sea,' *si'sitsha* 'it is a dish,' etc.

Or it may be omitted altogether.

SWAHILI: *Hamisi mpagazi:* 'Hamisi (is) a porter.'
ZULU: *ngi-lapa:* 'I (am) here' (*lapa* = here);
Ku-njalo-ke 'it (is) so.'
HERERO: *Owami omuhona:* 'I (am) a king.'

Sometimes 'is,' 'are,' are rendered by an invariable particle: Swahili *ni*, Nyanja *ndi*, Chwana *ke*.

NYANJA: *Nyalugwe ndi chirombo choopsya:*
'The leopard is a terrible beast.'

CHWANA: *Boshwa jwa tau ke letlalo:*
'The lion's inheritance is the skin.'
(Proverb.)

SWAHILI: *Dalili ya mvua ni mawingu:*
'The sign of rain is clouds.' (Proverb.)

As stated above, the inseparable pronoun of the class to which the noun belongs can be substituted for this invariable copula, as *Hii i nyumba* (instead of *hii ni nyumba*) 'this is a house'; *hizi zi nyumba*, 'these are houses'; *mti u mzuri*, 'the tree is fine' (Swahili); *l'itanga*, 'it is a pumpkin' (for *li(li)tanga*); *l'ulwandhle* (*lu(lu)lwandhle*) 'it is the sea'; *b'utywala* 'it is beer'; *zinkomo* (contracted from *z'izinkomo*), 'they are cattle' (Xosa); *lo' muntu l'idaka*, 'that man is a sot'; *waba l'ukuni*, 'he was (like) a log' (Zulu). But we sometimes find forms which cannot be thus accounted for, as in Zulu: *nguwena*, 'it is you'; *nguyena*, 'it is he'; *y'imina* (or *umina*) 'it is I'; *ng'umuntu*, 'it is a person'; *ng'amehlo*, 'they are eyes,' etc.

The truth seems to be that this copula is the old demonstrative root supposed by Meinhof to have been originally *γà*, which being placed before nouns gradually assimilated its vowel to their prefixes, became *ngu*, *nga*, *ngi*, etc., and finally dropped its consonant or became a mere duplicate of the prefix (as in Gisu *ba-ba-ndu*). In Swahili *ngu* survives in the form *yu* as a copula, in such phrases as *yu mzuri*, 'he is handsome'; though before the verb it has generally been replaced by *a*. Ila has retained the copula to a greater extent than many other languages,

THE COPULA AND THE VERB 'TO BE'

and it may be of interest to give the forms for the different classes here:

(1) *Ngu muntu:* 'it is a person.'
(2) *Mbo bantu:* 'they are people.'
(3) *Ngu munzhi:* 'it is a village.'
(4) *Nji minzhi:* 'they are villages.'
(5) *Nd'isamo:*[1] 'it is a tree.'
(6) *Ngu masamo:* 'they are trees.'
(7) *nchi chintu:* 'it is a thing.'
(8) *nshi shintu:* 'they are things.'
(9) *nimpongo:* 'it is a goat.'
(10) *nshimpongo:* 'they are goats.'
(11) *ndu lumo* or *ndumo:* 'it is a razor.'
(12) *ntu tushimbi:* 'they are girls.'
(13) *nku kashimbi:* 'it is a girl.'
(14) *Mbuxane*, or *mbu buxane:* 'it is meat.'
(15) *nku kufuna:* 'it is love.'
(16) (not found).
(17) *nku kutwi:* 'it is an ear.'
(18) (not found).

Most languages combine the copula with the personal pronouns (in the 'prepositional' or 'enclitic' form) for such expressions as 'it is I,' 'it is he,' etc. In Swahili *ndi* is used instead of *ni* for this purpose.

---

[1] This is a very exceptional word for 'tree,' as puzzling as the Chwana *setlare*. In the plural it is hard to see why assimilation has not taken place: one would have expected nga masamo.

	Swahili	Nyanja	Ila	Giryama	Gisu
'It is I'	ndimi	ndine	ndime	ndimi	isono
'It is this'	ndiwe	ndiwe	ndiwe	ndiwe	niwe
'It is he'	ndiye	ndiye	inguwe	ndeye	niye
'It is we'	ndiswi	ndife	ndiswe	ndiswi	nifwe
'It is you'	ndinyi	ndinu	ndimwe	ndinwi	ninywe
'It is they'	ndio	ndiwo	imbabo	ndo	nibo
Class 3	ndio	ndio	inguo	ndo	nikwo
4	ndiyo	ndiyo	injiyo	ndoyo	nikyo
5	ndilo	ndilo	indidio	ndoro	nilyo
6	ndiyo	ndiwo	ingao	ndogo	niko
7	ndicho	ndicho	inchicho	ndocho	nikyo
8	ndivyo	ndizo	inshisho	ndozho	nibyo
9	ndiyo	ndiyo	injio	ndoyo	niyo
10	ndizo	ndizo	inshisho	ndozho	nitso
11	ndio	—	indulo	ndolo	nilwo
12	—	ndito	intuto	—	niko
13	—	ndiko	inkako	ndoko	niko
14	—	ndiwo	imbubo	ndo	nibwo
15	ndiko	ndiko	inkuko	ndoko	nikwo
16	ndipo	ndipo	—	ndoho	niho
17	ndiko	ndiko	—	ndoko	nikwo
18	ndimo	ndimo	—	ndomo	nimu

This form does not seem to be used in Ganda, where 'it is I" is *nze*, 'it is we,' *fe*— the same as the pronoun standing alone.

The above must be distinguished from what is sometimes called the 'adverbial demonstrative,' meaning 'here he is,' etc., as in Zulu 1 *nanku*, 2 *nabo*, 3 *nangu*, 4 *nansi*, etc., with three forms, corresponding to degrees of distance, like other demonstratives.

The copula is sometimes prefixed to adjectives used predicatively (that is, in sentences like 'the man is good' as distinguished from 'the good man') as in Ila *bantu mbabotu* 2 'the people are good.' Most of the other prefixes, however, have dropped or absorbed it, as *masamo malamfu* 6 'the trees are tall,' or 'the tall trees.' This point is worth noting in connection with the difference (to which we shall refer in the next chapter) between the treatment of adjectives when used as predicates and as epithets. Another, and somewhat unexpected use of the copula is to introduce the agent after passive verbs. We find, in Zulu, *e.g.*, *kutshiwo ng'u Ngoza loko*, 'that is said by *Ngoza*'; and the obvious explanation is that *ng'* is the preposition *nga*, which usually indicates instrumentality. Or it would be the obvious explanation, were it not for the disturbing fact that *nga u Ngoza* should normally become *ngo Ngoza*, instead of eliding its final vowel and leaving the *u* intact, as is done here. Furthermore, if this were so, why should we find *ngilibele y'imisebenzi*, 'I have been delayed by works,' and not *ngemisebenzi?* In Swahili, the construction which the foreigner would expect, and which is sometimes heard, is *nimepigwa na huyu*, 'I have been struck by this (man)' (*na*, literally 'with' or 'and'). But the more usual and idiomatic form is *nimepigwa ni huyu'*—*i.e.*, literally: 'I have been struck—it is this man.' So the Zulu sentences given above are really equivalent to: 'It is said—it is Ngoza (who said it).' 'I have been delayed—it is works (which have done it).'

As already said, there is an actual verb equivalent to 'to be' in most, at any rate, of the Bantu languages, though its sphere is much more restricted than a knowledge of European speech alone would suggest. There are several roots common to a number of languages, which do not, however, all use them in the same way. They are all monosyllables, and therefore classed by most grammars among 'irregular verbs'—though that is hardly a satisfactory way of describing them.

Thus, in Swahili, we have *ku-wa*, used in the past (*a-li-ku-wa* 'he was') and the future (*a-ta-ku-wa* 'he will be') but never in the present. This is the same root as the Zulu *uku-ba*, which also is not much used in the present, except as an auxiliary. Nyanja prefers *li* (or *ri*),[1] which in Swahili is only found as a particle indicating the past tense. Ganda has both *ba* and *li*, and Herero has *ri*. These seem to be the two commonest forms. Kongo uses what Bentley calls 'the defective verb' *na*,[2] as in *kina vava* 'it (Cl. 7) is here,' and also *kala*, which 'is much more definite, and . . . means to be habitually or generally.'

But *kala* is also found in Nyanja and (as *kaa*) in Swahili. Its primary meaning is 'sit,' and thence 'stay' or 'live' in a place: in Nyanja its use is so extended that sometimes it is really equivalent to a verb 'to be.' The

---

[1] The pronunciation varies with the preceding vowel: *ndiri, uli, ali, tiri*, etc.

Nna is 'to be' in Chwana.

Zulu *hlala*[1] seems to be the same word, but its meaning is not quite so widely extended. This verb is an excellent illustration of the way in which the abstract notion of 'being' may be developed out of such a simple concrete one as 'sitting' or 'staying.' *Kara* is similarly used in Herero.

---

[1] As a rule, Zulu *hl* corresponds to *s* in Nyanja; *-hlanu*, *-sanu*, 'five'; *in-hlatu*, *n-satu* 'python': *hlamba*, *samba* 'bathe.' There is, however, a Nyanja word *sala* 'remain' (of which the use is somewhat more restricted than *kala*) but it is more properly *tsala*, and *sala* is also found in Zulu (as in the parting salutation *sala kahle*.) Ila has *kala* 'sit,' and *shala* 'remain,' side by side.

CHAPTER VIII

THE ADJECTIVE

THERE are very few real adjectives in Bantu. Their place is often supplied by nouns and verbs. Thus Nyanja has no adjective to express 'bad' or 'black'; but there are verbs 'to be bad' (*ku-ipa*) and 'to be black' (*ku-da*), and the place of the adjective is taken by a kind of participle formed of the infinitive with the possessive particle prefixed to it. 'Black' is *wa ku-da* 'of being black,' or, more literally, 'of to-be-black,' and 'bad' *wa ku-ipa*, usually contracted into *woipa*.[1] This construction, which has a genitive or partitive force, as the Chwana participle in *ng* has a locative force, sometimes replaces a relative pronoun. We can say, for instance, *mnyamata wosaka* (for *wa-ku-saka*) *nyama*, 'the youth who hunts

---

[1] Monosyllabic verbs do not contract, so it is *wa -ku-da*, never *woda*.

game,' *mzungu wosakala* ' the white man who never sits down.' (*Sa* is a negative particle, to be explained in a later chapter.)

Or the idea may be expressed by a tense of the finite verb. ' He is fat ' is *a-li-ku-nenepa*, from *ku-nenepa* ' to be fat '; ' there are too many fowls ' *nkuku zi-churuka* (*ku-churuka* ' to be too many '). So, too, in Zulu: *uku-lamba* ' to be hungry,' *uku-tshisa* ' to be hot,' *uku-godola* ' to be cold,' *uku-lunga* ' to be straight ' (and thence ' upright,' ' good '), etc.

Nouns are usually made to do the work of adjectives by having the possessive particle prefixed to them. So, in Nyanja, *wa mpamvu* is ' strong ' (literally ' of strength '); ' good ' *wa bwino*, ' many ' *wa mbiri*, ' new ' *wa tsopano*. *Bwino* and *mbiri* are not at present used by themselves; *tsopano* is an adverb of time meaning ' now ' (so that ' a new thing ' is, literally, ' a thing of now '); but all three may once have been nouns.

Zulu seems to prefer a relative construction in similar cases; ' a strong man ' is *umuntu onamandhla* (*a-u-na-amandhla*); literally ' a man who he (is) with strength.' And a very common and curious idiom in Swahili is the use of *mwenye* ' owner,' in the sense of 'having': *mwenye nguvu* 'strong,' literally 'owner (of) strength.'

The genuine adjective roots (to be distinguished from the derivative adjectives, which will be mentioned presently) are few in number and should probably be reckoned among the most primitive elements of Bantu speech. Some of them can be traced through many if not most of the Bantu languages hitherto studied; others might seem to be confined to one or two; but it would be very rash to dogmatize when so much still remains to be known. Sometimes, when present-day forms seem quite unrelated, the parallel is found to have existed in an older stage of the language; and sometimes the cognate word is found to have different senses in two languages, like *-kulu*, which is used almost everywhere for 'large,' but in Kongo and Herero has come to mean 'old.' The following list is not complete but comprises the most important of these root-adjectives.

Adjectives derived from verbs have various endings, of which, perhaps the commonest are *-u* (*-fu*, *-vu*) and *-e*. So, in Swahili, we have *nyama-vu* 'silent' from *ku-nyamaa*, and *-tuli-vu* 'gentle' from *ku-tulia*. With regard to *ere-vu* 'cunning' and *vi-vu* 'idle,' it does not seem certain that they can be traced to verbs, and *-refu* 'long, compared with *le* and *-de* in other languages, suggests that it is the same root, with the termination *-fu* suffixed to it.

In Herero, we have *-potu* 'blind,'[1] *dhorodhu* 'black' (from the verb *dhorera*), *taradhu* 'damp' (from *tarara*).

Of adjectives in -e, Herero has *-kohoke* 'clean,' from the verb *kohoka*, and *-pore* 'just,' 'gentle,' 'kind,' from *pora*, of which the primary meaning is 'to be cool.'[2]

In Ila, a language of the Middle Zambezi, there are a large number of adjectives ending in *-shi*, usually derived from verbs in *-ka*:

-dimbushi 'foolish,' from *ku-dimbusha* 'to be foolish.'
-komoshi 'broken,' „ *ku-komoka* 'to be broken.'
-zapaushi 'ragged,' „ *ku zapauka* 'to be ragged.'

Some of these adjectives can scarcely be

---

[1] Phonetically the same as the root of the Swahili noun *ki-pofu*; but *-pofu* is not used in Swahili as an adjective, in the sense of 'blind.'

[2] A widely distributed root, which usually has the secondary meaning 'recover' (from illness)—probably with reference to the reduction in temperature. But in Herero, the notion of 'cooling' seems to suggest that of being, or becoming 'moderate'—and so 'reasonable,' 'just,' gentle,' etc.

	Zulu	Chwana	Herero	Nyanja	Swahili	Ganda	Gisu	Kongo
Good	-hle	-ntle	-ua	—	-ema	-lungi[1]	-lahi	-weti
Bad	-bi	-ve	-vi	—	-baya[2]	-bi	-bi	-bi
Long	-de	-lele	-re	-tari	-refu	-wamvu	-lehi	-la
Short	-futshane[3]	-khutshane	-thupi	-fupi	-fupi	-mpi	-mbi	-kufi
Other	-nye	-ng'we	-kuao	-ina	-ngine	-lala	-ndi	-ake
Old	-dala[4]	-χoloχolo	-kuru	—[5]	-kukuu[6]	kade[7]	-gore	-kulu
New	-tsha	-sha	-pe	-pea[8]	-pya	-gya[9]	-'kya	-mpa
Many	-ningi	-ntsi	-ingi	-nyinji[10]	-ingi	-ngi	-ngi	-ingi
Large	-kulu	-χolo	-nene[11]	-kulu	-kuu[12]	-nene[13]	-gali	-nene[13]
Small	-ncane	-nyenye	-titi	-ng'ono	-dogo[14]	-tono	-ke'ke	-kete
Raw (unripe)	—[15]	-tala[15]	-vihu	-wisi	-bichi	-bisi	-bisi	-mbisa
Female	(-kazi)[16]	-χali	-kadhe[17]	-kazi	(-kazi)[18]	-kazi	-kasi	—

THE ADJECTIVE

[1] Probably connected with the verb *lunga*, which (*e.g.* in Zulu) means 'to be straight,' and so 'to be right,' 'good,' etc.

[2] Old Swahili has *-wi* (*-bi*, *vi*).

[3] Diminutive of *-fupi*, which appears in the adverb *kufupi*.

[4] This word is also found in Nyamwezi, Shambala, Bondei and some other East African languages.

[5] Instead of an adjective, Nyanja has the verb *kalamba* 'to be old,' and *-a kale*, which means 'of long ago.'

[6] *-kukuu*, in the sense of 'worn out' applied to things. Of persons, *-zee* is used, or in some dialects *-zima*, properly 'whole,' and so 'grown up.' *Kale* is also sometimes used, as in *Mji wa kale*, 'the old town,' at Mombasa.

[7] *eda* 5, a noun, meaning 'age' has perhaps the same root as *-dala*, but there does not seem to be an adjective of this form.

[8] Used in some dialects.

[9] This modification returns to its original form after a nasal, as *mpya* in Cl. 9.

[10] Preferred to *-a mbiri* in some dialects.

[11] This is found, *e.g.*, in Swahili, with the meaning 'thick,' 'stout.' I doubt whether the Zulu *-nene* 'generous' is from the same root.

[12] More commonly used in a figurative than in a literal sense; the usual word for the latter is *-kubwa*.

[13] *-kulu* is used in the sense of 'mature' or 'important,' etc.

[14] When used with the simple prefix *-nene* means 'too large'; to make it mean merely 'large' it requires another prefix. This very curious point in Kongo grammar will be touched on later.

[15] In the Lamu dialect *-titi* and *-toto* are used.

[16] Perhaps the root which we find in the other columns exists in the Zulu *u-bisi* and Chwane *le-vese*, 'fresh milk.' With *-tala* compare Herero *taradhu* 'damp';—'wet' is one of the meanings of *-wisi* in Nyanja.

[17] Only found as a suffix, in *inkosi-kazi*, etc.

[18] Herero has no *s* or *z*: the former is represented by the sound of *th* in 'thin,' the latter by that of *th* in 'there' (here written *dh*).

[19] Only found as a suffix in one or two words; the root *-ke* has taken its place.

distinguished from passive participles, as the Ila *komoshi*, 'broken,' given above, and, in Sango[1]:

fi-nhu fi-teleχe[2] 'cooked food,' from *teleχa* 'cook.'
umu-pixi mu-hongole 'a hewn tree,' from *hongola* hew.'

The *Concord of the Adjective* is often something of a puzzle. *A priori*, nothing could be simpler: you have your adjective root, and you place before it the prefix of the noun with which it is to agree. This happens, in fact, with most of the classes in Swahili.

1. *m-tu m-zuri* 'a handsome man.'
2. *wa-tu wa-zuri* 'handsome men.'
3. *m-ti m-zuri* 'a fine tree.'
4. *mi-ti mi-zuri* 'fine trees.'
5. *tunda zuri* 'a fine fruit.'
6. *ma-tunda ma-zuri* 'fine fruits.'
7. *ki-ti ki-zuri* 'a fine chair.'
8. *vi-ti-vi-zuri* 'fine chairs.'
9. *nyumba n-zuri* 'a fine house.'
10. *nyumba n-zuri* 'fine houses.'
11. *u-pindi m-zuri* 'a fine bow.'
15. *ku-shona ku-zuri* 'fine sewing.'
16. *pahali pa-zuri* 'a fine place.'

[1] The Sango (or Lori) people live to the north-east of the Konde, some distance north of Lake Nyasa.

[2] The Greek χ is used to indicate the Scottish sound of *ch* in 'loch.'

THE ADJECTIVE

Adjectives do not seem to be used, in Swahili, with the locatives of the seventeenth and eighteenth classes, though they are *e.g.* in Nyanja.

The above is perfectly plain sailing, with the exceptions of Class 11 which has taken the concord proper to Class 3, the contracted form *u* being doubtless associated with that class through its pronoun, though the *u* has disappeared from the third prefix. (Of course the old form for 11 would have been *lu-pindi lu-zuri.*) Phonetic laws have produced some modifications in Classes 9 and 10 (such as the change of *n* into *m'* before a labial and its loss before *k, t,* and some other sounds) but these need not concern us here.

In Nyanja, the case is different. Here the principle seems to be that the inseparable pronoun is prefixed to the adjective root and the Possessive Particle to it as *chachikulu* 7 *zazikulu* 8, etc. It is not quite consistently carried out in the First Class, for there the noun-prefix takes the place of the pronoun: *wa-m-kulu,* not *wa-u-kulu;* perhaps in order to preserve the distinction between it and Class 3, which is *wokulu* (contracted from *wa-u-kulu*).

This applies to all real adjectives in Nyanja:

any which do not take the concord as above are treated either as nouns or as verbs. But in Zulu a distinction is observed, to which we shall now come.

The real adjectives, in Zulu, prefix (1) the relative particle *a*, (2) the noun-prefix. (1) coalesces with the initial vowel, *i.e.*, when followed by *u*, it makes *o*, when followed by *i*, *e*. The contracted prefixes return to their original form.

Thus we get *omu-hle* (*a-umu-hle*), *eli-hle* (*a-ili-hle*), *olu-hle* (*a-ulu-hle*), etc.

But there are some other adjectives, which take shortened prefixes in Classes 1, 3, 4 and 6 (*i.e.*, *o- e- a-*, instead of *omu*, *emi*, *ama*) as *umu-ntu o-nsundu* 'a brown man,' *imilomo e-banzi* 'wide mouths,' *ama-hashi a-mhlope* 'white horses'—not *omu-nsundu*, *emi-banzi*, *ama-mhlope*. The reason for the distinction is not very clear, but some at least of the adjectives so treated are originally nouns, as *-lukuni* 'heavy' (*u(lu)-kuni* 'a log of wood'), *-luhlaza* 'green' (*u(lu)-luhlaza* 'green grass').

Then, in Chwana, both the Pronoun and Noun-Prefix are added to the Adjective, but in the reverse order from that in which we find them in Nyanja.

THE ADJECTIVE

It will be sufficient to illustrate this by examples from these three languages and Ganda. In dealing with a Bantu language which has not been much studied, the learner should pay special attention to this point, as the system followed may be different from any of those which have been enumerated. We must not too hastily assume—having studied the theory of the Alliterative Concord, not wisely but too well—that we can apply the noun-prefixes, as they stand, to the adjectives; which, so far as it has taken place, is probably a late development.

The adjective selected for the illustrations is *-kulu*, which is found in most Bantu languages, though in Ganda it does not seem to be used quite in the sense here implied.

Many languages make no distinction between the form of an adjective when used as an epithet or as a predicate; but some, as Zulu, Xosa and Ganda, drop the initial vowel in the latter case.

ZULU: *Umu-ntu omu-hle* 'a good man'—but
umu-ntu mu-hle 'the man is good.'

GANDA: *ebi-gambo ebizibu* 'difficult words,'—but
ebi-gambo bizibu 'the words are difficult.'

	Zulu	Chwana	Nyanja	Ganda
1	umu-ntu om-kulu	mo-tho eo mo-χolo	mu-ntu wa-m-kulu	omu-ntu omu-kulu[1]
2	aba-ntu aba-kulu	va-tho va va-χolo	a-ntu a-kulu[2]	aba-ntu aba-kulu
3	umu-ti om-kulu	no-re[3] o mo-χolo	m-tengo wo-kulu[4]	omu-ti omu-kulu
4	imi-ti emi-kulu	me-re e me-χolo	mi-tengo ye-kulu[5]	emi-ti emi-kulu
5	i-zinyo eli-kulu	le-ino je le-χolo	dz-ino la-li-kulu	eri-nyo e'kulu[7]
6	ama-zinyo ama-kulu	meno a ma-χolo	ma-no a-kulu[8]	ama-nyo ama-kulu
7	isi-ntu[9] esi-kulu	se lo se se-χolo	chi-ntu cha-chi-kulu	eki-ntu eki-kulu
8	izi-ntu ezi-kulu	di-lo tse di-kχolo[10]	zi-ntu za-zi-kulu	ebi-ntu ebi-kulu
9	im-buzi en-kulu	puli e-kχolo[11]	mbuzi ye-kulu[5]	em-buzi en-kulu
10	izim-buzi ezin-kulu	di-puli tse di-kχolo[10]	mbuzi za-zi-kulu	em-buzi en-kulu
11	u-limi olu -kulu	lo-leme lo le-χolo	lu-lime la-li-kulu[12]	olu-limi olu-kulu
12			tulo ta-ti-kulu[13]	otu-lo otu-kulu
13			ka-ntu ka-ka-ng'ono[14]	aka-ntu aka-tono
14	ubu-kosi obu-kulu	vo-χosi jo vo-χolo[15]	u-ta bu-bu-kulu[16]	obu-lungi-obu-kulu
15	uku-tanda oku-kulu	χo-rata mo χo-χolo[17]	ku-konda kwa-ku-kulu	okw-agala oku-kulu
16			pa-mudzi pa-pa-kulu[18]	wa-no wa-lungi
17			ku-mudzi kwa-ku-kulu	ku-no ku-lungi
18			m'mudzi mwa-mu-kulu	mu-no mu-lungi

It has not been thought necessary to make the table include Classes 19 and 20. Ganda is the only one of these four languages which has either, and 20 is not much used even there.

THE ADJECTIVE

[1] *-kulu* in Ganda is generally used in the sense of 'grown-up.'

[2] Contracted from *a-a-kulu*.

[3] The usual word for 'tree' is *se-tlhare*, but *more* is sometimes used with the meaning of 'herb' or 'medicine,' or in a figurative sense.

[4] Contracted from *wa-u-kulu*.

[5] Contracted from *ya-i-kulu*.

[6] The particle *je* seems anomalous here, like *tse* in 8 and 10 and *jo* in 14. Meinhof thinks these forms may be relatives (*Grundzüge einer vergleichenden Grammatik der Bantusprachen*, p. 32), but does not fully explain them.

[7] The full prefix is only found in Ganda with some monosyllabic adjectives, such as *eri-ngi* 'many,' *eri-mpi* 'short,' etc.

[8] Shortened from *a-a-kulu*. In the Likoma dialect this class has the pronoun *ya*, and the adjective has the form of *ya-i-kulu*. The *y* is an almost extinct remainder of the initial consonant to which the Giryama *ga* is a nearer approach.

[9] *Isi-ntu* does not mean 'a thing,' as the other words in this row do, but has been inserted because it is the same word, though changed in meaning.

[10] χolo hardens into *k*χolo after the *di-* (*li-*) prefix, which is the same as *zi* in many other languages.

[11] The same hardening (see last note) takes place after *e*, which also is contracted from *e-e*.

[12] The occurrence of the forms *lulime, lulimi,* along with *lilime,* in Nyanja, shows that the 11th class is not quite merged into the 5th, though in process of disappearing. Pronunciation seems to fluctuate, as in *lipenga* 'trumpet,' which is sometimes heard as *lupenga* and in Yao definitely belongs to the *lu-* class. In Nyanja words beginning with *lu* have their agreements according to Cl. 5, as is the case here.

[13] *Tulo* still survives in these two languages, and its adjectives would agree as above, if they were used.

[14] Of course *-kulu* cannot be used with this class.

[15] Some dialects have *vo vo*-χolo or *vyo-vo*-χolo.

[16] Some concords of *uta* in *bu-* are given in Scott's *Dictionary*, and though the above may not be in use, this would be the correct form.

[17] I do not know how to explain this *mo-*.

[18] See the remarks on the Locative Class in Chapter V.

I

The distinction may seem a slight one, but it must not be overlooked.

(The copula is not used in Zulu before adjectives, as it is before nouns and pronouns.)

We mentioned on a previous page a *number of adjectives which are derived from verbs*. But there are also verbs derived from adjectives—at least it is difficult to see how the Yao *kulungwa* 'to be great' can be anything else; though, curiously enough, the adjective *-kulu* is not found in this language. And, again, there are some cases where it is difficult to tell whether the verb or the adjective should have the priority. Mr. E. W. Smith, in his *Handbook of the Ila Language*, says (p. 61): 'Many of the adjectives proper have corresponding verbs which may be used in place of them as predicates,' and gives a list which we need not reproduce in full. Some of them seem to be formed with the suffix *-u*, as *-lemu* 'heavy' (verb *ku lema*), *-botu* 'good' (verb *ku bota*), but *ku fwimpa* 'to be short' seems just as likely to be formed from the adjective *-fwafwi* (or its root *fwi*) as *vice versa*. We are reminded of the Nyanja verbs *fini-mpa* 'to be short' and *tani-mpa* 'to be long'; but there are no adjectives *-fini* and *-tani*. There is the root *ta* in *-tari*, however, and *fi* may be akin to the *fu* in *fupi*. At any rate the possibility suggests itself that either the verb or the adjective, or both at the same time, may be derived from one of those 'interjectional roots,' which will be discussed in a later chapter.

There is no need to waste any time on the Degrees of Comparison. They do not exist, as grammatical forms. There are various ways of expressing comparison—the commonest, perhaps, is the use of some verb meaning ' pass,' ' excel ' or the like.

NYANJA: *Ndi ichi ndi icho cha-pambana ndi icho:* 'that is better than this.' (Literally: 'it is this it is that—that (which) excels is that.')

ZULU: *indoda idhlula umfana emandhleni:* 'a man is stronger than a boy' ('passes a boy in strength').

Or, *kuna* is used (the pronoun of the eighth class followed by *na*, equivalent to ' there is '); *indoda inamandhla kunomfana (kuna umfana)*. The idiom is not quite easy to explain, but the idea underlying it may be somewhat similar to the Swahili *kuliko* ' where there is,' as in *nyumba hii ni nzuri kuliko ile* ' this house is finer than that '—literally, ' is fine where that is '—*i.e.*, so fine that it would attract attention when the other was in view, and therefore superior to it.

In Kongo, the simplest form of the adjective implies that the quality is possessed *to excess*; an additional particle has to be inserted for the ordinary or what we should call the positive form.

Sometimes it almost seems as if the notion of comparison were absent till imported into a language by European speakers. Thus, the author of *Elements of Luganda Grammar*, after mentioning the use of the word *singa* ('surpass'), says (p. 58) '*Singa* in this sense is rarely heard among the peasants until they have come in contact with European thought . . . thus . . . they would say'—for 'Bring a longer stick,' 'This stick is short, bring a long one,' and so on.

What we mean by the Superlative is expressed either by some equivalent to 'very,' 'exceedingly,'—or by some such phrase as 'surpassing everyone else,' 'excelling all.'

CHAPTER IX

The Numerals

Numerals, of course, are a kind of adjective; but, in Bantu, their agreements are not always the same as those of other adjectives, and in any case they are important enough to deserve a section to themselves.

They are so convenient for the purpose of comparing different languages, that perhaps more attention has been given to them than to any other part of speech; and being among the easiest words to ask for, they are found in the vocabularies of all the early travellers.

The numerals from one to five, and the word for ten are, with few exceptions, common to the whole of the Bantu area. The numbers six, seven, eight and nine present considerable differences. Some have no separate words for these numbers at all, but call six 'five and one,' seven 'five and two,' and so on. This does not facilitate arithmetical operations and children in mission schools are usually taught the English names of the numbers before entering on the mysteries of addition and subtraction. 'Eighty-seven' is certainly easier to deal with, at least for the instructor, than 'five tens and three tens and five and two.'

Where the numerals from six to nine exist, they are sometimes nouns, with an unmistakable reference to the practice of counting on the fingers. Thus, the Zulu for six is *isi-tupa*, 'the thumb'—showing that the counting begins with the little finger of the left hand— seven is *isi-kombisa*, 'the forefinger.' Eight and nine are expressed, rather cumbrously, by 'leave two fingers' (or 'bend down two fingers') and 'leave one finger' respectively, It is curious that Xosa, which is so closely related to Zulu, has *-tandatu* for six, which is also found in some of the Eastern languages— Pokomo, Giryama, Nyamwezi, etc.

This is probably a modified reduplication of *-tatu* 'three' (contracted from *tatu na tatu*), just as *-nane*, sometimes used for 'eight,' seems to be a doubling of *-ne*, 'four.'

The numbers up to five sometimes (as in Zulu) agree like ordinary adjectives, sometimes (as in Nyanja) they take the inseparable pronoun. 'Ten' seems to be a noun—it is usually invariable, but sometimes, when it has kept its prefix, it is treated as a noun, and preceded by a connective particle, as in Zulu: *abantu abay' ishumi*—literally 'people who are ten.'

The following table shows these six numerals in ten languages. Konde is spoken at the head of Lake Nyasa, on the eastern side.

	Zulu	Chwana	Herero	Nyanja	Konde	Swahili	Ganda	Gisu	Kongo	Duala
1	-nye	-nwe	-mwe	-modzi	-mo	-moja	-mu	-twera	-moshi	-wo
2	-bili	-vedi	-vari	-wiri	-bili	-wili	-biri	-biri	-ole	-ba
3	-tatu	-raro	-tatu	-tatu	-tatu	-tatu	-satu	-taru	-tatu	-lalo
4	-ne	-ne	-ne	-nai	-na	-ne	-na	-ne	-ya	-nei
5	-hlanu	-tlhano	-tano	-sanu	-hano	-tano	-tano	-nano	-tanu	-tanu
10	ishumi	shome	omu- rongo	kumi	mlongo	kumi	ekumi	kikum	kumi	dom

Zulu (but not Xosa) omits the initial vowel in the prefixes of *nye*: *mu-nye*, *li-nye*, *si-nye*, not *omunye*, *elinye*, etc. (which would mean 'some,' 'other').

The roots as given here are sometimes modified when preceded by noun-prefixes, *e.g.*, in Swahili, *-wili* becomes *mbili* when agreeing with a noun of the tenth class. We may also notice that there is often a distinct set of numerals without any class-agreement, used in counting where no particular things counted are specified. Thus, in Swahili, we count: *mosi, pili, tatu, nne, tano*, whereas the same numbers applied to people would be: (*mtu*) *mmoja*, (*watu*) *wawili, watatu, wane, watano;* to trees: (*mti*) *mmoja*, (*miti*) *miwili, mitatu, uine, mitano*; to nouns of the seventh and eighth classes: *kimoja, viwili, vitatu*—and so on.

Yao (an important language occupying a considerable area in Nyasaland and the Portuguese territory) has *mcheche* (invariable) for four, the root of which is found in Makua as *-cheshe*. Yao has another peculiarity, in treating five (*msanu*) as invariable.

Some dialects of Chwana use *mphecho* 'completion' instead of *-tlhano*, that is 'the whole hand'—the five fingers.

The root *-rongo* or *-longo* sometimes serves to form multiples of ten: *e.g.*, in Pokomo 'ten' is *kumi*, but 'twenty' *mi-ongo mi-wii*. In Swahili *mwongo* survives, meaning 'a decade'; in the older reckoning (now mostly superseded by the Muhammadan Calendar) a month was divided into three *miongo* of ten days each. Twenty, etc., are usually expressed by *makumi* followed by the number required; but sometimes, though rarely, there is a special word for twenty. Such is *du* in

Isubu,[1] which seems, however, to be borrowed from the Sudan languages. Konde occasionally, along with *amalongo mabili*,[2] has *umundu* 'a man'—*i.e.*, both hands and both feet. Swahili uses the Arabic word for 'twenty'—*ishirini*.

Sometimes there are distinct words for 'hundred' and 'thousand,' but in other cases these are only treated as multiples of ten. The Lower Kongo people and the Baganda have the completest systems of numeration, because they have been used, for many generations, to deal with a cowrie currency, and the latter in particular have an ingenious plan of varying the prefixes for tens, hundreds, thousands, tens of thousands: thus, 10 is *kumi*, 100 *ekikumi*, 1,000 *olukumi*, 10,000 *akakumi*, beyond which this form of numeration does not seem to go. At least I find in the Rev. G. R. Blackledge's *Luganda Vocabulary* a word for 'a million,' which is quite distinct—*akakada*. Kongo does not use this

---

[1] Isubu is spoken in the Cameroons delta, by people living between the Duala on the south and the Bakwiri on the north.

[2] Or *imilongo mibili*, as would be expected from the usual singular. There is also the curious form *tu-longo tu-bili*.

system of prefixes, but has words for 100, 1,000, 10,000, 100,000 and 1,000,000.

The numbers in the following table, if not preceded by a hyphen, are invariable, except in so far as they are treated as nouns, and behave like *ishumi* in Zulu. These are marked*. Those with a hyphen prefixed agree like those in the first table.

	Xosa	Chwana	Herero	Kongo	Duala	Ila
6	-tandatu	-rataro	hambomwe[4]	sambanu[5]	mutoba	*chisambomwi[6]
7	-sixenxe[1]	-shupa[2]	hambombari	nsambwadi	samba	*chiloba
8	-sibozo	—[3]	hambondatu	nana	lombi	*lusele
9	-litoba	—	muviu	vwa	dibua	*ifuka

Continuation of above.

	Hehe[7]	Nyamwezi	Giryama	Kikuyu	Gisu	Ganda
6	mutanda	-tandatu	-handahu[11]	-tandatu	-sesaba	omukaga
7	mufungate[8]	mpungati	-fungahe	mugwanja	musafu	omusamvu
8	munane	munane	-nane	-nana	kinane	omunana
9	igonza[9]	kenda[10]	chenda	kenda	kyenda	omwenda

THE NUMERALS

¹ Though the forms for 7, 8 and 9 look identical with the preceding ones (*aba-hlanu, aba-tandatu,*) they are really nouns (*isi-xenxe, isi-bozo, i (li)-toba*) and the prefix is preceded by the relative particle. Otherwise it would be *aba-xenxe*, not *aba-si-xenxe* and so for the others. *-xenxe* (the *x* stands for the 'lateral click') and *-bozo* seem to be borrowed Hottentot roots. *i(li)-toba* is evidently a noun formed from the verb *toba* 'bend down' (*cf. tob'umunwemunye* for 9 in Zulu.)

² From the verb *shupa* 'show,' 'point.'

³ These numbers are not given, as they are similar to the Zulu: 'bend down two fingers,' 'bend down one finger.' There is, however, in some dialects an almost obsolete word for 8, *seswai,* of which the derivation is curious: *swaya* means 'to mark' (with paint), and as this is usually done with the middle finger of the right hand, it comes to be synonymous with 'eight.'

⁴ *hamba* (the same word as the Zulu for 'go') means 'jump over' (*i.e.,* from the thumb of the left hand to the thumb of the right) —*hambo-mwe* 'jump over (and take) one.'

⁵ Kongo numerals have a double system of agreement (for the details of which see Bentley, pp. 567-570); in the 'primary form' 7, 8, 9, and 10 are invariable, in the 'secondary' they take prefixes.

⁶ This looks like a variant of the Herero word; but the only meanings given for *samba* in Mr. Smith's vocabulary are 'wash, bathe, swim.'

⁷ The Wahehe are to be found some distance N.E. of Lake Nyassa and to the south of the Wagogo.

⁸ *Fungate* is still used in Swahili, meaning 'a period of seven days'—but only in connection with a wedding (see Krapf, s.v. and Steere's *Handbook*, p. 91). It was, no doubt, the old word for 7, but has long been replaced by the Arabic *saba'a*.

⁹ I have found no other example of this form.

¹⁰ Also found in Swahili, though not so often as the Arabic *tissa* or *tisia*.

¹¹ 'Cerebral *t*' becomes *h* in Giryama. The difference between the two *t*'s is very important in Swahili : *-tatu*, with 'cerebral *t*' becomes in Giryama *-hahu*, but *-tano*, with dental *t*, *tsano*. 'Cerebral' *t* is pronounced by pressing the tongue against the hard palate, 'dental' by pressing it against the teeth; our ordinary English *t* is between the two, being 'alveolar'—*i.e.*, the tongue touches the gums or 'tooth-ridge.' The two *t*'s in Swahili may be distinguished, if necessary as t (-tatu) and -ṭ (-tano) or the cerebral, as the commoner, may be left unmarked. The Rev. W. E. Taylor, in his *African Aphorisms*, prints the dental *t* in italic; but in his version of the Psalms it is underlined. The difference is more important at Mombasa than at Zanzibar, where most of the words which at Mombasa have dental *t* are pronounced with *ch*, —*mato* = *macho* 'eyes'; *teka* = *cheka* 'laugh.'

Some of the words for 'hundred' and 'thousand' are as follows:

	Zulu	Herero	Kongo	Duala	Ila	Nyanja	Hebe	Kikuyu	Gisu
100	ikulu	ethere	nkama	ebwea	mwanda	dzana[a]	igana[4]	igana	litondo
1000	inkulungwane[1]	eyovi	ezunda	ikoli	chulu	chikwi[3]	imbirima	ngiri	—[5]

The Ordinal Numbers are usually expressed by turning the cardinal number into a noun preceded by the possessive particle of the noun with which the number is to agree.

Thus in Nyanja *muntu wa chi-modzi, wa chi-wiri, wa chi-tatu* 'the first, second, third person.' *Chintu cha chi-modzi* 'the first thing'; *nyumba ya chimodzi* 'the first house,' etc., etc.

But the first ordinal is not always an actual

[1] This looks like a diminutive of *ikulu*, but I do not know how to explain it.

[2] Also in Ronga. In some dialects *zana*.

[3] *Kikwi* was formerly used in Swahili, but is now seldom if ever heard. The usual word is the Arabic *elfu* (*mia* for 100).

[4] This (or *gana*) is also used in Nyamwezi, Shambala, Zigula, Giryama, Pokomo, etc.

[5] Gisu has no special word for 1,000, *kamatonda kikumi* 'ten hundreds' being used.

Konde expresses 'a hundred' by 'five people.'

Xosa has the same word for 'hundred' as Zulu; but 'thousand' is *iwaka*. Nyamwezi has *kihumbi* for 'thousand.'

numeral. In Swahili *mtu wa kwanza* is literally 'the man of beginning,' from *kwanza* (*ku-anza*) 'begin'; and similarly in Zulu *umuntu wokuqala* (*wa uku-qala*).[1]

Invariable numerals, as a rule, simply have the possessive particle prefixed to them, and in Ila this particle is prefixed directly to the stem even of the variable ones. In Herero a somewhat curious system is adopted: the inseparable pronoun followed by the verb *tya* 'say,' is prefixed to the stem of the numeral: 'the second man' is *omundu utya vari*—literally 'the man he says two,'—'the third tree' *omuti utya tatu*, 'the fifth name' *ena ritya tano*.

The way in which the variable numeral is changed into a noun is not everywhere the same, and no general rule can be given. Zulu, like Nyanja, uses the seventh prefix for this purpose; Chwana and Ronga the fourteenth, Ganda the fifteenth; and sometimes, as in Swahili, the isolated forms of the numerals (those which serve for counting when no objects are specified) are used. In this language 'the first man,' as already stated, would be *mtu wa kwanza*.

---

[1] Q represents the 'cerebral' click.

The second tree	*mti wa pili.*
The third name	*jina la tatu.*
The fourth thing	*kitu cha nne.*
The fifth house	*nyumba ya tano.*

'Twice,' 'thrice,' etc. are formed in many languages by prefixing *ka-*, which will be noticed later on, as it forms adverbs from other adjectives as well as numerals.

Special features to which attention should be directed are the dual pronouns and the distributive numerals in Ganda, and the forms in Zulu expressing 'both,' 'all three,' etc.: *bobabili, bobatatu.* But these belong to the study of particular languages, and cannot be dealt with here.

Some Bantu grammarians include the numerals among the adjectives; others (because of the difference in their agreement, already referred to, observable in some languages) place them among the pronouns. This difference usually extends to the words for 'all,' 'only,' and one or two others, sometimes called 'indefinite adjectives' or 'indefinite pronouns.'

The most logical plan appears to be to give the numerals a separate chapter as we have done.

CHAPTER X

THE VERB

The Bantu verb normally consists of two syllables and ends in *a*, e.g.:

ZULU: *lima* 'cultivate'; *hamba* 'go'; *tanda* 'love'; *lala* 'lie down.'

CHWANA: *lema* 'cultivate'; *eta* 'go'; *rata* 'love' *roma* 'send.'

NYANJA: *manga* 'tie'; *enda* 'go'; *konda* 'love'; *tenga* 'carry.'

There are a few monosyllabic verbs, most of which are used as auxiliaries: some are now only found in composition, as tense-particles. They are seldom fully conjugated, and have some other peculiarities which have led to their being described as 'irregular verbs.' Sometimes, as we shall see more fully later on, it seems probable that they have been worn down from a dissyllabic stem. In other cases they may be original roots, perhaps traceable in the monosyllabic Sudan languages.

Verbs of more than two syllables are practically certain to be either 'derived forms' or foreign importations (as Swahili *fikiri* 'consider,' *kubali* 'agree,' which come from the Arabic). In the former case, the fact is sometimes disguised by the loss of the simple form. In Zulu there is a verb *kumula* 'untie,' 'undo'; this has the 'reversive' termination *-ula*, showing that it is the opposite of a verb *kuma* 'fasten'—but there is no such verb now to be found in Zulu. A very common verb in Swahili is *simama* 'stand'; now in other languages we have *ima, yima, yema, jima, zhima ema* (or *ma*) with this meaning; and *ima* is even found in old Swahili. *-Ama* is a termination implying 'to be in a position,' as *ang-ama* 'be suspended,' *in-ama* 'stoop' (be in a stooping position,)[1] etc.

---

[1] But sometimes we may get a verb which looks like a derived form, though it is not really one. Meinhof gives an instance of a Konde word *hov-ela*, 'hope,' which would naturally be taken for the applied form of *hova*. But there is no such verb as the latter, and the word is ultimately derived from the Arabic through the Swahili *subiri* 'be patient.' Other verbs of more than two syllables, formed direct from adjectives, nouns or

Verb stems beginning with a vowel are not very common, and usually produce some modification of the prefix, owing to the contact of two vowels, which necessitates a special paragraph or section being devoted to them in most grammars. Comparative study makes it appear likely that these "vowel verbs" once began with a consonant, and Meinhof thinks this consonant was the voiced velar fricative, γ. This is not an easy sound to pronounce at the beginning of a word, and would very soon tend to disappear, or at least to become modified. In the above examples, where it has not been dropped altogether, it is represented by *y*, *j*, or *zh* (pronounced like *z* in 'azure').

In Zulu we find several verbs which may or may not have an initial e : *ema* (or *ma*) 'stand,' *eza* (or *za*) 'come'; *emba* (or *mba*) 'dig,' *epa* (or *pa*) 'pull up' (as weeds, etc.). These, we can see, are reduced to monosyllables by dropping the vowel, after the loss of the original initial consonant. The vowel

---

the invariable roots called ' sound pictures ' or ' vocal images' will be noticed later. Some diacritic marks have been omitted from *hovela*—most Konde words bear more than could be printed here without confusion.

being retained where it happens to be more easily pronounced, keeps the real state of the case before us; otherwise it might be thought that these were true monosyllabic verbs.[1]

Verbs which do not end in a are very rare (unless borrowed from other languages) and chiefly monosyllables. *Ti* 'say' is found in nearly every Bantu languages, and so is *li* 'to be,' in composition if not independently. The Zulu *hlezi* from *hlala* 'sit' being a perfect, does not count in this connection, yet even as a perfect it is irregular, since it should end in -e not -i. I have never seen it satisfactorily accounted for.

The 'Derived Forms' of the verb, to which we have already referred, might perhaps be most accurately described as 'Voices.' We, in Europe, have the Active and Passive, to which, in Greek, is added the Middle: we also have traces of a Causative, as in 'fall'—'fell'(=make to fall) 'sit'—set (=cause to sit), etc. The Bantu languages have all these, and several others as well.

---

[1] It is possible that in some of these cases the *e* may have been adopted by analogy—*e.g.* in *eza*.

The PASSIVE is formed by means of the suffix -*wa*: *pig-wa* (Swahili) from *piga* 'strike,' *bon-wa* (Zulu) from *bona* 'see.' Sometimes the suffix is -*iwa*, (as in Ronga), -*edwa* or -*idwa*[1] (Nyanja), -*ebwa* or -*ibwa* (Ganda), -*igwa* (Konde). Duala has the very peculiar form -*be*. The suffix may cause considerable modification in the stem of the verb, as in Zulu, where *w* cannot follow *p*, *b*, or *m*.

The NEUTER-PASSIVE, usually ending in -*eka* or -*ika* (sometimes in -*uka*, -*aka* or -*akala*) is distinguished from the Passive by expressing a *state*, or the possibility of being subjected to an action, rather than the actual undergoing of the action on some definite occasion. Thus, in Swahili, *kamba yafunguka*[2] is: 'the rope is (in a state of being) unfastened,' but *kamba yalifunguliwa* is: 'the rope was unfastened' (by some person or persons). In Zulu,

---

[1] Whether it is *edwa* or *idwa* depends on the vowel contained in the verb stem. This 'Law of Vowel-Harmony' will be noticed in a later chapter.

[2] *Fung-uka* is really a compound form, being the intransitive (or neuter passive) of *fungua*, the reversive (see p. 150 below) of *funga* 'fasten.' *Funguliwa*, the passive of *fungua*, is formed from the original *fung-ula*, *l* between two vowels being usually dropped in Swahili, and verb-stems ending in *l* making their passive in -*iwa*.

inkanyezi ya-bonakala is: 'the star was visible,' but 'the star was seen' (by A. or B.), *inkanyezi ya-bonwa*.

The APPLIED (sometimes called the 'Relative' or 'Prepositional') form of the verb gives rise to numerous idioms, some of which have no exact European equivalents; but the most general rule which can be laid down for its use implies that the action is done with reference to some person or thing other than the direct object of the verb. If the verb is intransitive, and therefore has no direct object, this form makes it transitive, and enables it to take one. The ending is usually *-ela* (*-ila*) or *-era* (*-ira*); in Swahili *-ea* (*-ia*). Ex.:

ZULU: *hamba* 'go'; *hambela* 'go to' anyone, and so 'visit.'
hlala 'wait'; *hlal-ela* 'wait for.'
lima 'cultivate'; *lim-ela* 'cultivate for' some one else.

NYANJA: *dula* 'cut'; *dul-ira* 'cut for' anyone.
nena 'speak'; *nen-era* 'speak to' or 'for,' etc.

The CAUSATIVE, as a rule, has the ending *-isa* or *-isha*, or some easily recognisable modification of the same[1]. Its meaning needs no further explanation.

ZULU: *vala* 'shut,' *val-isa* 'make to shut,' *hamb-isa* 'make to go,' *tand-isa* 'cause to love,' etc.

NYANJA: *dul-itsa* 'make to cut,' *lim-itsa* 'make to cultivate,' *nen-etsa* 'cause to speak.'

SWAHILI: *funda* 'learn,' *fund-isha* 'teach' (*i.e.* 'cause to learn'), *soma* 'read', *som-esha* 'make, or help, to read.'

HERERO: *rara* 'sleep,' *rar-itha* 'make to sleep,' *thura* 'swell,' *thur-itha* 'cause to swell.'

An INTENSIVE form is sometimes found, identical in form (though not in origin) with the Causative. Thus, in Nyanja, *mang-itsa* (from *manga*, 'tie') may mean, either 'cause to tie' or 'tie tightly,' *end-etsa* either 'make to walk' or 'walk far.' This is also the case in Zulu, but here, the intensive sometimes reduplicates the causative termination and ends in *-isisa*: *buza* 'ask,' *buz-isisa* 'inquire thoroughly.' There is another intensive, in Zulu, ending in *-ezela*, which belongs to the

[1] It has not been thought necessary to take any notice here of the causatives in *-za* and other variations arising from the presence of certain consonants in the stem. The causative in *-ya* is a distinct form, sometimes found side by side with the others.

applied form. In Rundi[1] and probably elsewhere, the Intensive is a combination of the Applied and Causative endings: *rira* 'weep,' *riririsha* 'weep continually'; *saba* 'ask,' *sab-irisha* 'ask persistently.'

In Luganda, the Applied termination is reduplicated: *tonya* 'drip,' 'rain,' *tonyerera* 'drizzle incessantly.' Sometimes the root of the verb is wholly or partly reduplicated, to convey an intensive, or sometimes, rather, a repetitive force, but this is not the same thing as the verbal forms we are considering.

The REVERSIVE form has the ending *-ula* (*-ura*, in Swahili *-ua*)—sometimes *-ulula*, e.g.:

NYANJA: *tseka* 'shut,' *tseg-ula* 'open,' *pinda* 'fold,' *pind-ula* 'unfold.'
GANDA: *simba* 'plant,' *simb-ula* 'dig up,' *jema* 'rebel,' *jem-ulula* 'submit.'
KONGO: *kanga*, 'tie,' *kang-ula* 'untie.'
ILA: *amba* 'speak,' *amb-ulula* 'retract' (unspeak), *yala* 'shut,' *yal-ula* 'open,' *soma* 'sheathe,' *som-onona* 'pull out.'[2]

---

[1] Spoken in the country near the north end of Lake Tanganyika.

[2] Ila and Herero both have two additional reversive endings, *-ona* and *-onona*. These are found when the stem contains a nasal (*m* or *n*). Kongo also has *-ona* and *-una*.

HERERO: *patá* 'shut,' *pat-urura* 'open,' *yonya* 'be crumpled,' *yony-onona* 'smooth out,' etc.

This form is made intransitive by changing *l* to *k* : *tseg-uka* ' be open,' *simbuka* ' be dug up.' The Reversive form is not usually enumerated in Zulu grammars, but certainly exists in the language : *jaba* is ' be mortified, disappointed,' etc., *jab-ula* ' rejoice,' and there are words in *-ula* like *kum-ula* ' unfasten ' which distinctly have a reversive meaning, though the primitive verb may have been lost.

The RECIPROCAL, in *-ana*, implies, as may be gathered from the name, an act done by two or more people to each other :

SWAHILI: *pend-ana* ' love one another.'
NYANJA: *meny-ana* ' fight ' (' beat each other,' from *menya* ' beat ').
ZULU: *ling-ana* ' vie with one another,' ' be equal,' from *linga* ' strive.'

There are some variations in the ending. Kongo has *-ajiana*, or *-asajiana*, as well as *-ana* ; Ganda *-agana* or *-ang'ana*, as *kyaw-agana* ' hate one another,' *wulir-agana* ' hear one another,' etc.; and Herero *-asana*, as *mun-asana* ' see each other,' from *muna* ' see.'

The idiomatic uses of the Reciprocal form are curious: we may give some examples.

ZULU: *sa-bon-ana nomgani wami*, 'we saw each other (I) and my friend.'

NYANJA: *akulu a-bvut-ana mlandu* 'the headmen contend in a quarrel' (*bvutana*, reciprocal of *bvuta* 'be difficult.')

In Swahili this form enters into several expressions where its force is very difficult to render in English: *kupatik-ana* 'to be obtainable,' *kujulik-ana* 'to be knowable.' These are not quite the same as *kupatika* and *kujulika*, and the difference, probably, is in the implication that something is obtainable or knowable by everybody, the acquisition or information being, as it were, mutual.

The STATIVE form in *-ama* has left traces in most languages, even if it is not expressly recognised in the grammars. Verbs in *-ama* usually express an attitude:

NYANJA: *er-ama* 'stoop,' *kot-ama* 'be in a crouching position.'

SWAHILI: *in-ama* 'stoop' (*in-ua*, the reversive of the same root, means 'lift up') *ang-ama*, 'be suspended' from *anga* 'float' (in the air)—*angua*, the reversive, means 'take down,' and *ang-uka*, its intransitive, 'fall.'

Kot-ama is found in Zulu, with the same meaning as in Nyanja, and we also find *lul-ama* 'rise up a little from a recumbent position,' *fuk-ama* 'sit, as a hen hatching' and *pak-ama*, 'be elevated,' which may be verbs of the same kind. Compare,

HERERO: *themb-ama* 'be straight,' *pik-ama* 'be aslant' (from *pika* 'pull to one side').

CHWANA: *el-ama* (or *al-ama*) 'sit on eggs.'

KONGO: *lal-ama* 'be afloat,' *lamb-ama* 'be clenched' (said of a nail), *kok-ama* 'be hooked on to,' etc., etc.

Some languages have a REPETITIVE form in *-ulula*—others express the same idea by wholly or partly reduplicating the stem. Ila has *ula* 'buy, trade' (*cf.* Nyanja *gula*), *ul-ulula* 'trade a thing over and over again'; *nenga* 'cut,' *neng-ulula* 'cut up again and again'; Kongo: *sumba* 'buy,' *sumb-ulula* 'buy again.' Kongo also has the suffixes *-ununa*, *-olola* and *-onona*.

These two languages have, in addition, a 'Persistent Repetitive,' which in Kongo has the suffix *-ujiola*, with various modifications. Ex.:

Tunga 'build,' *tung-ujiola* 'keep on rebuilding.'
Kuna 'plant,' *kun-ujiona* 'keep on replanting.'

Ila has no suffix for this form, but inserts *a* before the final syllable of the verb.

sotoka ' jump,' *sotaoka* ' hop, as an insect.'
sandula ' turn over,' *sandaula* ' turn over and over.'

There are some other endings of which the functions do not seem as yet to be very clearly ascertained: *-ala*, *-ata*, *-nga* (found in Herero) and a few more.

The PERFECT IN -ILE is sometimes reckoned among the Derived Forms of the verb, because it is not a tense, strictly speaking— that is, it does not refer to *time*, but to ' the condition or progress of the action ' (Bentley), and because, unlike the real tenses, it is formed by a suffix.

Verbs formed from adjective-stems (as mentioned in a previous chapter) by the addition of *-pa* or *-mpa*, cannot be reckoned among the Derived Forms. Such are the Zulu *de-pa* ' be tall,' Nyanja (and Swahili) *nene-pa* ' be stout '; probably the Nyanja *i-pa* ' be bad ' is so formed from the root *bi*, originally *vi*, which has dropped its initial consonant. In Zulu we have a second form *-pala*, as *kulu-pala* ' be fat ' (or ' big ').

In conclusion, we may remark that all

these forms of the verb can be compounded with each other to almost any extent. So in Zulu: *hamb-ela* 'visit,' *hamb-el-isa* 'came to visit,' *hamb-el-is-ana* 'cause to visit one another,' *hamb-el-is-an-wa*, passive of the last named. Extreme instances of this kind of cumulative composition are given in Bentley's *Dictionary and Grammar of the Kongo Language*, pp. 640, 641. There is no need to say more on the subject here.

CHAPTER XI

THE VERB (*continued*)

MOODS AND TENSES

IF we ask ourselves what we mean by the term 'mood,' and find that it may be explained as 'manner of being,' it might seem that the distinction between the Derived Forms discussed in the last chapter, and Moods is not very clear. However, on considering some examples of each, it becomes evident that *moods are the various conditions under which some particular act is manifested:* the action, say, of writing is contemplated as *actually taking place* (whether in past, present or future time)—or as *possibly taking place* under certain conditions—or as *being desirable*, and so on. But it is always the same action of writing. In the Derived Forms, *the action itself is in some way modified:* it is looked on from the point of view of the sufferer instead of the doer, or as reversed, caused, intensified, applied to someone or something, etc., etc. And each separate form is carried unchanged through all the moods and tenses.

Moods are only marked to a limited extent in English. We have the Indicative, Infinitive, Imperative and Subjunctive, though the last is going out of use (that is, as shown by the form of the verb itself: 'if I be,' 'that he love,' etc.). In Latin, the distinctive inflections of the Subjunctive are more strongly marked, and in Greek we have an additional mood, the Optative.

The definition of '*Tense*' is simple enough, if we keep to European languages, where the word can be used in its strict etymological meaning. It refers to the *time* at which an action is performed—past, present, or future, with the sub-divisions of 'complete' and 'incomplete,' or 'perfect' and 'imperfect,' etc. But even here the matter is not quite so simple as it seems—should we, for example, call the French conditional a mood or a tense? For practical purposes, no doubt, the distinction matters little—yet it is worth thinking over in connection with our present inquiry.

When we leave Europe, we find—*e.g.*, in the Semitic languages—that the word 'tense' no longer applies, or rather, it has to be used with a somewhat conventionalised meaning, for the distinction of *time* is not kept in view so much as that of completed and of incomplete or continuous action. We saw in the last chapter that the Bantu so-called 'Perfect' tense does not necessarily imply a past state of things. It is very often equivalent to the Present, indicating an action completed in the past, whose effects still continue: thus, 'he is asleep' is rendered by an expression meaning: 'he has lain down' (and is still lying).

If we bear in mind that both terms are elastic as to *meaning*, we can draw a very clear distinction of *form* between moods and tenses in Bantu. The former are distinguished by *suffixes*, the latter by *prefixes*.[1]

On this showing, the Perfect in *-ile* should count as a *mood*, and it appears to me that there is no good reason against its doing so. We have seen that some reckon it as a Derived Form, or Voice.

---

[1] This cannot be taken quite absolutely: for instance, it does not apply to the Infinitive. (The Imperative, consisting of the bare stem, might be looked on as the ground-form whence the others are derived). But this, in spite of the prefix *ku-* (which marks neither person nor time) differs essentially from the tenses proper.

Some writers recognise (*e.g.*, in Zulu and Chwana) Optative and Potential Moods; but these, by their structure, are really tenses, and, since we cannot adhere to the strict definition of that word, they may very well pass for such.

We might reckon in Bantu eight moods, four of which, the Imperative, Infinitive, Indicative and Subjunctive, correspond, on the whole, with the notions expressed by those terms in European languages. The others are the Negative, the Perfect in *-ile*, the Continuative and the Relative.

The *Imperative*, as we have seen, consists of the bare verb-stem[1] in the singular, and suffixes *-ni* (really the pronoun of the second person) in the plural.

The *Infinitive* (which, as we have seen, is identical with the fifteenth noun-class) is distinguished, as a rule, by the prefix, *ku-*[2] This,

[1] Perhaps it is better to follow Meinhof in using this term instead of 'verb-root,' for we cannot tell that these verbs are not ultimately made up of monosyllabic roots, going back to a pre-Bantu stage of speech.

[2] This prefix has been quite lost in Kongo, except in the case of the two vowel-stem verbs, *kw-iza* and *kw-enda*. Duala shows traces of having had a different infinitive prefix. (See Meinhof, *Grundzüge, einer vergleichenden Grammatik der Bantusprachen*, p. 10.)

the Indicative and the Imperative all, in the present state of Bantu speech, end in -*a*, except in Herero and some of its cognates, and in the languages of the extreme north west (Duala, etc.).[1] Bleek seems to have considered this -*a* a later accretion, and supposed that the verb originally ended in some other vowel. But this matters little to our present purpose.

The *Subjunctive* ends in -*e*. Its uses are much like those of the European subjunctive, though more extensive; they can be better illustrated from the specimen texts at the end of the volume, which contain numerous examples, than by any explanations given here.[2]

The *Negative*, which on our definition we must reckon as a mood, ends in -*i*. It is a feature not found in any European language, where the addition of some invariable adverb

---

[1] Herero has one present tense which assimilates its final vowel to that of the stem, as *me piti* 'I go out' (from *pita*) *ma munu* 'he sees' (from *muna*). Some of the Congo languages, such as Ngala, Poto, etc. (not Kongo itself) seem to possess presents ending in -*e* and -*o*, which are probably to be explained by the same principle of Vowel-Harmony.

[2] Ex.: Zulu: *ngi-hambe* 'let me go'; Swahili: *ni-jenge* 'let me build"; Herero: *nge-mune* 'let me see'; Ganda: *a-lime* 'let him cultivate,' etc.

meaning 'not' is quite sufficient to negative any tense of the verb. The only difficulty that could arise is from the position of the negative, which, in a compound tense, has to be inserted between the component parts of the verb; and the two particles in French (*ne . . . pas*), by doubling this difficulty make it necessary to learn a negative as well as an affirmative conjugation. But 'not,' *nicht, non*, and *ne . . . pas* do not affect the form of the verb itself.

It is otherwise in Bantu. There are several different ways of forming the negative, but the main principle appears to be that a negative particle is prefixed and the final vowel of the verb altered to *i*. This is usually (though not in all languages) the Negative Present. The Negative Past is formed in a different way; and moreover there is not, as one might expect, a Negative tense corresponding to every Affirmative one. On the other hand, there are some negative tenses with no affirmative corresponding to them. This looks as though the Bantu mind conceived of 'not doing' a thing—just as the still more primitive mind conceives of 'more than one thing'—as a distinct and separate entity.[1] And perhaps this is borne out by the fact that languages of relatively advanced development, like Kongo, have lost the final inflection, and express the negative merely by invariable particles. Kongo has one of these particles before the verb and one after, like *ne . . . pas*.

Betonda = 'they love.' *Ke betonda ko* 'they do not love.'

In Duala, the negative particle *si* is used for all tenses, but is placed after the subject pronoun.

na loma 'I send'; *na si loma* 'I do not send.'
ba mende jipe 'they will cook'; *ba si mende jipe* 'they will not cook.'

The normal Negative Present is as follows:

Zulu	Chwana	Swahili	Ganda	Gisu
a-ngi-hambi	χa ke reke[2]	si-pendi[3]	si-laba	hi-n-teka
'I do not go'	'I do not buy'	'I do not love'	'I do not see'	'I do not cook'
a-si-hambi	χa re reke	ha-tu-pendi	te-ba-laba	hi-ba-teka
'We do not go'	'We do not buy'	'We do not love'	'They do not see'	'They do not cook'

[1] See *Language Families*, pp. 38, 39.

[2] This *e* in Chwana is the 'narrow e,' approximating in sound to i.

[3] The negative particle in Swahili is *ha*, which is

THE VERB

In Nyanja, the negative used throughout is *si* (contracting in the second and third persons singular to *su* and *sa*), and *i* is sometimes (not always) suffixed to the verb-stem : as *si-ndi-dziwa-i* ' I do not know,' but *si-ndi-dziwa* is also heard.

We need not enumerate all the different negative particles in use, *e.g.*, Ila *ta*, Yao *nga*, Zigula *nka*, etc., but we must say a word in passing as to the negative in the other tenses of the Indicative. Swahili has a negative past formed by means of the infinitive: *si-ku-penda* ' I did not love ' ; *ha-tu-ku-penda* ' we did not love.' This serves as negative both to the Past Tense (*ni-li-penda*) and the Perfect Tense (*ni-me-penda*).[1] Now, as -*mę*- indicates that the action is finished, complete, the sentence *ni-me-penda* cannot be negatived merely by the addition of a particle.[2] So another form is used : *si-ku-penda* is a negation

---

prefixed to the three plural pronouns, but contracts with those of the singular : *si* (originally ha+ni), *hu* (ha+u) *ha* (ha+a). *Te*, the Ganda negative particle, is in some dialects, used for all three persons alike as it is in Nyoro.

[1] Modern Swahili has disused the Perfect in -*ile* and the one which has replaced it is, by its structure, a tense, not a mood.

[2] See Meinhof, *Grundzüge* (p. 64).

of the Infinitive; literally 'not—I to love.' (This is different from the form actually in use as the Negative Infinitive, which is *ku-to-penda*, a contraction of *ku-toa ku-penda*, literally 'to take away loving.')

But Zulu negatives the Perfect by simply prefixing the Negative Particle: *a-ngi-tandile* 'I have not loved'; *ka-tandile*[1] 'he has not loved.' This is what might be called a mechanical formation; which means that, the original force of the inflections having been more or less forgotten, the prefixes and suffixes used with some tenses, etc., are applied to others, without reference to their abstract congruity.

There is, in Zulu, a Negative Past, made by prefixing *a-* as for the Present, and suffixing *nga* : *a-ngi-hamba-nga* 'I did not go.'

The Negative Future is, as Professor Meinhof points out, a recent formation,[2] and, as such, entirely mechanical.

---

[1] *Ka* sometimes, in Zulu, replaces *a*, which is never used, *e.g.* with the 3rd person singular (if the subject is of the first class), or with a noun of the 6th class: *umfana ka-hambile* ' the boy has not gone '; *ama-hashi ka-gijimi* ' the horses do not run.'

[2] *Grundzüge*, p. 65.

THE VERB

Swahili:

ni-ta-penda 'I shall love'; *si-ta-penda*, 'I shall not love.'

tu-ta-penda 'we shall love'; *ha-tu-ta-penda*, we shall not love.'

This, of course, as it does not change the final vowel, is indistinguishable from the tenses we shall have to consider later on. But the Zulu Negative Future is different. It is recognizably a compound tense, made up of the verb *ya* 'go' and the infinitive; and the first part of the compound is negatived in the same way as the Present.

ngi-ya-ku-tanda 'I shall love' (*lit.* 'I go to love').
a-ngi-yi-ku-tanda 'I shall not love.'

In all these indicative tenses, the negative particle comes first, but in the Subjunctive, the Participle, and the Relative Tenses, it comes after the subject-pronoun.

Subjunctive:

ZULU: *ngi-nga-tandi.* SWAHILI: *ni-si-pende* 'I may not love.'

Relative:

aba-nga-yi-ku-tanda   *a-si-po-sema*
'they who will not   'if he does not
love.'   speak.'[1]

[1] These forms were explained in Chapter VI. As to the reason for the difference in the position of the negative particle, see the reference in the last note.

It will be noticed that the Negative Particle here is different from that used with the Indicative. In Swahili, *si* is used all through the Subjunctive, and not with the first person only.

The Perfect in -ile is found in a great many Bantu languages. Swahili, as remarked above, has lost it—except in some of the northern dialects—and it seems to have disappeared altogether from Nyanja, though not from the neighbouring Yao. It is sometimes shortened to *i* or *e*, and assumes various modified forms—*e.g.* it may change the vowel instead of adding the suffix, as Zulu *lele* from *lala*,[1] *pete* from *pata*, and in the verbs of the Reciprocal form, as *hlangana* 'meet,' perfect *hlangene*. Derived forms, especially the Applied, very frequently shorten the termination to *e*: *sond-ela* 'approach,' perfect *sondele*.

It is not surprising that missionaries and others engaged in the reduction of a new language should sometimes have failed to recognise this 'Perfect' when they came across it, as its use did not correspond with

---

[1] *Lalile* is also used, but with a somewhat different meaning.

their notion of a tense. Yet that use is not without parallels nearer home. The Greek οἶδα 'I know,' is really the perfect of the **verb** meaning 'to see,' and Latin perfects used in a present sense, like *coepi, memini, odi* (which have lost their presents), and *novi*, (the perfect of *nosco*) 'I have come to know'='I know,' are really exemplifications of the same thing.

The *Continuative Mood*, with the suffix -*ga*, is less frequently met with. It implies that an action is done habitually, or that it continues for a long time. It is found in Yao, Kinga, Konde, Sango, Ganda, Kongo, Benga, Duala and elsewhere—sometimes in one of the forms *ka, nka, nga*, or with other modifications. It is used in more than one tense, and is even sometimes added to the Imperative, to make it more emphatic. This, and the fact that Kongo suffixes it also (in the form *nge*) to the Perfect, might seem to negative its being counted as a mood; but, though we do not as a rule find moods superadded on one another, after the fashion of the Compound Derived Forms, there does not seem to be any reason why we should say it is impossible in these two cases. Or, again, it is conceivable that the imperative -*ga*, at least (which is not exactly continuative, though it might, on occasion, be so) may not be the same suffix. The following are a few examples of this form, which does not exist in Zulu (unless—which I doubt —we could count the Negative Past), Nyanja, Herero or Swahili.

YAO: *na-tawa-ga* 'I was binding,' or 'I kept on binding' (*tawa* 'bind')
ni-ndawa-ga 'if I am binding.'
ni-nga-tawa-ga 'I should be binding' (if something else had happened).

GANDA: *a-fumba-nga omupunga bulijo* 'she cooks rice every day.'
a-na-soma-nga 'he will read continually.'
omu-ntu eya-kola-nga ebi-bya 'the man who-used-to-make bowls.'

KONGO: *o unu n-tunga-nga e-nzo ame* 'to day I am building my house.'
o unu n-tungidi-nge enzo ame 'to-day I-have-been-building my house.'
e lumbu kina ya-tunga-nga enzo ame 'the other day I-was-building my house.'

KINGA: *ndi-tova-ga* 'I keep on striking' (*tova*, 'strike.')[1]

SANGO: *vuχa-ga* 'go, do!' (*vuχa* 'go.')

The *Relative Mood* may take, as in Zulu, an

[1] O underlined, in Meinhof's notation (used in the book whence this example is quoted), is the 'broad o,' like the sound of *ou* in 'ought.'

invariable suffix for all persons and classes, or as in Swahili, a suffix varying with the class to which the subject belongs (*a-penda-ye*, *u-anguka-o*, *li-vundika-lo*, etc.). This applies to the first and simplest form of the Relative given in Chapter VI, which is (in Swahili at least)[1] without distinction of tense. But the other Swahili forms, if analysed, are found to follow the same principle: the first part of the word is an auxiliary (*li* or *na*) in the Relative Mood, followed by the Infinitive without *ku*: *a-li-ye-penda*, *a-na-ye-penda*, *ki-li-cho-anguka*, *vi-li-vyo-vundika*, etc., etc. As the Relative Pronouns were pretty fully discussed in Chapter VI., we need say no more about them here.

Before passing on to the Tenses, it may be well to say a few words about *Participles*.

We have, on previous occasions, referred to the quasi-participial forms existing in the Bantu languages: the very common one formed by prefixing the Possessive Particle to the Infinitive, and that with a locative termi-

---

[1] Zulu also suffixes -*yo* to the Perfect. The other verbal relative formations (those without -*yo*) are different in principle from the Swahili ones given in the text; but they need not be discussed here.

nation, found only (so far as I am aware) in the various dialects of Chwana (including Sutu). But Zulu has something like a real Participle, which 'may be formed for all the Tenses' (Colenso, *First Steps* § 232), but, unlike our participles is preceded by a pronoun and found in all three persons, singular and plural. Except in the third person (where the pronouns are *e* for the singular and *be* for the plural, instead of *u* and *ba*), and when agreeing with a noun of the sixth class (when the pronoun *a* is changed to *e*) the forms are identical with those of the finite tenses; and a participle is often only to be recognised by the difficulty of construing it as a finite verb in the context.

I shall not attempt anything like a complete enumeration of tenses. The simple ones are few and well marked, but there are endless compound tenses, built up with auxiliaries and other particles, which are not always easy to classify. The principle of their structure once recognized, however, they need present no great difficulty here.

The tense-particles not immediately recognizable as verbs may have existed as such in former times—indeed, it is practically certain that this was the case with most of them.

The simplest form of the Indicative Present (in some languages, as in Swahili, it exists only in theory) is formed by prefixing the Inseparable Pronoun directly to the Verb-Stem.

'See'		Zulu	Nyanja	Ganda
Si.	1st pers.	ngi-bona	ndi-ona	ndaba (for n-laba)
	2nd ,,	u-bona	u-ona	o-laba
	3rd ,,	u-bona	a-ona	a-laba
Pl.	1st ,,	si-bona	ti-ona	tu-laba
	2nd ,,	ni-bona	mu-ona	mu-laba
	3rd ,,	ba-bona	a-ona	ba-laba

This tense seems, as Junod says of it in Ronga, not to convey any precise indication of time. The more usual Present, in Zulu, is one compounded with the verb *ya* 'go': *ngi-ya-bona* ' I am seeing' or, more literally ' I go seeing.'

In some languages, a tense with similar meaning is formed by means of the prefix -*a*-, of which the exact force is uncertain. It usually contracts with the pronouns. The Swahili tense given below is that used at Mombasa; the corresponding one at Zanzibar is *ni-na-ona*, *u-na-ona*, etc.

Na is one form of the verb ' to be'; and in

Ronga	Chwana	Swahili	Zigula
nda-bona (ndi-a-bona)	ke-a-vona	na-ona (ni-a)	n-a-ona
wa-bona (u-a)	wa-vona	wa-ona	w-a-ona
a-bona (a-a)	wa-vona	a-ona	a-ona
ha-bona (hi-a)	re-a-vona	twa-ona (tu-a)	ch-a-ona
ma-bona (mi-a)	lwa-vona	mwa-ona	mw-a-ona
ba-bona (ba-a)	va-a-vona	wa-ona	w-a-ona

some languages, instead of the above tense, we have one compounded with this auxiliary in one shape or another. Thus, in Nyamwezi, *ndi-wona* (for *n-li-wona*), *u-li-wona*, etc.; in Nyanja *ndi-ri-ku-ona*, literally 'I am to see (= 'I am seeing'), and so on.

Some languages (Zulu, Konde, Ganda and others) have a Past Tense identical in form with the Present in -a-. Others use *na* to form a Past Tense, *e.g.*, Nyanja *ndi-na-ona*, etc.

The Future is very often formed with the auxiliaries meaning 'come' or 'go'—Nyanja *ndi-dza-ona*, Chwana *ke-tla-vona*, Zulu *ngi-ya-ku-bona* (or *ngi-za-ku-bona*). Swahili has *ni-ta-ona*: *ta* at present means nothing by itself, but it may be shortened from *taka* ('wish' or 'want.') In Ganda, the Near Future is formed with the prefix *na*, and the Far Future with the prefix *ri*. Both of them mean 'to be.'

The most peculiar Future is that in the Likoma dialect of Nyanja, which is identical with the Negative Past in other dialects—*e.g.*, *si-ni-fe* 'I shall die.' The explanation seems to be that what one has not yet done is still in the future, and, therefore, to say one has not yet died is the same as saying that one will die.

In Swahili, as already stated, there is a Perfect Tense differing from the form in *-ile* discussed under the Moods. It is formed with the particle *-me-* (which may be connected with *mala* 'finish')—*ni-me-ona* 'I have seen.' A similar tense is formed in Pokomo with *-ma-*.

Giryama has two Perfects—the Perfect Mood, which is the older form, ending in *-ere* or *-ire* (*ni-onere* 'I have seen,' *ni-fik-ire* 'I have arrived'—from *fika*) and the tense, formed with *dza*: *hu-dza-m'-ona* 'we have seen him.'

Compound Tenses are very numerous in Zulu, chiefly built up on the verb 'to be' (*uku-ba*) and the particle *nga*, which mainly implies potentiality (*e.g.*, *nga-ngi-be-ngi-bona*, 'I would have been seeing,' etc.), and Chwana has a still greater variety, introducing several other verbs. But these, and the particles which play so great a part in Nyanja (*ma*, *ta*, *ka*, *ngo*, etc.), must be left to the students of the respective languages. It only remains to say a few words more about auxiliaries and about monosyllabic verbs. (The latter are not always auxiliaries, and there are some auxiliaries of more than one syllable).

The auxiliaries which we have mentioned so far are employed as tense-prefixes, and inserted between the subject pronoun and the verb. But there are others which are grammatically separate from it, but necessary to its meaning. Some of these are defective, only used in one or two tenses and never apart from a principal verb; others are independent verbs, which have a peculiar use as auxiliaries. Thus in Zulu *ponsa* 'throw' means, as an auxiliary 'to be on the point of doing'—*ngiponse ukuwa* 'I was on the point of falling.' In Ganda *yagala* 'like, love, want' is similarly used to express that something is about to take place: *enyumba eyagala okugwa* 'the house is likely to fall.' *Va* 'go out' conveys that something has just been done, or that an act results from something mentioned before; in the latter case it is equivalent to 'therefore.'

Tu-va ku-kola 'we have just been working.'

Sometimes the auxiliary is followed by an infinitive, as in the last examples, and as we should expect in European languages. But it is just as often followed by a finite verb, and this construction gives rise to some of the most curious and difficult idioms—*e.g.*, in Zulu: *u-buye u-hlangane nabo*, 'do thou after that join with them.' Literally 'do thou return (*buya*) that thou mayest join with them.' In Ganda, *mala* 'finish' is used in various unexpected ways. It may denote, with a negative, 'non-completed, though intended action.' *Ya-mala na-ta-kola* 'as a matter of fact, he did not do the work.' Or we may find it in such sentences as *mala ga-lya* 'eat it just as it is'—whether you like it or not; (perhaps the idea is 'eat it and have done with it!')—*mala ga-genda* 'never mind, go!'

In Ronga, *dyuleka* neuter-passive of *dyula* 'seek' is employed as an auxiliary to express 'it is necessary,' and *chuka* 'start' (with surprise) to convey the notion of 'perhaps' 'by any chance,' or to emphasize a negative imperative.

Ku-dyuleka ndi-famba 'I have to go.' *U-ta-mu-khoma loko u-chuka u-mu-bonile* 'You will seize him if by any chance you have seen him.' *U-nga-chuke- u-hlaya* 'Don't go to say. . . .' = 'Don't think of saying. . . .'

The use of the verb *ti*, properly meaning 'say' is very important. It will be mentioned again in the next chapter, as it occurs so frequently in conjunction with the 'descriptive adverbs' or 'sound-pictures' so common in the Bantu languages. But besides this use, it enters into a variety of characteristic idioms.

It is found in most languages (except perhaps those of the Congo), though now disused in Swahili. In Chwana, it has the form *re*[1], in Herero *ty-a* (*ti* + *a*) otherwise it scarcely varies. Its infinitive is often used as a conjunction, equivalent to 'that' (*cf.* our 'that is to say,') as in Nyanja:

Antu a-ganiza   kuti   ndi   mfiti
'People think   that (they) are   wizards (who)
zi-sanduka   makoswe
'change-themselves (into) rats.'

Sentences like this, where it is equivalent to 'saying,' show the connection quite clearly:

[1] Where *e* in Chwana corresponds to an *i* in Zulu, it is the narrow *e*—intermediate between French *é* and *i*.

Tambala   a-lira   kuti   'kukuluku!'
'The cock   crows   saying   "*kukuluku!*"'

Other tenses, simple and compound, are used more or less as conjunctions, *e.g.*, Nyanja *nga-ti* 'if' Ila *a-no-ku-ti* 'whereas,' Zulu *ku-nga-te, ku-nga-ti-ti*. Ila has *a-tela* 'lest,' *antela* 'perhaps,' which may be applied forms of it. A very common idiom is to use it as an auxiliary at the beginning of a sentence, with some such meaning as 'when,' 'as soon as,' or 'it came to pass that. . . .'

Irregular Verbs. Bantu verbs can be irregular in two ways, neither of which need cause much difficulty. They may be of one syllable only, or they may end in some other sound than *a*. *Ti* and a few others are irregular in both ways at once.

Genuine Bantu verbs of more than one syllable which do not end in -*a* are so rare that we need do no more than mention them.

The monosyllables are more important, but of these a certain number must be eliminated, which are not original monosyllables, but have only become so by attrition. The case of the Zulu *ma* or *ema* 'stand' (Swahili *sim-ama*) was referred to in the last chapter, and there is a whole number of verbs in Zulu, found either with or without an initial *e*. Such are (*e*)*mba* 'dig'[1] (*e*)*ba* 'steal,' (*e*)*pa* 'thin out'[2] (as seedlings) (*e*)*zwa* 'hear.'

Some have more than one syllable, and these (like (*e*)*muka* 'go away' (*e*)*tula* 'take off') look like Derived Forms.

It seems clear that these (or most of them, for some might have been formed later, by 'false analogy') originally began with a consonant which was dropped, and then the initial vowel, when it could not easily be contracted with the pronoun, was elided also.[3] It is interesting to see that Nyanja, while keeping the initial vowel in *ima* 'stand' has incorporated the infinitive particle with *mba* 'dig,' which is now *ku-kumba*. Perhaps this is to avoid confusion with *imba* 'sing,' as it has not been done in the case of *ku-ba* 'steal.'[4] Nyanja has no objection to the contact

---

[1] Probably the Swahili *j-embe* 'a hoe' comes from the same root.

[2] To be distinguished from *pa* 'give,' which seems to be an original monosyllable.

[3] 'Vowel verbs' are usually reckoned among 'irregular verbs,' on account of this contraction, which is not always applied in the same way.

[4] Cf. Swahili *iba* (Mombasa) and *jepa* (Lamu).

between two vowels, and, as a rule, sounds them both distinctly, not often contracting them into an intermediate sound, as is done in Zulu; and perhaps this is why it retains the original *i* in *ima*, which in Zulu is altered to *e*.

When we come to primitive monosyllables —or what we may fairly presume to be such— we find, apart from tense-particles and recognised auxiliaries, several verbs expressing simple and universal notions (such as 'eat,' 'drink,' 'die,' etc.), in so many Bantu languages that they are likely enough to have formed part of the original common stock. The following table exhibits some, but by no means all, of these.

The great interest of these primitive verbs lies in the fact that it may be possible to trace them in the Sudan languages, as indeed, I think, has been done with one or two. But such questions lie outside the scope of this book.

	Zulu	Chwana	Herero	Nyanja	Ila	Zigula	Swahili	Giryama	Ganda	Gisu	Kongo	Bangi	Duala
Eat[1]	dhla	ya	rya	dya	dya	dya	la	rya	lya	lya	dia	le	da
Drink[2]	—	nwa	nwa	mwa	nwa	nywa	nwa	nwa	nywa	(nyuwa)	nua	nua	nyo
Fall[3]	wa	wa	wa	gwa	wa	gwa	(gwa)	gwa	gwa	gwa	bwa	(ku)	ko
Die[4]	fa	shwa	ta	fa	fwa	fa	fa	fwa	fa	fwa	fwa	wa	wo
Fight[5]	lwa	lwa	rwa	—	lwa	—	(wa-na)	—	(lwa-na)	—	—	—	(a-na)
Give[6]	pa	ha	pa	(pa-tsa)	pa	—	pa	pa	wa	ha	va	pe	—
Dawn[7]	sa	sa	tya	cha	cha	cha	cha	cha	kya	—	kia	—	—
Rain[8]	na	na	—	nya	—	nya	nya	nya	—	—	—	—	—

¹ The Kongo form of this word is spelt as given here in Bentley's *Dictionary*, but I have no doubt that it is pronounced *dya*, as it is in Nyanja, where many of the printed books have *dia*. The same applies to the spelling *nua* (for *nwa*) and *kia* for *kya* in Kongo and Bangi. Bangi is spoken in the district near the junction of the Kasai with the Congo.

² The old root has been lost in Zulu, probably for *hlonipa* reasons*; the word now used is *puza*. Zanzibar Swahili has *nywa*, like Ganda, etc. Note the tendency of Duala verbs to end in *-o*.

³ *Gwa* is found in old Swahili: the modern word is *anguka*. The usual word in Bangi is *kita*, but *kū* is given as an 'indeclinable adjective' suggestive of falling. It may be the root of Duala *ko*.

⁴ A dissyllabic form of this word is found in Yao (*uwa*) and Kikuyu (*kua*). The former must not be confused with Swahili *ua* 'kill,' which is the same word as Zulu and Kongo *bula* ' strike.'

⁵ Nyanja Zigula and Swahili have lost this, and use words meaning 'strike each other' (*menyana, towana, pigana*). Giryama and Ganda use the reciprocal *lw-ana*, and Kongo has *nw-ana*, evidently another form of the same ro

⁶ *Ha* in Chwana is used in the special sense of "giving food." The word used in Kongo is *vana*, reciprocal of *va*, which could correspond etymologically with *pa*.

⁷ *Kia* and *kya* (which should probably be spelt alike) may be the same sound as that indicated by *cha* and *tya*. See Noël-Armfield, *General Phonetics*, p. 91.

⁸ This is only found in some dialects of Nyanja; it is not used at Blantyre, probably to avoid confusion with a similar word, tabooed as vulgar.

---

* This word in Zulu expresses what anthropologists call 'taboo.' People are said to *hlonipa* a word, if they avoid it (1) as improper or vulgar, (2) because it is the name—or part of the name—of a deceased chief, or (in the case of women) the head of the family. Thus, the wives and daughters of a man named u-Langa would have to find some other word when speaking of the sun (*i-langa*).

CHAPTER XII

ADVERBS AND PARTICLES

I have preferred the term 'Particles' for the invariable parts of speech—except adverbs, which are somewhat more clearly defined—because the words which act as prepositions and conjunctions may be—and often are—used in other ways, and, in fact, they usually prove, on examination, to be different parts of speech altogether.

Pa, ku, mu, which, as sometimes employed, are genuine prepositions, and treated as such in all the older grammars, are really pronouns, as we saw in an earlier chapter. In fact, Meinhof says there are no such things as prepositions in Bantu. The Zulu *nga* 'with' (in an instrumental sense, as *watshaywa ngomcibitsholo* 'he was hit with an arrow') at one time seemed to me a possible exception, but its use after the passive[1] shows that it is really identical with the copula, as explained

---

[1] See above, pp. 114, 115.

above. *Na* 'with,' in the sense of 'along with,' is really the conjunction 'and,' perhaps the only undoubted conjunction.

We have already remarked that infinitives and even finite tenses of verbs may be used as conjunctions: *e.g.* (*u*)*kuti* in Zulu and Nyanja; χo-*hitlha*—literally 'to arrive' (at) for 'until' in Chwana; Swahili *kw-amba* 'that' literally 'to say' (*kuti* not being used), Lala *k-umfwa* 'and so' literally 'to hear.' Nyanja -*ngakale* 'although,'—used with a pronoun, *a-nga-kale*, *chi-nga-kale*, *i-nga-kale*, etc., from *kala* 'sit,' 'stay, be in a place,' and so, literally, 'it may be (that. . . .')

There is also an interesting use of nouns as conjunctions, as, Nyanja, *chi-fukwa* 'because,' which really means 'fault,' 'blame,' etc.; Duala *onyola na*, contracted from *o nyolo a na*, 'through the body of' ('the fact that . . .' also meaning 'because.') In Swina *pa musoro pa* 'on the head of' and *pa musana pa* 'on the back of,' are used prepositionally for 'because of,' 'on account of.'

The ease with which these locutions change places is illustrated by the fact that some adverbs are turned into prepositions by the addition of a particle.

Thus *pa-nsi* (it is found in a great many languages, even where, as in Zulu, *pa* by itself has gone out of use) means 'on the ground,' 'down,' but *pansi ya* is 'under' 'below.' *Tini* (*chini*) which takes the place of *pansi* in Swahili is treated in the same way.

It would serve no useful purpose to attempt enumerating all the possible words or combinations of words which might serve as prepositions and conjunctions: the above is a sufficient indication what sort of thing to look out for in any particular language.

With regard to Adverbs we have several possibilities to consider. First, there are the regular adverbs, formed from adjectives with the prefix *ka-*; to which we have already adverted in the chapter on the Numerals. These are found in Zulu, Nyanja (only with numerals), Ila, Nyamwezi (with numerals), Zigula.[1] They do not occur in Swahili, Ganda, Gisu or Kongo. *Kale* or *kade* 'long ago' found in almost every language, even those which have no other adverbs in *ka*, seems to be the adverbial of the root for 'long.'

---

[1] Besides the numeral adverbs this language has *ka-ngi* 'often' (from -(*e*) *ngi* 'many') and perhaps other words of the same kind.

Then we have nouns preceded by a possessive particle, as in Swahili *kufanya kwa uzuri* 'to do beautifully.' Here the possessive particle agrees with *kufanya*, but it would also be used with a finite verb—I suppose still with reference to the infinitive; or perhaps because its real relations had been forgotten, so that it could be placed indifferently after any form of the verb.

Another way is to use an adjective with the prefix of the seventh or the eighth class—as Hereo *tyi-nene* 'very,' from *-nene* 'great'; Swahili *vi-baya* 'badly'; Duala *bu-bi* 'badly' which last might also be classed as a noun. Other nouns are used, by themselves, or with a particle prefixed, as Zulu *na-muhla* 'to-day,' Nyanja *mawa* 'to-morrow.'

Then we have the locative Adverbs—not merely those already mentioned, which are preceded or followed by a locative particle, as *pezulu*, *pansi* (some languages have also *kunsi* and *munsi*), *tini*, etc., but such as *pano*, *muno*, *kuno*, or *hapa*, *pale*, or *mumona*, *kukona*, (Ila) and *momwemo*, *pomwepo* (Nyanja), with other variations, too many to be enumerated. These, however, are rather a kind of demonstrative pronoun. And it should not be forgotten that the Derived Forms of Verbs, in many cases, render adverbs unnecessary.

There are some invariable Adverbs, which do not seem to be derived from other parts of speech, as *lero*, *leo*, *lelo* 'to-day,' Nyanja *tsopano* (Yao *sambano*) 'now,' *kati* 'in the middle' (sometimes with added prefixes), Yao *soni* 'again,' Nyanja *-nso* (suffixed to almost any other part of speech), 'also,' 'again'— and others, which can be found by consulting the lists in various grammars. It may be that the etymologies of these are only as yet untraced, and they may be assigned to their proper position in time; but some of them possibly belong to the class described in the next paragraph, though they have settled down to a more assured position in the language than those we are about to mention.

These are what are sometimes called 'Sound-pictures'; other terms for them are 'onomatopoetic vocables' (Stapleton), 'descriptive adjectives' (Junod), 'onomatopoetic substantives' (Torrend), 'indeclinable adjectives' (Whitehead), 'interjectional roots,' etc.

The importance of these has been more and more recognized of late years. They occupy a very prominent place in the Sudanic languages, and Westermann has devoted a good deal of attention to them in his *Ewe Grammar*.[1] There is also a very interesting passage dealing with this feature of primitive language in Lévy-Bruhl's *Les Fonctions Mentales dans les Sociétés Inférieures*.[2] Dr. Hetherwick (Handbook of the Yao Language, p. 76) says:

'Certain words onomatopoetic in their character may be classed as adverbs. They represent the action or the idea referred to and may be used either with or without the descriptive verb; thus *chum* signifies the sound of falling into water, like our English "splash." *Wa-gwile m'mesi, chum!* "He fell into the water, splash!" *Myu*, with the fingers drawn across the lips, or accompanied by a peculiar motion of the hands, one over the other, signifies completion; *Ngondo jaiche nekumala wandu myu!* "The war came, and the population was completely destroyed." An idiomatic use of the verb *kuti* "to say," is used in conjunction with such words. To the form *-ati* is prefixed the characteristic pronoun of the

---

[1] See *The Language-Families of Africa*, pp. 43, 66.
[2] Paris, 1910.

object described, and joined with the onomatopoetic has the force and application of an adjective. *Ngo jati pyu* " red cloth " (literally the cloth which says *pyu* or red), *Nale, ngope jakwe jati bi* " Look, his face is black " (says *bi*—i.e., he is angry).'

Here we see one of the expressions noted accompanied by a gesture. In fact we may suppose them to have arisen out of the gestures which preceded speech—to be, as it were, gestures translated into sound. To quote M. Lévy-Bruhl (p. 183):

'It is not even necessary that these " auxiliaries " of description should be exclusively gestures or movements.' (The previous paragraph deals with the use of gesture, not in the absence of speech, but to help it out and make it more expressive.) 'The desire to describe may also try to find satisfaction by means of . . . a kind of pictures or reproductions of what one wants to express, obtained by means of the voice. Among the Ewe tribes, says M. Westermann, the language is extraordinarily rich in the means of directly reproducing an impression by sound. This richness arises from an irresistible tendency to imitate all that is heard, seen, or generally perceived, and to imitate it by means of one or more sounds. . . . What is imitated, in the first instance, is apt to be movement; but we also have these imitations or vocal reproductions—these "vocal images," for sounds, odours, tastes, tactile impressions. There are some which accompany the expression of colours, abundance, degree, pain, enjoyment, etc. It is beyond doubt that many words in the real sense (nouns, verbs, adjectives) have originated in these vocal images. They are not, properly speaking, onomatopœias, but rather descriptive vocal gestures.'

Stapleton, therefore, defined them somewhat too narrowly in calling them imitations of sounds[1]—in fact this is contradicted by the very examples he gives a few lines further back:

NGALA: *mai mabandakani* **lilili** 'the water has quieted down peacefully.'
butu boindi **pi** 'the night darkens darkly, or silently on all the heavens at once, etc.'
LOLO: *ntso* **kwi kwi kwi** 'go quickly.'

This writer goes on to say: 'These forms

[1] *Comparative Handbook of Congo Languages*, p. 130.

are used very largely as interjections, and some are evidently amongst the most primitive elements of these languages. Some appear to be the roots from which nouns, etc., are formed,—*sanja abameli* **bu** *o mai* (Ngala) "the moon shines on the water brightly" (*cf. bo-bu*, "light"). *Ndako* **foi foi** (Kele) "the house is lit up brightly."'

It is a pity that the author did not illustrate this point a little more fully, as he does not tell us what noun is formed from *foi foi:* by analogy we should expect *bo-foi*. In the cognate Bangi language (which does not seem to possess the *f* sound) *poipoi*[1] expresses the brightness of a shining surface, such as polished wood or metal. It makes a verb *poibana*. A glance through the Dictionary shows numerous other examples: *pioka* 'beat with a stick or whip,' from *pio*, the sound made by a switch; *tsakana* 'be dispersed' from *tsa; zonga* 'surround,' from *zo*. These are given in the Dictionary as derived from

---

[1] As printed in Whitehead's dictionary, this word has diacritic marks indicating that o is the narrow o with the 'raised' tone, and i has the 'lowered' tone. This is important, as there are other words quite similar except for the tones.

verbs, but it is not fair to mention this without quoting the passage from the Grammar (p. 18) which relates to them :

'For the most part these are derived from verbs, or the verbs from them. For practical purposes it is here assumed' (but why?) 'that they are derived from verbs. Those who maintain that the verbs are derived from them have the best of the argument, for these indeclinable adjectives are the most elementary parts of the language, and many may be traced to an onomatopoetic origin. These words are the most graphic in the language, they are the "colouring" words, the stories and common speech of the people are full of them, and often they have such force that sentence after sentence can be constructed by means of them, without the use of a single verb, the verb being indicated by these indeclinable adjectives. They take the place of adjectives to a very large extent, and in the dictionary their meaning will often be found indicated by an English adverb, yet in Bobangi they are adjectives.'

These languages of the Middle Congo and its northern affluents tend to shade off towards those of the Sudanic family. This would seem to account—I do not say for the abundance of these roots, for Ronga, Nyanja, Zulu, Yao, etc., are very rich in them,[1] but for the frequency of nouns and verbs formed from them, and the ease with which they can be recognised.

In Zulu (which in many ways seems to be one of the younger Bantu languages), a number of verbs are plainly derived from these particles, though they are more usually introduced by *ukuti*. See § 298 (p. 128) of Colenso's *First Steps in Zulu-Kafir*—a most instructive passage, though the author did not quite appreciate the character of these 'vocal images.' The remark (p. 129) that 'others are probably imitations of the sounds referred to' shows, however, that he was on the right track.

Some of the examples given to illustrate this derivation of verbs incidentally show that some verbs may seem to be Derived Forms which are not so in reality; thus *hlepula*

---

[1] And probably other languages, where no special attention has been called to them. In Velten's Nyamwezi grammar, *e.g.* (Velten's books are practically useful, but he is scarcely a safe guide in philology) we find *bu* 'abundantly,' and *po* or *pe* 'also'—perhaps others. It is rather surprising to find no indication of such 'adverbs' in Gisu—but the work done on that language is admittedly very tentative as yet.

'break off' looks like the reversive of a (non-existent) *hlepa*, whereas it comes straight, so far as one can see, from *ukuti hlepu*. So, too, *boboza* 'pierce,' which looks like a causative, is from *ukuti bobo* 'to have a hole in it'; and the same root gives us the nouns *im-bobo* and *isi-bobo*. Perhaps some of us have not left our childhood too far behind to feel in a dim way that *bobo* somehow suggests a hole (and it does so quite as much as the same word, in French nurseries, expresses 'something that hurts')—but even these will not be able to explain why it is so.

Some of the Zulu examples are so delightful for their own sake, that I make no apology for quoting them.

Ngaziti shwangalazi lezo' zinto zonke.

'I said *shwangalazi* to all those things—swept them away with a swish.'

'He says *xafuxafu*'[1]—eats like a dog.

'It (the sky) said *namanama* (rained very gently) this morning."

'He said (or went) *gigigi* down the slope'—*i.e.*, ran down—'and crossed over to the other side.' (Evidently getting impetus for the upward effort).

'The sun said *tetete*'—was low down in the sky.

---

[1] *x* indicates the lateral click.

Mr. E. W. Smith (*Grammar of the Ila Language*, p. 66) mentions 'certain particles suffixed to adjectives which express a superlative or absolute idea. They do not seem to be used with all verbs.

'NE. *Menzhi a la tontola-né*, the water is very, very cold.'

'BU. *Muntu u la tuba-bú*, the person is very, or altogether white.

'NSWA. *Menzhi a zuma-nswá*, the water is altogether dried up.'

The acute accent (which is not explained in the text) may indicate a raising of the tone, or (more probably) that it is accented independently of the verb, and does not, as enclitics in Bantu usually do, draw the accent forward. In that case, it would surely have been better not to connect the two by a hyphen.

It would seem as if Ila had limited the scope of the Vocal Image to a mere expression of intensity. Or perhaps the author has to some extent mistaken its nature; for it seems clear—even without an inside knowledge of the language—that they do not mean 'very' or anything of the sort; but *ne* is 'cold, *bu* 'white'; *nswa* 'dry,' *piu* 'red' (as in Yao), and so on. Mr. Smith goes on to say: 'These particles are also used interjectionally, the verbs being omitted, *e.g.*, *Nda ka ya ku menzhi. Nswa!* I went to the water. Quite dry!' This could not be explained on the supposition that *nswa* simply means 'very.' We should also like to refer back to the parallel columns of verbs and adjectives given by Mr. Smith on p. 61—already adverted to in Chapter VIII. The adjectives there given look to me like developments (*-biabe* and *-fwafwi* are imperfect reduplications; all the others ending in *o* or *u*)[1] from roots of this kind, and the verbs as if they had been formed directly from the roots. Of the 'superlative particles' I have only been able to trace one which has given rise to a verb: *-pi*, whence *pia* 'to be hot.' (This, as *pya*, *psya*, *swa*, etc., is found in most Bantu languages with the same, or some closely connected meaning. Meinhof thinks the Proto-Bantu stem was PIA.) But I have no doubt that careful search would be able to discover a great many.

We shall recur to this point in the next chapter.

In Swahili these particles are not conspicuous, yet I do not know how otherwise to account for *tu* 'only,' *pia* 'also,' 'altogether,' 'entirely,' (*watu wote pia*), *hima* 'quickly.' A few are heard as expletives ('When the doctor pulled out my tooth, I felt—*bu!*'—*lo-o-o!* expressive of surprise, *chub!* of impatience, etc.), but they are not used otherwise and do not seem to have given rise to any verbs or nouns. Perhaps the influence of Arabic, which has supplied some useful adverbs, prepositions and conjunctions, has favoured the disuse of the Vocal Image.

The late Revs. D. C. Scott and W. A. Scott, of Blantyre, collected, in a valuable little pamphlet—*The Mang'anja Unit of Thought*—some interesting specimens of what they have somewhat enigmatically called 'Buds or Thorns?' I take this title to imply a doubt whether such particles were really roots whence speech was developed, or outgrowths of developed speech—atrophied 'fragments of verbs.' A few of the sentences may be here given in illustration.

'The lion did not spring—he just came, *kuputu! kuputu! kuputu!*—like a horse.'

'The eagle has swept past—*kwā*.'

'A man with a lame leg goes *timpya, timpya, timpya*.'

'The soldiers stood *nda, nda, nda*' (in line).

'The stars are shining *ng'ani, ng'ani, ng'ani*.'

'He got into the mud and fell *tapwi !*—he got out and fell into the water, *pabva !*'

'The guinea-fowl has run away *njo ! njo ! njo !*' Here the verb used is *njonjola*, clearly formed from the particle.

Further quotations are unnecessary, and would take up too much space, but I would direct the reader's attention to M. Junod's paragraphs (§§ 378, 379) on *Adverbes descriptifs* (pp. 196, 197 of his *Grammaire Ronga*.)[1] He strongly insists on the importance of these adverbs' and on the great number of verbs derived from them.

One point to notice, in conclusion, is that Vocal Images frequently contain sounds not otherwise found in the language, just as we use clicks not found in any articulate English words to express surprise, regret or (to a horse) encouragement. *Chum* (Yao and Nyanja) and *chub* (Swahili) have unwonted final consonants.

---

[1] His *Elementary Grammar of the Thonga-Shangaan Language* (in English) is more generally accessible. The section on 'Descriptive Adverbs' will be found on pp. 84-86.

In Shambala, quite a number of these words begin with *p*—a sound which in that language is (except when preceded by *m*) changed to *h*. This matter would evidently repay further study.

CHAPTER XIII

WORD BUILDING

WE saw, at the outset, that *inflexion by prefixes* was a great and striking characteristic of the Bantu speech-family. We have seen, also, that *suffixes* play by no means a negligible part, as they distinguish both the Derived Forms and the Moods of Verbs. Further, some languages have the suffixed Locative; and we just remarked in passing that a good many adjectives are formed by suffixes. What more there is to say about these, and the other cases not already noticed, can best find a place here.

Nouns may end in any one of the five vowels.[1] Any one of these may be a suffix.

---

[1] I am using this expression for convenience sake. They may, for aught I know, end in any of the fifty or so vowel-sounds recognised by phoneticians which exist in Bantu. But the old original five will serve the purpose of this exposition.

but is not necessarily so; *e.g.*, in *mbwa* 'dog,' *nyati* 'buffalo,'[1] the final vowel seems to belong to the stem.

Taking, first, nouns and adjectives formed from verbs, and going through the classes in order, we find that one of the commonest derivatives of this kind is the noun-agent, where the verb-stem takes the prefix of the first class, and changes its final *-a* to *-i* (in Herero to *-e*).

ZULU: *um-fiki* 'one who arrives,' from *fika* 'arrive.'
um-fi 'deceased person,' from *fa* 'die.'
HERERO: *omu-tarere* 'overseer,' from *tarera*, applied form of *tara* 'look.'
CHWANA: *mo-dihi* 'worker,' from *diha* 'work'; *mo-ruti* 'teacher' from *ruta* 'teach.'
NYANJA: *m-weti* 'herdsman' from *weta*; *m-pambi* 'robber' from *pamba*.
GANDA: *omu-zimbi* 'builder' from *zimba*; *omu-somi* 'reader,' from *soma*.

Other nouns prefix the first-class prefix to the unchanged verb-stem, as Swahili *m-chunga* (*m-tunga*) 'herdsman,' from *chunga* (*tunga*) to 'herd'; *m-gema* 'one who taps palm trees' (for

[1] These words are Swahili, but they are found (sometimes in the same form) in many other languages.

wine), from *gema*. But these are really a species of participle, and their verbal character is still so far felt in Swahili that they are usually (not always) followed by an object: *mchunga mbuzi* 'a goat-herd' ('one who herds goats') *mfanya biashara* 'one who makes trade,' *i.e.*, 'a merchant.' But both in Swahili and in other languages we also find nouns of this kind without an object, which shows that there is a tendency to lose sight of their verbal character. *E.g.*, Yao *m-langa* 'herdsman,' Nyanja *m-londola* 'one who tracks game,' from *londola* 'follow up' and the Swahili *mgema* already given.

There are some verbal nouns in -*e* as Swahili *m-tume*[1] 'messenger,' from *tuma* 'send.' We have already pointed out that adjectives in -*e* are frequently derived from verbs, and from these we get names of the first class, like *m-ume* 'husband,' the adjective -*ume* 'male being derived from an almost obsolete (in this sense) *luma* 'cohabit.' Ganda has a set of nouns ending in -*e* with a passive significance— *omu-fumite* 'wounded man,' from *fumita* 'stab,' *omu-sibe* 'prisoner' from *siba*, 'bind.'

---

[1] Not often used except in the sense of 'apostle.'

Verbal nouns of the first class in *o* do not seem to be so common, but are found in Yao, as *m-jiganyo* 'teacher,' from *jiganya* 'teach.' (Dr. Hetherwick, however, says that 'in actual use, the relative forms *juakwiganya*,' etc. —*i.e.*, the infinitive preceded by the possessive particles—'are more frequently employed'). And, in general, it is so easy to make these forms for oneself that it is well to remember the warnings of experienced writers, and never venture on any not ascertained to be used by the natives themselves. Bishop Colenso says:

'The above words, however,' (*i.e.*, *um-fundi* 'learner' and *um-fundisi* 'teacher') 'and most of the above kind which appear in the printed books, are formed by *Missionaries*, not by the *Natives*, who employ these derivatives much more sparingly, but may form them at pleasure, so that they cannot be entered in the Dictionaries as standard Zulu words.' Examples of the latter kind are *um-ondhli* 'nourisher' used in an *isibongo*[1] of Mpande,

---

[1] *Isi-bongo* (from *bonga* 'praise') is a song (generally a string of laudatory epithets) composed by the professional bards or 'praisers' of the Zulu chiefs, and handed down by tradition.

so that it may be regarded as a kind of poetical license, and *um-hambi* 'traveller,' which occurs in a proverbial expression. Some such words, however, 'belong to the language'; and indeed we might add that even of the others, some (such as *um-fundisi*) have been found so useful that they are by this time fully naturalized.

And the late Dr. Scott, in the Preface to his *Cyclopædic Dictionary of the Mang'anja Language*, says:

'Yet no word can be formed at pleasure: it must bow to usage and wont. However clear the formation. . . . is . . . one must serve the language, not create it.'

But I cannot refrain from adding to this a remark I once heard from Professor Meinhof, to the effect that no one knows a language really well, until he can play tricks with it. The application of this, in connection with the previous quotations, must be left to the individual conscience of the linguist.

Adjectives, as we have seen, often end in -*u* when derived from verbs (-*fu* and -*vu* are common terminations in this case) and sometimes when their derivation is not so clear. Meinhof derives -*kulu* from *kula* 'grow,' but it is open to question whether the derivation is not the other way about. Nouns in *-u* derived from verbs, do not seem to be so common,— unless they are verbal adjectives used as nouns: *e.g. m-tulivu* 'a quiet, peaceable sort of person,' from *tulia*.[1]

There is in Swahili another suffix to personal nouns, which denotes habitual action: *-ji*, as *m-sema-ji* 'orator' from *sema* 'speak'; *m-pa-ji* 'a generous person' (but see note on this word in Madan's *Swahili-English Dictionary*), from *pa* 'give.' I do not know if this particular ending is found anywhere else.

Nouns of the third class are sometimes formed from verbs with the ending *o*; Nyanja *m-pepo* and Herero *om-bepo* 'wind,' from *pepa* 'blow,' (this verb and its resulting noun are found in most Bantu languages, but the latter is sometimes of a different class); Herero *omu-hapo* 'shape,' from *hapa* 'grow'; Nyanja *m-kotamiro* 'lintel of a door' from *kotamira* 'stoop'; *m-duliro* 'mode of cutting' (the

---

[1] Chatelain says that, in Mbundu (Angola) *-u* and *-o* have, in general, a passive 'or inactive' force and *-a*, *-e* and *-i* an active one.

hair); Swahili *m-teremo* 'cheerfulness,' from *terema* ' rejoice'; *m-pako* 'plaster' from *paka* ' smear,' *m-chezo* (*m-tezo*) ' dance,' ' game,' from *cheza* (*teza*), *mw-endo* 'journey' from *enda* ' walk' (the same word is found in Nyanja, meaning ' leg '). Duala has in this class a peculiar suffix *-ko* : *mu-anga-ko* ' roast meat ' from *anga* ' roast,' *mpoko* ' gimlet,' from *poa* ' bore.'

Verbal Nouns of Class 5 ending in *o* are common. They often mean the place where anything is done, as Ganda *e-fumbiro* 'a place to cook in' from *fumba*; Bangi *ebombelo* ' hiding place,' from *bomba*, ' hide.' In Kongo nouns of this kind, end in *u*: *esumbilu* ' place for buying' from *sumba* ' buy.' Sometimes these are only used in the plural, as Nyanja *matero* ' limits,' from *tera*, applied form of *ta* ' finish '; *malowero* ' place where the sun sets,' from *lowera*, *lowa* ' go in.'

Another kind of noun in *o* belonging to this class indicates the result of an action, or sometimes the way in which it is done. Swahili *chezo* (*tezo*) ' game,' etc. (used as well as *mchezo* 3, but more frequent in the plural, *ma-chezo*); *pendo* ' love,' ' liking ' from *penda*. Also *mapenzi*, not used in the singular: in fact, many of these nouns only exist in the plural, *e.g.*, Nyanja *maganizo* 'thought' from *ganiza* 'think'; *matyolo* 'breaking' from *tyola*, 'break'; *majebo* 'notches cut round a stick' from *jeba;* Swahili *ma-choro* 'carving,' *ma-patano* 'agreement' from *ku-patana*, reciprocal of *pata* 'obtain': 'get (from) each other' = 'agree.'

Some have taken these nouns as plurals to the infinitive (*ku*) class; but they should have been warned by the termination and the slight, but quite distinct, difference in meaning. *Ku-chora, e.g.*, is the *act* of carving, *ma-choro* the carving itself (our English participle is ambiguous) *ku-teza* the act of dancing, *matezo* the dances (or games) themselves.

I may repeat here that the coining of words for oneself is apt to be a dangerous experiment. Because *matezo* comes from *teza*, and *taka* is 'wish' it is not safe to conclude that *ma-tako* means 'wants,' 'wishes': if you do, the result will be embarrassing.

The seventh class has a good many nouns formed from verbs, sometimes without change in the final vowel, sometimes with the endings *e, i* or *o:* perhaps the last is the commonest. The chief meaning is (1) the instrument with which, or the place or time where, anything is done, but we also find (2) a person who does a thing habitually, or excels in it. Some, however, can scarcely be distinguished in meaning from those mentioned in the last paragraph, as (Swahili) *kitendo* 'action,' *kicheko* 'a laugh'; Yao *chi-nyengo* 'deceit' from *nyenga*. Ganda: *eki-gambo* 'word,' from *gamba* 'speak.'

(1) ZULU: *isi-bongo* from *bonga* 'praise,' *isi-fo* 'disease' (that by which one dies).'

CHWANA: *se-reko* 'a thing to buy with,' from *reka* 'buy'; *se-aparo* 'clothing' from *apara* 'put on.'

YAO: *chi-lindo* 'watch-hut,' from *linda* 'guard'; *chi-gono*, 'sleeping-place' from *gona*.

SWAHILI: *ki-fo* 'place of dying'; *ki-funiko* 'lid,' from *funika* 'cover.'

HERERO: *otyi-dhera* 'sacred place,' from *dhera* 'avoid for ceremonial reasons'; *otyi-kunino* 'garden,' from *kuna* 'plant.'

(2) ZULU: *isi-lauli* 'habitual jester,' *isi-hambi* 'traveller.'

RONGA: *shi-di* 'great eater' (from *da*), *shi-yaki* 'skilled builder,' from *yaka* 'build.'

Nouns in -*e* are

NYANJA: *chi-ponde* 'a mess of pounded food, from *ponda* 'pound,' *chi-kalidwe* 'nature of a thing.'[1]

Chwana has a large number of verbal nouns belonging to the ninth class, which in form (as this class in Chwana has no prefix) and meaning are much like those of the fifth already mentioned: *tiho* 'work,' from *diha* 'do'; *kepo* 'digging' from *epa* 'dig'; *picho* 'assembly' from *bitsa* 'call.' These usually have a more and a less concrete meaning— *e.g.*, *picho* may mean the act of calling, or the assembly which is called; and there is another *kepo*, with a difference in the quantity of the final vowel, meaning 'a digging-stick.' The differences in the initial consonant follow the special laws of sound to which Chwana is subject, and we may remark that, in *kepo*, *k* is not prefixed to the root, but is a modified restoration of a lost consonant.

---

[1] From *kalidwa*, passive of *kala* 'sit,' 'stay,' 'be'— verbs which with us cannot have a passive. *Chikalidwe* means, I suppose, 'the way in which a thing is,' as regarded by an outsider, and not from its own point of view—this might make its 'being,' in some sense, passive.

In Herero we find some personal verbal nouns of this class: *o-ndodhe* 'an artful, crafty person'[1] from *rora* 'test,' 'examine,' *o-hodhe* 'spy,' from *hora* 'spy out.' They are not so common elsewhere, but Meinhof derives the Zulu and Chwana word for chief *in-kosi*, *kχosi*, from *koka*, *χoγa* 'draw,' 'lead'—like *dux*, from *duco*.

We find some nouns of the eleventh and fourteenth classes derived from verbs, though the latter oftener come from nouns and adjectives. Yao, however, has a great many in *u-*, which seem to belong to this class.

GANDA: *olu-tindo* 'bridge' from *tinda* 'bridge over'; *olu-talo* 'battle' from *tala* 'set in array'; *olu-imba* 'song' from *imba* 'sing'; (in other languages this ends in o: Swahili *w-imbo*, Ila and others *lw-imbo*); *olu-gendo* 'journey' from *genda* 'go' (Nyanja *ul-endo*), *olu-gero* 'a proverb' 'story,' from *gera* 'tell' (a story, etc.).

KONGO: *lu-keselo* 'how the cutting-down came about,' from *kesela*, applied form of *kesa*, 'cut'; *lu-vangilu* 'the manner of

[1] 'One who will take nothing on trust' is the sense suggested by the derivation.

being made'; 'manufacture,' from *vanga* 'make.' Of Cl. 14, *umbangu* 'skill,' from *vanga*; *undoki* 'witchcraft,' from *loka* 'bewitch.'[1]

ILA: *lufuno* 'love,' from *funa*; *lufuko* 'dust,' from *fuka* 'rise' (said of smoke, etc.), *lubeta* 'judgment,' no doubt from *beta*, but the verb now in use is the derived form *beteka*.

SWAHILI: *u-funguo* 'key,' from *fungua* 'unlock'; *u-fagio* and *u-peo* 'broom,' from *fagia*, *pea* 'sweep'; *u-pito*, 'passage,' from *pita* 'pass'; *u-puuzi* 'nonsense,' 'folly,' from *puuza* 'talk foolishly.' The last two are probably of Cl. 14, which is not now to be distinguished from 11 in Swahili.

GANDA: Cl. 14, *obu-sera* 'flour,' from *sera*, applied form of *sa* 'grind,' *obu-ganza* 'favouritism,' from *ganza* 'be fond of.'

NYANJA: *u-limbo* 'bird-lime' (*obu-limbo* in Ganda: probably from *limba* 'be firm, hard, tough,' also 'stick fast,' etc.), *u-bvundo* 'decay,' from *bvunda* 'rot'; *u-sokedwe* 'manner of sewing,' from *soka*; *u-endedwe* 'manner of walking,' from *enda*.

YAO: *u-lindi* 'watching,' from *linda*; *uwii*

---

[1] Both these words have their initial stem-consonant modified by contact with the prefix,

'theft,' from *iwa* 'steal'; and a number indicating the way of doing things, like the last two Nyanja examples: *u-tawe*[1] 'plan of building,'[1] *u-panganye* 'mode of making,' from *panganya* 'make,' etc.

XOSA: *ubu-xoki* 'falsehood' from *xoka* 'tell lies' (also Zulu); *ubu-lumko* 'prudence,' from *lumka*; *ubu-sika* 'winter' (*i.e.*, 'the cutting time'), from *sika* 'cut,' (also Zulu), etc., etc.

In Kele (Congo) we have, *e.g.*, *bo-lio* 'door,' from *lia* 'shut.'

The Locative Class sometimes has a kind of relative form based on a verb-stem in the applied form; as in Nyanja: *po-gonera, mo-gonera*[2] 'a place to sleep at' or 'in.' The latter implies that it is an enclosed place, and can therefore be used as an equivalent for 'bedroom'; so, too, *mo-dyera* 'dining-room' (from *dya*) and *mo-sambira* 'bath-room,' from *samba* 'wash.'

This does not exhaust the ways of forming

---

[1] *Tawa* 'tie' is used to mean 'build' (as *manga*, with the same meaning in Nyanja) because in erecting the framework of a native hut, a great part of the work consists in tying the poles, or withes, together—and, again, in tying on the thatch.

[2] From *gona* 'sleep.'

nouns; but these are the principal ones to be found in most languages. The passage on the Derivation of Nouns in Bentley's *Kongo Grammar* (pp. 528-538) is both interesting and instructive, but it should be remembered that the system is not everywhere so elaborate. See also the section headed 'Formation of Nouns,' in the Rev. A. J. Wookey's *Secwana Grammar*, pp. 10-14.

Before leaving the subject of noun-suffixes, it is necessary to notice the diminutive in *-ana*, which Zulu, Chwana and Ronga have substituted for the diminutive formed by the thirteenth prefix (*ka-*). It is probably like the suffix *-kazi* (*-kχali*), which forms something like a rudimentary feminine gender, due to the influence of the suffix-inflecting 'Hottentot' language—or languages.

We must say a few words about *Denominative Verbs*—*i.e.*, verbs derived either from nouns or adjectives. They were mentioned in connection with the Derived Forms, but they are distinct from these, and probably of later formation. They are exceptional, in that they consist of more than two syllables, without going back to a simple verb; but they often look like derived forms; *e.g.*, Swahili *chafu-ka* 'be dirty,' which is not the neuter-passive-reversive of a verb *chafa*, but comes from *chafu* 'dirty.' So, too, *toroka*, 'run away' from *m-toro* 'deserter'; *pevu-ka* 'be grown-up' from *-pevu* 'full-grown.'

Verbs are also formed in this way by the suffix *-pa*, as *nene-pa* 'be' or 'grow stout' (also found in Nyanja, where the adjective *-nene* is not used). In Herero we have *handu-ka* 'be impudent,' from the noun *e-handu* 5; *raru-ka* 'be greedy,' from *e-raru* 5 'gluttony,' *dhandu-pa* 'become young' from *-dhandu*; and others with the suffix *para*, as *potu-para* 'be blind,' *re-para* 'be long.'

In Zulu there are a few verbs in *-pa* and *-pala*; *de-pa* 'grow tall,' *kulu-pala* 'be fat' (or 'big'). In Yao, verbs are often formed from Vocal Images by the suffix: *-ma*, as *sisima* 'be cold,' from *si* or *sisisi*.

Herero has a somewhat peculiar class of compounds, which we must not leave unnoticed. We saw, quite early in this book, that names of trees have practically everywhere the prefix of the third class. In Herero they are sometimes still further distinguished by suffixing the root *-ti*: *omu-hama-ti*, *omu-tendere-ti*, *omu-ngwa-ti*. (I am unable to say what these trees are, except that the last of the three is called by Brincker 'wild tamarisk.' *Umu-nga*, in Zulu, is a common species of mimosa.) Again, we have a number of words compounded with *-ndu* (the root of *omu-ndu*, *umu-ntu*).

omu-kadhe-ndu	'woman'	(*-kadhe* = 'female')
omu-rume-ndu	'man'	(*-rume* = 'male')
omu-hepu-ndu	'widow'	(Meinhof suggests a derivation from *-hepu* 'discontented'!)

Also:

on-dume-wa 9	'male dog'	(*on-rume-ombwa*)
omu-kuru-kadhe 1	'old woman'	(*-kuru* = 'old')
omu-dhoro-twa 1	'Hill Damara,' from *-dhoro* 'black' and *omu-twa* 'Bushman.'

Another curious feature is the insertion of the interrogative particle *ke* between prefix and stem, as *imu-ke-ndu*.[1] 'What sort of person?' *omu-ke-ti* 'What sort of tree?'

Professor Meinhof says that compound nouns are unusual in Bantu[2] and that perhaps

---

[1] The initial vowel *i* is sometimes substituted for *o* in Herero—as in the Demonstrative Pronoun (Cl. 1) *ingwi*.

[2] *Lautlehre*, p. 135.

those in Herero are due to the influence of Nama, in which they are very common. If he is referring to the compounds enumerated above, he is probably right; but he goes on to give a number of compounds consisting of a verb and a noun, which could easily be paralleled elsewhere.

Some of these are:

omu-rara-nganda 1   'neighbour'; that is 'one who sleeps (*rara*) in the same village' (*onganda*).

oru-pit' onganda 11   'vagrancy,' from *pita* 'go out' and *onganda*.

omu-dhemba-tima 3   'forgetfulness,' literally 'forgetting heart' (*dhemba* 'forget,' *omu-tima* 'heart'—Nyanja *mtima*, etc.).

otyi-dhuma-we 7   'noise made by the fall of a meteor'—strange that this should be a common enough occurrence to have a word to itself—from **dhuma*[1] 'roar' and *e-we* 5 'stone' (the verb *dhuma* does not seem to be in use. Zulu has *duma* 'thunder,' but the word corresponding to the

---

[1] An asterisk prefixed to a root or word means that it is not actually used in that form.

Herero one should be *zuma*, which has a different meaning).

It would not be difficult to make a long list of similar compounds.

ZULU: *in-dhlula-miti* 9 'giraffe,' from *dhlula* 'pass' and *imiti*: it is 'higher than the trees.'

in-swela-boya 'a horrible portent' (sometimes 'a corpse')—literally 'a thing without hair,' from *swela* 'lack' and *ub-oya* 'hair,' 'wool,' etc.

u-mahamba-nendhlwane 'caddis-worm,' etc., from *hamba* 'go' and *indhlwana* 'little house.'

kwa' Mamangalahlwa 'the Back of Beyond' —literally: 'At (the place of) "Mother! I'm lost!"'

Many Zulu proper names are such compounds, sometimes very curious and suggestive.

NYANJA: *kokalupsya* 'early rains' which 'sweep away' (*koka*) the 'burnt grass' (*lupsya*); *mpinganjira* 3 'obstacle in the way,' from *pinga* 'lie across,' and *njira* 'road' *fulagombe* 'the bee-eater' (which builds its nest in a bank, like our sand-martin) from *fula* 'dig out' and *gombe* 'river bank.'

ILA: *chi-zhinga-lula* 'intestinal fat' ('that which surrounds the bowel').

mu-dima-ku-bushu 'small-pox' ('what digs (holes) on the face') and numerous others.

In fact the compounding of words (there are numerous examples of two nouns connected by the possessive particle forming an inseparable compound[1]) seems—if not so fully carried out as in Greek—to be by no means alien to the genius of the Bantu languages. It is oftenest found in proper names (as already remarked) and in the names of animals and trees.

[1] ZULU: *inja-yo-mSutu* ('dog of the Mosutu')—a hairy caterpillar.

iso-le-nkosikazi ('lady's eye')—a flower (a kind of jasmine).

CHAPTER XIV

Some Phonetic Laws

I think I have sometimes been asked—by persons whose philological science was somewhat more imperfect than my own—whether Grimm's Law was applicable to the Bantu Languages. Of course, as the law in question is only a statement of what happens to certain consonants in the Indo-European languages, the answer must be no. But the principle on which it is based, that of the permutation of consonants, holds good, and seems to work out with unfailing regularity. That is, if we meet with any apparent irregularities, they are probably due, either to imperfect observation of the sounds, or to the operation of some law not yet ascertained: in either case, they will disappear in the light of further knowledge.

'In investigating the relations of any dialect with its kindred dialects, the first step

SOME PHONETIC LAWS

is to determine to what sounds in the latter its own sounds regularly correspond."[1]

This was done to a limited extent by Bleek —with remarkable thoroughness considering the number of languages at his disposal, and the small amount of material available for some of them. But the work can never be satisfactorily completed till the nature of all Bantu sounds has been determined with scientific exactitude. Meinhof, for instance, after working for years in order to discover the Bantu sounds regularly corresponding to the clicks in Zulu and Xosa[2] was obliged to give up the task as hopeless for the present, chiefly because 'the method followed in these comparisons was a very rough one. The question whether the clicks were or were not aspirated, was never taken into account, and the tones were not investigated at all. Therefore, in cases where it seemed as if we had found two or three instances going to prove a particular sound-shifting, it is not certain that

---

[1] Whitney, W. D., *Language and the Study of Language* (1884), p. 97.

[2] Most of these clicks occur in borrowed (Hottentot and Bushman) words; but some are found in words which have parallel forms in other Bantu languages.

even these were valid, and . . . . the results of infinite trouble are worthless from a philological point of view.'

But, even now, some broad principles of correspondence can be set down as certain, though we must await the exacter definitions of phonetic science before filling in the details. As this book does not concern itself with phonetics, I should be straying beyond my province, if I attempted to do more than indicate these in the most general way; but a few hints on the subject may fitly close our survey.

The difficult sounds called 'laterals' (written *hl*, *dhl tl*, *tlh*) are confined to Zulu, Chwana and Thonga.[1] They are absent even from Herero and the Venda languages of the North Transvaal. The following table will illustrate the various sounds in which they correspond with other languages.

Here we find that *hl* (which seems to be the

---

[1] Here 'Zulu' includes Xosa and the various subordinate dialects spoken by the AmaBaca, Swazis and others; Chwana comprises Sutu and Pedi (besides Rolong, Khatla, etc.) and Thonga (the *h* is necessary to prevent confusion with at least three other Tongas), Ronga and other languages of the Delagoa Bay region.

	Zulu	Chwana	Herero	Venda	Nyanja	Swahili	Ganda
Five	-hlanu	-tlhano	-'ano	-tanu	-sanu	-tano	-tano
Python	in-blatu	tlhware	—	—	n-satu	chatu	—
Elephant	in-dhlovu	tlou	on-dyou	n-dou	n-jobvu	n-dovu	en-jovu

same sound as the Chwana lateral in the corresponding word, though written differently), is represented in the other languages either by *s* or (dental) *t*, except in the case of the Swahili for 'python,' to which we must return presently. *dhl* or *tl*, on the other hand are represented either by *j* (*dy* is probably in some cases nearer the sound) dental *d*, or (in languages not included in the table) *z*, *dz*, or *s* (Pokomo *nzovu*, Giryama *ndzovu*, Konde *i-sofu*).

(The names for 'python' used in Herero and Ganda seem to come from a different root, and I have not been able to get the Venda word. Ronga *n-hlaru* keeps the lateral and, like Chwana, substitutes *r* for *t*.)

The apparent anomaly of the Swahili *-tano* and *chatu* requires a little further explanation. In the Mombasa dialect there are two kinds of *t*, in that of Zanzibar only one is recognised in practice. They may be distinguished here (though this book, on principle, tries as far as possible to avoid diacritic marks) as *t̪* and *ṭ*. In Mombasa printed books—the former, as the more usual sound, is left unmarked, the latter is underlined, or printed in italics, or distinguished in some other way. *ṭ* is pronounced with the tip of the tongue against the hard palate, *t̪* with it touching—or even between—the front teeth. Get a Mombasa native to pronounce, first -*t̪at̪u* and then -*t̪ano*, and, if you have even a moderately good ear, you cannot help hearing the difference.

Now many words (but not all) which at Mombasa have *t̪*, as *fit̪a* 'hide,' *t̪eza* 'dance,' *jit̪o* 'eye,' are at Zanzibar pronounced with what (with apologies to the I.A.P.) I will write *ch*: *ficha*, *cheza*, *jicho*. Therefore *chatu* is the Zanzibar form, which, logically, at Mombasa, should be *t̪atu*. But I am not sure that it is so, never, to my remembrance, having heard the latter pronunciation. In fact, the only time I can recall hearing a python mentioned in Swahili was by a Lamu man, and I think—but would not swear to it— that he said *chatu*. Krapf gives *chatu*, but as a quotation from Steere: it is possible that some other word is used at Mombasa.

But, looking again at our table, and taking it backwards—*nj*[1] in Nyanja does not always correspond to a Zulu lateral. We have *njoka* ' snake,' *njati* ' buffalo,' and *njuchi* ' bee,' which in Zulu are *in-nyoka, in- nyati, in-nyosi*. And sometimes we find Zulu words containing *ny* not only in Nyanja, but other languages as well, such as *in-nyama* ' animal,' or ' meat '—which only in one or two cases that I have come across is *nama* (in Chwana and in Venda). Before coming to a conclusion in a case like this, one would want to be sure whether all the *ny* sounds were the same. Some may, perhaps, be quite properly written *ny*, while others require the symbol which for typographical reasons is banished from these pages—and as to the sound, see Mr. Noël-Armfield's *General Phonetics*, p. 63.

The comparative tables of words given in the preceding chapters will already have called attention to some correspondences, such as that between Zulu *t* and Chwana *r* (*which t* and *which r* are important points to be dealt

---

[1] The presence or absence of a nasal before a consonant makes some difference as regards sound-shiftings.

with by the phonetician), the tendency of Chwana (which it shares with Makua) to prefer a voiceless stop to the same sound voiced and preceded by a nasal (*e.g.*, *rata = tanda* and *podi*[1] = *mbuzi*); the curious absence of *p* from a large group of East African languages, etc.

In most of these latter, the place of *p* is taken by *h*, in Ganda by *w* and in Pokomo, by ' bilabial *f* '—written *bf* by the German missionaries who have chiefly cultivated this language, and who spell the name of the people 'Wabfokomo.' Chwana, curiously enough, shares this tendency to a certain extent, though having no objection to the p-sound *per se*. The word usually found as *pa-nsi* is *le-hatse* or *le-fatse*, (the *pa-* prefix being incorporated with the noun-root) and *p* appears (as we saw just now) where one would not expect it— instead of *mb* or *mv*. There is no *v* in Chwana, but ' bilabial *v* ' is a common sound, and—at any rate in some dialects—takes the place of

---

[1] Here the o is an extra-narrow o (written in Meinhof's notation o) which approaches u in sound : the word is sometimes written *poli*, in which case it must be remembered the l is 'cerebral l.' If you try to sound l by turning the tip of the tongue up against the palate, you will find that it approaches very nearly to the sound of d similarly pronounced.

b also. P, unless nasalised (*i.e.*, preceded by *m*) is not common in Kongo: perhaps the words in which it unquestionably occurs might on examination prove to be borrowed.

Herero has no *s* or *z*,—the sounds substituted being those of *th*, voiced and voiceless (*i.e.*, as in 'there' and 'thin') for which I have written *dh* and *th* respectively. Makua, too, and Kikuyu, have no *s* sounds: the reason in all three cases is supposed to be the custom of extracting—or chipping away part of—two front teeth. On the other hand, Nyanja, Yao, and some others have no *h*, while Swahili seems to have an exceptional preference for the sound—as in the pronouns. (It should be noted that it frequently arises, in this language, from a contraction which one would scarcely expect to produce it: *e.g. ha-* for *ni-ka*—not to be confused with the negative *ha-*—and *hi-* for *ni-ki-*[1] Conversely, *si-*, in the negative of the first person singular, is a contraction of *ha-ni*.)

There are three main principles[2] which we

---

[1] Steere, *A Handbook of the Swahili Language*, pp. 134, 137.

[2] See Meinhof, *Lautlehre*, pp. 12-16.

must keep in mind when examining the structure of any language and its relation to others of the same family. These are:

(1) ASSIMILATION.
(2) DISSIMILATION.
(3) TRANSPOSITION.

We might add FALSE ANALOGY, which often accounts for phenomena otherwise inexplicable, as when in Swahili we have *julika* 'be knowable,' from *jua* 'know,' which never can have contained *l*, as we see by the noun *mjuvi*, formed from it, and the parallel forms Nyanja *dziwa*, Pedi *tzeva*. But, as most Swahili verbs in *-ua* have dropped *l*, which reappears in some of the derived forms (*e.g. pindua* 'turn over,' applied form *pindulia*, passive *pinduliwa*) *jua* has been made to 'follow the rule,' like many modern English verbs ('helped,' 'worked,' etc.).

(1) Assimilation may be (a) Incomplete, or (b) Complete, and is applied both to vowels and to consonants.

In Complete Assimilation, two different sounds occurring in succession are made exactly alike, for greater ease in pronunciation. Sometimes the second is assimilated to the first, sometimes the first to the one following it. Thus, in Konde, the verb *fisa* 'hide' (Zulu *fihla*, Swahili *ficha*, *fita*) is sometimes heard as *fifa*. Shambala, having borrowed from Swahili the word for 'paper,' *kartasi* (itself borrowed from the Arabic) makes it into *talatasi*: the first consonant being influenced (in spite of the intervening $l=r$) by the *t* in the next syllable but one.

If a sound becomes, not exactly the same, but only *similar* to that which precedes or follows it, we have Incomplete Assimilation. This is shown in Bantu when the prefix *in-* is followed by a labial (*p*, *b*, *f*, *v*)—when the dental nasal *n* is changed to the labial nasal *m*. *N*, again (except in a few languages, *e.g.*, Kongo and Makua), cannot be followed by *l* or *r* and changes these sounds to *d*; this is why the plural of *u-limi* 'tongue' in Swahili is (*zi*)*n-dimi*, instead of (*zi*)*n-limi*.[1] In the same way, verbs whose stem contains *o* or *e* take the

---

[1] Another case of Assimilation is when the two sounds unite to form a third, different from either. We have already met with the union of *a* and *u* to form *o*, and *a* and *i* to form *e*. In Chwana, if *n* is followed by *v*, the two together become *p*. See *Lautlehre*, p. 13.

termination *-eka* instead of *-ika*, because the position of the tongue for *e* is nearer to that for *o* than is that for *i*. But these terminations are in most (not in all) languages governed by the *Law of Vowel-Harmony*, which rests partly on Assimilation, and partly on Dissimilation and may be stated thus: If the verb-stem contains *a*, *i*, or *u*, the termination has *i*: if *o* or *e*, it has *e*. So, in Nyanja *ang'-ana* 'look' makes *ang'an-ira*, *ang'an-itsa*, *lira* 'weep,' *lir-itsa; funa* 'seek,' *fun-itsa*; but *yera* 'be white' *yer-etsa* and the passive *yer-etsedwa*, and *omba* 'strike' *omb-era*, *omb-etsa*. In the case of *e*, *i*, and *o* the sounds are made quite identical, or at any rate brought nearer together; in that of *a* and *u* they are put further apart.

This last process belongs to Dissimilation. This arises when two similar sounds occur in close conjunction, and the speaker, to avoid confusing them, lays special emphasis on one and tends to slur the other, in order to make a difference between them. Some Yao verbs, whose stems contain *l*, have a perfect in *ite-* instead of *-ile*, as *lolite*, from *lola* 'look.'

Under this heading, special attention should be directed to the law discovered by Dahl, a missionary in Unyamwezi, and prevailing in many East African languages—among others that usually written as 'Kikuyu.' As a matter of fact, the people call themselves *A-gikuyu;* just as the infinitive prefix for certain verbs is *gu,* not *ku,* and the word for a stool is *gi-ti,* not *ki-ti.* All these words, and many more, are illustrations of Dahl's Law, which may be stated thus:

When a voiceless stop (k, t, p) is followed by another voiceless stop, it becomes voiced. In other words, if *k* is followed by either *k, t,* or *p,* it becomes *g; t* becomes *d,* and *p* becomes *b.*

This principle, if it had been clearly recognised by those who have dealt with Kikuyu, would have saved them a good deal of trouble. In Mr. Barlow's *Tentative Studies* (p. 5) it is mentioned as the 'Euphonic Change of *k*,' and no doubt the fact that Kikuyu has neither *p* nor (except nasalised) *d* helped to obscure the real bearings of the case. But the matter stands exactly as it does in Shambala, Bondei and Nyamwezi—probably also in Yao, where we have *nguku* 'fowl' (Nyanja, *nkuku*) *mbeko* 'fire-stick,' which elsewhere would be *mpeko.*

NYAMWEZI: *mbeho* 'cold' (*mpepo:* the second *p* has become *h*).

deka ' cook ' (elsewhere *teka*).
-datu for *-tatu* ' three.'

SHAMBALA: *m-gate* ' bread ' (Swahili *m-kate*).

Transposition may occur in two forms: syllables may be transposed, as in Venda, where *gidima* 'run' is sometimes heard as *digima*, and Nyanja, where 'cough' is either *sokomola* or *kosomola*. Or a vowel in one syllable may intrude into another, as in the Konde perfect of *-elupha*[1] ' be white,' which is *-elwiphe*, for *-eluphile;* the *l* being dropped and the *i* taken into the previous syllable. Other interesting examples of this and similar changes may be found in the sections of Meinhof's *Lautlehre* already referred to.

A study of General Phonetics is indispensable to anyone taking up an African language. As already stated, this is a subject with which I have not attempted to deal, my object being merely to give an outline of such grammatical features as are common to the Bantu speech-family. A list of the most useful grammars, dictionaries, and other helps towards the acquisition of particular languages will be found in the Bibliography.

[1] This *ph* is an aspirated *p*.

After embarking on the study of some one language, it will be well (though I am aware that, till the English edition is published, this is more or less a counsel of perfection) to go systematically through Meinhof's *Lautlehre der Bantusprachen* or, at any rate, Chapters I. to III. and the one dealing with the language nearest to that on which the student may be engaged. But it is a book that cannot be used to much profit, unless one has some little notion of at least one Bantu language to begin with.

As the readers which a book of this kind can hope to meet with are necessarily limited in number, and (in one way or another) somewhat specialised in outlook, we may be excused if, feeling a sort of personal interest and parting from them not without regret, we remind them in the words of Brother Hyacinth that:

'If any be desirous of learning . . . . beyond what is asserted in the preceding pages for the more easy understanding of beginners, and their careful recollection, he ought also sedulously to study and labour in learning what follows . . . *and the preludes of other matters worthy to be known.*'

APPENDIX I.

TEXTS

I. Zulu

(a) *Why the Rock-Rabbit has no Tail**

Ku-tiwa,[1] **im-bila**[2] **ya-swela**[3] **um-sila**[4]
It is said, rock-rabbit was-without tail

ngo-ku-yalezela[5] **ezi-nye**[6]. **Ngokuba**[7]
with-giving-a-message (to) others. Because

na-mhla[8] **kw-abiwa**[9] **imi-sila la-li-**
on the day (when) there were distributed tails it had

buyis-ile[10] **i-zulu;** **za-puma-ke**[11] **ezi-nye**
clouded-over the sky; they went out so (the) others

uku-ya-'u-tata[12] **imisila lapa**[13] **i-tatwa kona**[13];
to take tails where they were taken;

y-ahlul-eka[14] **e-nye uku-ba i-hambe**[15] **na-zo**[16],
he was prevented another that he might go with them,

ya-yaleza ezi-lwan-eni[17] **zonke ezi-ne-misila**[18]
he sent-a-message to-animals all who with tails,

ya-ti, **'O, nina ba-kwiti**[19], **a-no-ngi-patela**[20]
he said, 'O, ye our (people), do ye get-for me

owami[21] **umsila; ngi-kohl-we**[22] **uku-puma**
that which is mine tail; I cannot come-out

em-godi-ni, ngokuba izulu li-ya-na.'
from-hole, because sky is-raining.'

---

* From Callaway's *Nursery Tales, Traditions and Histories of the Zulus* (1868), p. 255.

APPENDIX I.

Za-buya-ke ezi-nye nemisila; leyo[23] yona
They returned, so, others with tails; that-one he
a-i-ba-nga i-sa-ba[24] na-msila ngo-ku-enqena[25]
he was not he still being with tail with being-disinclined
uku-puma, izulu li-buyisile. Ya-lahla konke
to come-out, sky it has clouded-over. He lost all
oku-hle ngomsila; ngokuba umsila u-ya-siza
good with a tail; because tail it helps
eku-zi-pung-eni[26]; ngaloko-ke
in-driving-away-from-oneself (flies); and so in this way,
imbila a-i-sa-zi-pungi nga'
rock-rabbit does not now drive away from himself
luto.[27]
with (any) thing.

Se-ku[28] izwi eli-kulu loko 'ku-libala kwe-mbila
Now it is word great that loitering of rock-rabbit
ku'bantu[29] aba-mnyama; ba-kuluma ngaloko
to people black; they say with that
'ku-tsho kwembila, ku-tiwa kw-aba-nga-zi-
saying of rock-rabbit, it is said to those-not-tiring-them-
katazi ngaloko oku-tandwa-yo aba-nye, n-aba-tsho-
selves with that which is liked (by) others, and those who
yo kwabanye, ku-tiwa, 'Bani,[30]
say to others (to act for them) it is said, 'So-and-so,

a-w-azi[31] ukuba loko 'kutsho kwako kw-okuti[32],
do you not know that that saying your of saying,
"A-no-ngi-patela"[33]— a-w-azi na ukuba umu-ntu
" Bring for me "— do you not know that a person
ka-pat-el-wa[34] omu-nye, uma into leyo
not is-carried-for (by) another, when thing that
i-lingene[35] abakona? O!
it is-enough (only for) those (who are) there? O!
imbila ya-swela umsila ngokuyalezela.
rock-rabbit went without tail by sending-message.

APPENDIX I.

Nawe, musa ukw-enza[86] **njenge-mbila**[87];
And you do not do like (the) rock-rabbit;
ku-yi-ku-zuza[38] **'lu-to ngokuyalezela; zi-hamb-ele**[39]
you will not get anything by sending-word; go for yourself
ngokwako.' I-njalo-ke in-daba ye-
as to what is yours.' It (is) thus, then, story of
mbila. A-i-kuluma-nga yona ngo-mlomo, ukuti,
rock-rabbit. He did not speak he with mouth to say,
'A-no-ngi-patela'; kwa-yela[40] **izwi kodwa**[41]
'Bring for me'; there came forth word only
ngokuba izi-lwane zi-ne-misila,[42] **kepa yona**
because animals they (are) with tails, but he
a-i-na 'msila[42]**; kwa-nga**[43] **ya-swela umsila**
not-(is)-with tail; it (was) as if he went without tail
ngokuyaleza, na ngokuba izulu imbila
by sending-word, and because sky rock-rabbit
i-ya-l-esaba[44] **uma li-buyisile; a-i-**
he is fearing it if it has clouded-over; he does not
pumi emgodini uma li-ng-enzi[45] **izi-kau**
come out from hole if it not making gleams
zoku-sa.
of sunshine.

NOTES

[1] *Tiwa*, passive of *ti* 'say'; the prefix is that of Class 15, which is used when there is no definite subject, like our 'it, or 'there.'

[2] A noun of Class 9, the prefix *in-* becomes *im-* before a labial.

[3] *Swela* 'want,' 'lack.' *Ya* prefix of the past tense, agreeing with *imbila*.

[4] *Umsila*, a noun of the third class; pl. *imi-sila*, found in next line but one.

[5] *Yalezela*, applied form of *yaleza*, ultimately from *yala* 'direct,' 'order'; *yaleza* means 'give a message,' and takes the

APPENDIX I. 235

thing, not the person, as its direct object, whereas *yalezela* takes a direct object of the person by whom, (not *to* whom) the message is sent. *Ngoku-* for *nga-uku- : nga* 'by means of,' prefixed to the infinitive.

[6] *ezi-nye* agreeing with *izi-lwane* 8 'animals,' understood.

[7] For *nga ukuba*, lit. ' with being '—*i.e.* ' because.'

[8] *namhla*, for *na umu-hla*, often used for ' to-day.'

[9] *abiwa* passive of *aba* ' distribute.' Monosyllabic verbs, and those beginning with a vowel, make their passive in *-iwa* instead of *-wa*.

[10] Agrees with *izulu*, which, by a not infrequent exception, follows its verb. Pluperfect tense ; the Perfect having both the Past (*la*) and present (*li*) prefixes before it. *Buyisa*, lit. ' bring back,' is the causative of *buya* 'return'; the idea being that the sky ' brings back ' the clouds from below the horizon.

[11] *ke* an enclitic particle, usually rendered ' then,' ' just,' ' so,' etc. Unlike the interrogative *na*, it draws forward the accent of the word to which it is attached, so that we pronounce *zapumáke*, instead of accenting the syllable *pu*, as would otherwise be done. It is the subjunctive of the auxiliary *ka* (Colenso, *First Steps*, p. 132).

[12] This is a future infinitive, for *ukuyakutata :* the *k* of *ku* is often dropped.

[13] *Lapa* ' here,' followed by *kona*, has a relative force, the two together being equivalent to ' where ' (not the interrogative ' where,' which is *-pi*). *Kona* is the pronoun of Class 15— or, more properly, of Class 17, which in Zulu has been merged in 15—and usually means ' the place,' ' there ' (not adverbially, like *lapo*, *lapaya*, but more in the sense of the French *y*).

[14] Neuter-passive of *ahlula* 'overpower '; the subject is *enye* 9 which seems to refer in a loose way to *imbila*, properly, it should be *esi-nye* 7 agreeing with *isi-lwane* ' animal,' which seems to be required by the sense.

[15] Subjunctive, agreeing with *enye*. There is no distinction of tense in this mood.

[16] *na-zo*, agreeing with *ezi-nye* (*izilwane*) above.

[17] *Ezi-lwan-eni*, locative of *izi lwane*. It is not very usual to have nouns denoting living beings in the locative, though we sometimes find *ebantwini* (more often *ku' bantu*). Here it is used because *yaleza* cannot take a direct object of the person : it is therefore equivalent to a dative. *Isi-lwane* for *isi-lo-ane* is the diminutive (suffix *-ana* or *-ane*) of *isi-lo* ' wild animal,' but generally used for ' leopard.' *Isilwane* means a

wild animal in general,—but more especially a carnivorous or noxious one, whereas *in-nyamazane* is 'game,' and more particularly 'buck.'

[18] Relative construction (*ezi=a+izi*; *nemisila=na+imisila*) literally 'which they with tails'—*i.e.* 'which have tails.'

[19] *bakwiti* or *bakiti* 'my' (or 'our') 'people'—*ki=ku*, followed by the 'prepositional' form of the personal pronoun (always in the plural). See Colenso, *First Steps*, §91.

[20] *a-no-ngi-patela*, Future Indicative, used authoritatively for Imperative (*First Steps*, §222), with *a*, prefix of Imperative; *no=niya'u=niyaku*: see *First Steps*, §241.

[21] *owami*, relative form of the possessive = 'that which is mine.' It is generally used for special emphasis, 'my own,' etc. *First Steps*, §137.

[22] Perf. passive of *kohla*, properly 'escape,' 'slip (the memory of)'—so that the usual meaning of *kohlwa* is 'forget' —*i.e.* 'be escaped' by the thing forgotten. The use here seems somewhat unusual, but probably means 'coming-out has escaped me'—*i.e.* is beyond my power.

[23] *leyo*, demonstrative of Cl. 9 'that one' (or rather 'the aforesaid one')—agreeing with *imbila*, though the antecedent is not expressed in this sentence.

[24] *aibanga* negative past of *ba* 'be'; *a* neg. prefix, *i* pronoun agreeing with *imbila* understood. *isaba* is best taken as a participle, *sa* here = 'still'; the two verbs together may be taken as a compound tense and translated 'he no longer had.' Cf. *First Steps*, §271.

[25] For *nga-uku-enqena*: *nga*, instrumental = 'with' or 'through.'

[26] Locative of the infinitive; *zi* is the reflexive pronoun.

[27] *U(lu)-to*, usually uncontracted, because of the monosyllabic stem. Here *nga'luto*, not *ngoluto*, because following a negative, when the initial vowel is always elided, never contracted.

[28] Verb 'to be' understood. The subject with which the pronoun agrees is *ukulibala*. Concerning *se* see the chapter on 'The Particles SA and SE' in Colenso's *First Steps*, pp. 112-116, especially §274.

[29] *ku' bantu*, more usual than *ebantwini*. A little later we find *kwabanye* (*u* becoming *w* before *a*), not *ku' banye*; but *ku' bantu* seems to be preferred,—perhaps because *kwa' bantu* is used with a different shade of meaning—'at (the house of) the people'—like *chez*.

APPENDIX I.

³⁰ *Ubani* 'who' (interrogative, not relative) is sometimes used in this way, 'when the name of a person is not known or not immediately remembered,' or in a familiar and slightly contemptuous style of address, 'You, sir!' 'you, fellow!' (*u* is always dropped in the vocative.)

³¹ *Awazı* for *a-u-azi*, *u* becoming *w* before the vowel-stem. *Azi* is one of the few verbs which end in *i* and therefore cannot change their termination in the negative.

³² *Kwokuti* for *kwa ukuti* 'of saying'—the possessive particle agreeing with the preceding *loko 'kutsho*.

³³ The sentence breaks off, and the question begins afresh.

³⁴ *Ka*, not *a*, is the negative for the third person singular, or nouns of the first class; *a* being used in the subjunctive and in some forms of the relative, as the pronoun of the third person singular. *Patela* applied form of *pata* 'carry' (in the hand or on the arm—not on the head, which is *twala*). This is an instance of the Bantu preference for the passive when European languages would have the active construction.

³⁵ *Linga* 'try,' 'test,' 'strive' (in some languages, *e.g.*, Nyanja, it means 'measure'); the reciprocal, *lingana* (perf. *lingene*) means 'try or strive with,' 'vie with,' 'be as large as,' and so 'be sufficient for,' as *umbila ulingene labo' bantu* 'the maize is sufficient for those people.' It may take a direct object, as in this sentence, and in the text (*abakona*), or be followed by *na*. *Kulingene*, without an object, means 'it is fair, fitting, reasonable.'

³⁶ The Negative Imperative is the Infinitive preceded by *musa*. I do not know that any satisfactory explanation of this has been given, but *sa* is a negative particle in some languages.

³⁷ For *njenga* ('like') *imbila*.

³⁸ Negative Future (2nd person sing.) of *zuza* 'obtain.' *Ku* instead of *a-u* (which would contract into *o*), probably to avoid confusion with the same person of the relative.

³⁹ *Hambela* here means 'go for,' and not, as most commonly, 'go to' (='visit'). *Zi* the reflexive pronoun. The Subjunctive is generally used instead of the Imperative, when an object-pronoun precedes.

⁴⁰ Past tense (*ku-a-vela*) with the indefinite subject *ku*; instead of saying *izwi la-vela*. This construction so exactly corresponds to our idiom of beginning with 'there' and letting the real subject follow the verb, that we can translate quite literally.

⁴¹ The adjective *-odwa* 'only' (which, like *-onke* 'all,' takes

the concords of a pronoun, not of an adjective), with the concord of the 15th class—*i.e.*, agreeing with an undefined subject. It is often used as here, adverbially for 'only,' and thence easily glides into the very common sense of 'but,' in which it is synonymous with *kepa*.

⁴² Note the difference between these two words: the first contracts because the verb (understood) is affirmative; the second elides because it is negative.

⁴³ *Nga* as an auxiliary is 'used to express a wish or likeness' and is followed by a finite verb. Compare *wanga angawela* ' he wished that he might cross.'

⁴⁴ An unusual order of words, but not unknown.

⁴⁵ *ng*' here stands for *nga*, the negative particle for the Imperative, Infinitive and Participles: see *First Steps*, §§259, 263.

Connected Translation

It is said that the rock-rabbit (*Hyrax*) is without a tail, because he sent a message through someone else (instead of going himself). For, on the day when tails were distributed (to all the animals), the sky clouded over; the others went out to get their tails where they were to be got, but he was prevented from going with them; he sent a message to all the animals who had tails (*i.e.*, all who subsequently received them), saying, ' O ye my people, do ye obtain my tail for me; I cannot come out of my hole, because the sky is raining.' So the others returned with their tails, but he had none, through being disinclined to come out when it was cloudy. He lost all the advantage of a tail, for a tail is useful in driving away flies; and so the rock-rabbit has nothing now with which to drive them away.

And so that loitering of the rock-rabbit has become a great proverb among the black people; they make use of that saying of his with regard to those who will not take any trouble about what other people like, or who tell other people to do things for them. ' So and so! As for that saying of yours " Just bring it for me," don't you know that you cannot have anything brought for you by another person, when there is only just enough for those who are on the spot? Oh!—the rock-rabbit had to do without a tail because he sent a message. Do not be like him; you will not get anything by sending word through another; go and attend to your own affairs for yourself.'

This is the story of the rock-rabbit; he did not (exactly) say, with his mouth, ' Bring it for me'; the proverb only arose because (the other) animals have tails, but he has none. It was as though he went without a tail by sending word and because he feared the threatening look of the sky; for he does not come out of his hole except when the sun shines.

(b) *Extracts from Native Letters**

Sa-fika	**e St. Helena,**	**kwa-t' uba¹**	**ngi-pume**
We arrived	at St. H.,	it befell when	I came out
em-kunj-ini²	**aba-kiti³**	**ba-jabula kakulu**	**uku-ngi-**
from the ship	our people	rejoiced greatly	to see
bona,	**nga-puma**	**ngi-nga-sa-tandi⁴**	**na kancane**
me,	I came out	I no longer wishing	even a little
uku-hlala pakati⁵	**kwomkumbi,**		**so-ku-ngi-**
to stay inside	of the ship,		it having already
gulisa.⁶	**Yebo-ke,**	**'Nkosazana**	**ya-kiti**
made me ill.	Yes, indeed,	lady	of our (country)

e-tandeka-yo,⁷   **ama-kosi lawa⁴ a-kwa' Zulu⁸**
who is worthy to be loved,   chiefs   these   of the Zulus

ay' etanda⁹   **kakulu**   **uku-finyelela¹⁰**   **England**
they are wishing   greatly   to reach   England

a-bone   **aba-ntu**   **nezwe**   **la-kona**
that they may see   the people   and country   of there

---

* Written from St. Helena, in 1896-7, by a Natal Zulu, employed as secretary and teacher to the exiled chiefs.

nomuzi[11] lowo o-dumile yo[12] was' e London.[13]
and town that famous of at London.

Ngezindaba e-zi-vela e-kaya[14] kiti, ngi-zwile
As to news which come from home our, I have heard

ukuti aba-ntwana bami ba-ya-gula[15] kakulu ngo-
that children my are ill greatly with

mkuhlane. Nokuti um-kuhlane w-andile[16]
fever. And that fever has increased

pakati kwezwe, kodwa-ke kuhle, nje,
in the midst of the land, but yet it is well, indeed,

noma[17] ku-njalo,[18] ngoba i-kona innyanga
even though it is thus, because there is a doctor

ya-kiti leyo o-y-azi-yo[19] nawe; yena
of our (people) that-one whom you know, you also; she

u-ya-b-elapa, kambe,[20] labo aba-gula-yo,
is treating them, of course, those who are ill,

njengokumiswa[21] kwake y'inkosi[22]
according to the being made-to-stand her by the chief

uyise, aba-ntu ba-ya-m-bonga kakulu,
her father, people are praising her greatly,

ba-ya-jabula nga-ye[23] ezwe-ni lonke las'
they are rejoicing on her account in the land all of

Ekukanyeni[24]. . . .
Ekukanyeni. . . .

Nkosazana—Omunye um-ntwana wenkosi yakwa'
Madam—One child of the chief of

Zulu, u Ndabuko, u-zwile kimi[25]
The Zulus, Ndabuko, he has heard from me (when)

ngi-m-xoxele[26] indaba[27] ngawe ya leso' sizwe[28]
I related to him story from you of that tribe

esi-mnyama o-wa-u-hlezi[29] pakati kwa-so,[20] na
black which you stayed among them, and

ngezinncwadi lezo o-wa-u-zinge[30] u-ngi-tsheleka
from the books those which you used you lending me

APPENDIX I.

zona uku-ba ngi-funde ngesi-kati leso e-nga-ngi-gula[81]
them that I might read at the time that when I was ill

nga-so kiti Ekukanyeni. Nga-loko
at it at our (home) at Ekukanyeni. Therefore

u-ya-tanda kakulu, u-ya-cela ukuba wena,
he wishes greatly, he asks that you,

Nkosazana, u-m-xoxele izin-daba za labo
Madam, you would relate to him affairs of these

'bantu. Ngi-m-landisile[82] **futi uku-ti aba-nye**
people. I have narrated to him also that some

baku lezo' zizwe[83] **ba-kuluma ngo-limi**[84] **lwakwa'**
of those tribes they speak with tongue of the

Zulu impela, ngitsho[85] **labo a-ba-biza u Nkulunkulu**
Zulus indeed, I mean those who call God

ngokuti 'Mulungu,'[86] **nabanye aba'lulimi lwabo**[87]
by saying 'Mulungu,' and others who tongue their

lu-sondele[88] **kwolwetu; a-nga-jabula**[89] **u-qobo**[40]
approaches to ours; he would rejoice in truth

u Ndabuko uma wena, Nkosazana, u-nga-m-tumela
Ndabuko if you, Madam, you could send him

in-cwadi etile[41] **(Book), kumbe**[42] **u-m-tumele**
book some or send him

in-cwadi (Note) yo-ku-m-xoxela[43] **indaba ya labo**
letter to relate to him story of those

'bantu noku-m-tshela ukuti lezo' zizwe z'ake[44]
people and tell him that those tribes they have built

kuyipi[45] **in-dawo, izi-zwe ezi-ngaki, za-vela-pi**[46]
in which place, tribes how many? (and) where did they

na?
come from?

Nkosazana, njengokutembisa kwami ukuti
Madam, as to promising my that

ngi-ya-ku-tuma[47] **ezi-nye izi-bongo zama-kosi akwa'**
I will send some praises of chiefs of the

Q

Zulu kuwe nga lesi 'sitimela,[48] **a-ngi-na-wo**[49]
Zulus to you with this steamer, I have not

ama-ndhla ukuba ngi-ku-tumele[50] **namuhla, kodwa**
strength that I might send you to-day, but

ngi-ya-ku-ku-tumela[50] **ngesitimela esi-za-yo.**[51]
I will send you by the steamer which comes.

Ngi-sa-hamba[52] **kahle em-zimb-eni wami, uku-gula**
I now go will in (as to) body my, illness

loko e-nga-ngi-na-ko[53] **Ekukanyeni a-ku-ka-ngi-**
that which I (was) with it at Ekukanyeni has not again

vuki[54] **lapa. . . .**
arisen (upon) me here. . . .

MAGEMA MAGWAZA.

NOTES

[1] *Kwati*, past tense, like the preceding *safika*, but with the indefinite subject *ku*, 15. An idiomatic use of the verb *ti* 'say' (cf. *First Steps*, §290), which may often be rendered, 'and so,' or 'once upon a time.' *Uba*, a contraction of *ukuba* 'to be,' is here equivalent to *uma* 'when.' (*First Steps*, p. 81.) It is followed by the subjunctive *ngi-pume*.

[2] *emkunjini*, locative of *umkumbi* 3 'ship.' *mb* becomes *nj* in accordance with the Zulu law that a labial is never followed by *w*. There is no apparent *w* here, such as we find in *endhlw-ini* (from *indhlu*, *u* becoming *w* before *-ini*, but the form endhl-ini is also in use); but it is probably introduced into the termination by analogy with the *u* of the stem: *umkumbw-ini*, for *umkumbu-ini*.

[3] *Abakiti* lit. 'those of at us,' cf. *First Steps*, §91, and *ante* p. 236, note 19.

[4] This is not the Potential Mood (*First Steps*, §247), but the Negative Participle (*ib.*, §269). *Sa*, 'when used with a negative verb, may be generally expressed by *any more*, *any longer*, *at all*, etc.' (*ib.* §271).

[5] This is an instance of a word compounded with *pa* (like *pansi*, *pezulu*, *pambili*, etc.), though that preposition (or rather pronoun) is no longer used in Zulu. *Um-kati* 3 'space inter-

APPENDIX I.

vening between any two things' preserves the root *kati* 'between,' which is still so used in Swahili, though not in Zulu. (There is an adverb *kati* 'although,' 'in spite of,'—which may have the same origin, though possibly a derivative of *ti*.)

⁶ This is not the infinitive, but a participle, having for its subject the pronoun *ku*, which may be the indefinite subject ('it,' or 'there') or may agree with *ukuhlala* 'the staying.' *So=se*, the vowel being modified under the influence of *u* in the next syllable. *Se* has the force of ' now,' ' by this time,' ' already,' etc. (*First Steps*, §§274, 275.) *Gulisa*, causative of *gula* ' be ill '; *-ngi-* is the object-pronoun, first person.

⁷ *Tandeka*, neuter-passive of *tanda* ' love ' (*First Steps*, §86); for the relative *etandekayo*, see *ib.*, §132. *e=a+i* is the Relative Prefix, because agreeing with *inkosazana* 9.

⁸ *A* possessive particle agreeing with *amakosi* 6 (exceptional plural of *inkosi* 9—see *First Steps*, §38). *Kwa 'Zulu : kwa* ' at ' (=French *chez*)—see *First Steps*, §92; *u Zulu* (the vowel elided is probably *u=ulu*) used for ' the whole Zulu nation '; *a kwa' Zulu* is used instead of the locative—*as' ezulwini* because the latter would mean ' in ' (or ' from ') ' the sky ' (*ib.*, §79).

⁹ *A* pronoun agreeing with *amakosi*. *A-ya-(ba) etanda*, lit. ' they are, they loving ': the verb *-ba* being understood.

¹⁰ *finyelela* (properly a double applied form of *finya*, but the latter does not seem to be used in any sense recognisable as cognate) ' reach, as a traveller a place,' followed by the locative. (' England,' as it begins with *e*, seems to be treated as a locative, without further modification.)

¹¹ *Nomuzi=na umuzi* 3, ' kraal; people of a kraal, family '; hence used for ' village ' and ' town.' (Nyanja *mu-dzi*, Swahili *m-ji*.)

¹² Literally ' that (town) which has thundered': *dum-ile* perf. of *duma :* the usual expression for ' renowned,' ' glorious,' etc. Cf. Psalm viii., 1: *igama lako lidume kangaka emhlabeni wonke*, lit. ' thy name has thundered how greatly in all the earth.'

¹³ *s* is inserted before the Locative when it follows a Possessive Particle. See *First Steps*, §69.

¹⁴ Locative of *ikaya* ' home,' ' dwelling.' The word is found among the ' Nyika ' tribes of East Africa (*e.g.*, the Giryama) to denote the principal (fortified) village of the Tribe. For the absence of the locative termination, see *First Steps*, §68.

¹⁵ ' Emphatic Present' (Colenso) or ' Present Progressive ' (Bryant) tense,

[16] For *u-andile;* *u* agreeing with *umkuhlane* 3, which is (Bryant) 'a general name for any acute disease accompanied by fever, such as ague, influenza,' etc., etc.

[17] *noma*=na *uma*. For *uma* 'if,' 'when,' etc., see *First Steps*, §81.

[18] *Ku* is here (as in the preceding *kuhle*) the indefinite subject, with the verb 'to be' understood.

[19] Objective Relative (*First Steps*, §134) *y* (=*yi*, for *i*) agreeing with *innyanga* 9. The reference is to Miss Agnes Colenso.

[20] For *kambe*, see *First Steps*, p. 75.

[21] For *njenga ukumiswa*. *Misa*, causative of *ma* 'stand,' means, in the first instance 'make to stand,' establish, 'ordain, as a law or custom,' etc., whence the present sense is easily inferred. The infinitive is here used as a noun of the 15th class (8th in Zulu grammars), with which the possessive *kwake* agrees.

[22] The Passive (*ukumiswa*) is followed by the Copula denoting the Agent (*First Steps*, §100 *et seq.*, and *ante*, p. 114). The 'Chief' is Bishop Colenso.

[23] *ye*, pronoun of the third person singular (*First Steps*, §104) following, and governed by, *nga* (*ib.*, §§93-99), and see *ante* p. 91.

[24] For this locative see *First Steps*, §69, and *ante*, p. 243, note 13.

[25] *kimi* for *kumi*, like *kiti*, etc.—*First Steps*, §90.

[26] X, in Zulu books, stands for the 'lateral click,' made by pressing the tongue against the side teeth and then withdrawing it suddenly. *Xoxele*, perf. of applied form, instead of *xoxel-ile*—*First Steps*, §236.

[27] For the various senses of *indaba*, see Colenso's or Bryant's *Dictionary*, s.v. *Daba* (*in*).

[28] *isi-xwe* 'tribe'—the root of *i(li)-xwe* 'country,' with the 7th prefix—see *ante*, pp. 45, 55.

[29] Relative, with object in an oblique case (*First Steps*, §134): viz., *pakati kwa-so* (*so* pronoun agreeing with *isi-xwe* 7).—*o-* is the Relative (2nd person singular) subject, *wa-* the subject-pronoun of the 2nd person combined with (Past) tense-particle.—*Pakati*, used prepositionally, is always followed by *kwa*.

[30] Relative construction similar to *owauhlexi*. *Zinge* is a

APPENDIX I.

(defective) auxiliary verb, used (*First Steps*, §334) 'to express "repeatedly," "continually," "habitually," etc.' *Zona* (agreeing with *izinncwadi* 10) is governed by *tsheleka*, which, like all verbs of giving, etc. (see *First Steps*, §340), takes a double accusative; but only one objective pronoun can be prefixed to the verb., *viz.*, here, that of the person, *-ngi-*.

[81] A similar relative, but with the subject in the first person (prefix *e-*). The tense is the Past, which when combined with a Relative (cf. *owauhlezi*, above) takes the prefixes both of past and present (*nga-*, *ngi-*). *Ngaso* agrees with *isi-kati* 7.

[82] Perfect of *land-isa*, causative of *landa* 'follow': 'make to follow'—hence 'narrate.'

[83] Literally 'of at those tribes,' one would have expected *ba lezo'zizwe*—but the construction is like *lwa kwa'Zulu*, a little further on, and cf. note 8 above. *Abanye* must be translated 'some,' or 'others,' according to the context.

[84] For *nga+u(lu)-limi*. The usual word for 'language.'

[85] Literally 'I say.'

[86] *Mulungu* is used by the Yaos, Anyanja and other eastern tribes. It is difficult to believe, with Bleek, that it is the same word as *Unkulunkulu*, since the latter is plainly derived from *-kulu*, a root existing in all the languages where *Mulungu* is found. Unless, indeed, some other form was anciently in use among the Zulus, which only became *Unkulunkulu* through an adaptation of popular etymology.

[87] Relative in the Possessive—see *First Steps*, §133.

[88] *lu*, pronoun agreeing with *ulimi* 11; *sondele*, perfect of *sondela* (see above, note 26). *Sond-ela* is properly an applied form of *sonda*, which, however, does not seem to be used.

[89] Potential Mood.

[40] *U(lu)-qobo* (*q* expresses the palatial click), properly 'substance of a thing,' 'self,' 'person,' 'reality,' is used adverbially to express 'really and truly' (Colenso).

[41] *Tile* is an adjective meaning 'certain, when the name or number is not known' (Colenso). It takes the prefix *o-* with Cl. 1, like *o-mnyama*, etc.; hence *inncwadi etile*, not *entile*. The original meanings of *inncwadi* (Colenso's *Dictionary*) are: 'mark, made to show whether any one has entered a hut in the owner's absence; mark or sign told to a person who enquires his way by which he will know whether he is going right or not; tribal token, as marks cut in the skin,' etc., and hence 'token generally, proof,' and, since the introduction of writing, 'paper, letter, book.' The writer has been compelled

APPENDIX I.

to distinguish between the two last-named senses by the addition of English words. The sense in which he here uses *etile* seems to be equivalent to 'some . . . or other.'

[42] *kumbe*, 'perhaps, with the idea of hope or expectation' (Colenso), but also equivalent to the conjunction 'or.' The latter is often expressed (as in Nyanja) by a word meaning 'perhaps'—the possible alternatives being set before the mind as conjectures.

[43] An example of the quasi-participle mentioned on p. 118, *yoku- =ya uku- : ya* referring to *innewadi*.

[44] *ake* perf. of *aka* 'build,' which is often used in the sense of 'live.' *Akelana* (reciprocal applied form) means 'to live near together,'—lit. 'to build for' (or 'with respect to') each other: hence *owakelene* 'neighbour.'

[45] *yipi*, interrogative, 'which'? (of two or more), agrees with *indawo* 9 following it. *-pi* means either 'where?' or 'which?' (see *First Steps*, §§169-171). *Yipi*, as used here is the object following *ku* : as subject it would have to be preceded by the copula (*iy'ipi*). *-pi* 'where?' takes the inseparable subject-pronoun as prefix: *upi? bapi? lipi? ipi?* etc.

[46] *-pi*, 'where?' is sometimes suffixed to the verb in this way, and draws the accent forward (*zavelápi*).

[47] This is the Future, 'I will send,' not the Present, with object-pronoun, 'I am sending you'; *tuma* in the simple form cannot take a person as object; to do this it must be put into the applied form (*tumela*), as will be seen a little lower down.

[48] An adaptation of the English word 'steamer.' *St* being a difficult combination in Zulu, *i* is inserted between the two consonants, and the first syllable being taken for the 8th prefix (*isi-*), the plural is *izi-timela*. (There is a genuine Zulu word *isi-timela*, meaning ' darkness '—see Colenso's *Dictionary*, *s.v.*, p. 587). The same tendency is observable in Swahili, where the Arabic *kitab* 'book' becomes *ki-tabu*, pl. *vi-tabu*. *Vi-mni* has even been heard at Zanzibar, as the plural of '(lamp-) chimney.'

[49] Literally, 'not I with it'— *-wo* 'prepositional form' of the pronoun of Cl. 6. *Amandhla* has no singular.

[50] Here *tumela* takes the direct object of the person, and, the verb being in the future, *ku* is repeated, or rather two different *ku*-particles follow each other. See note 47 above.

[51] *esi-*, Relative Particle agreeing with *isi-timela* 8.

[52] *sa* may be rendered by 'now,' 'still,' 'already.' See *First Steps*, chapter XVI.

⁵³ Relative—the construction like *engangigula* (see note 31), except that the verb is understood and the whole drawn into one word. The pronoun *-ko* refers to *uku-gula*.

⁵⁴ *Vuka* 'rise up from a recumbent posture; . . . rise in anger, be in a towering passion' (Colenso). The personal object *-ngi-* is unusual with this verb, but may be used because it is taken in the sense of 'attack,' which is perhaps not incompatible with the second meaning given above. In that case, however, one would have expected the Applied form, *vukela*, which is, in fact, so used; and *vuki* may be a mere slip on the writer's part. For the auxiliary *ka* see *First Steps*, §315.

Connected Translation

We arrived at St. Helena, and when I landed from the ship, our people were very glad to see me. I also was very glad to land, having no desire to remain on board any longer, as I had been very seasick. Yes indeed! dear lady coming from our country! these chiefs of the Zulus wish very much to come to England, to see that country and its people, and that famous city of London. . . .

As to the news which has reached us from home—I have heard that my children are very ill with fever. In fact, fever has been very prevalent in the country; but there is one very good thing, even though this is the case—for there is that physician of our people whom you also know, who is treating the sick according to the instructions received by her from the Chief, her father. The people praise her greatly, and they are rejoicing through her in all the country-side of Ekukanyeni. . . .

Madam,—One of the chiefs of the Zulus, Ndabuko, has heard from me a story which I related to him, having heard it from you, of that tribe of black people among which you (formerly) lived, and (gathered it) from those books which you used to lend me to read, at the time when I was ill, at our home, Ekukanyeni.

Therefore he wishes very much to ask that you, Madam, would relate to him the affairs of those people.

I have also told him that some of those tribes speak a
language exactly the same as that of the Zulus—I mean
those who call God by the name of *Mulungu*—and
others whose language resembles ours (though not quite
the same). He would be very glad if you could send
him some book or other, or perhaps a letter, to give him
an account of those people and tell him what place they
live in, and how many tribes there are, and where they
came from. Madam, as to my promise that I would
send you by this mail, some of the traditional songs
praising the Zulu Kings,—I am not able to do so to-day,
but I will send you (some) by the next steamer. I am
now very well in health, as that illness which I had at
Ekukanyeni has not again attacked me here. . . .

2. Herero.[*]

Story of the Old Woman with the Bag

Pa-ri[1] **omu-kadhe-ndu**[2] **omu-kuru-kadhe,**[3]
There was woman old,

ngu-ya-twa[4] **ova-natye**[5] **m'ondyatu.**[6] **E-yuva**[7] **ri-mwe**
who put children into bag. Day one

pa-rire[8] **ova-natye, ova-kadhona ov-engi,**[9] **va-ire**[10]
there were children, girls many, they went

k' oku-nyanda[11] **k' e-rindi,**[12] **n' a-rire**[13] **tyi**[14]
to play in pool, and it happened that

va-hukura otu-vanda[15] **n' omi-tombe**[16] **n'**
they took off little-skirts and necklaces and

ovi-mbakutu[17] **n' ou-ndyendye**[18] **n' odho-mbongora**[19]
(see note) and beads and (see note)

n' a-ve-pundu[20] **m' omeva. Kombunda**[21] **omu-atye**
and they descended into water. Afterwards child

---

[*] Published by C. G. Büttner in *Zeitschrift für afrikanische Sprachen*, Vol. I. (1887).

APPENDIX I.

u-mwe wa-tarere[22] kokure,   n' arire   ty' a-tara
one   she looked   far,   and it happened that she saw

omu-kadhendu omukurukadhe, ngu n' oka-ti m' eke
woman   old,   who with little-stick in hand,

oru-horo-ti,[23] n' ondyatu p' etambo.   Nu[24] ingwi
a-long-stick, and   bag   on back.   And   that

omu-kadhona wa-tyere k' ova-kwawo[25]: 'Indyee[26]
girl   said   to (the) others: 'Come

  tu-tupukee[27]   'ka-kurukadhe[28]   ingwina,
let us run-away-from   little old-woman   yonder,

ngu-twa ova-natye m' ondyatu.' Indino[29] ty 'a-tya[30]
who puts children into bag.   Now when she said

nai, avehe[31] arire tyi   va-piti[32] m' e-rindi oku-
so   all it happened that they came out from pool to

tupuka, nu auhe[33] wa-torera   oru-hira[34] r-omu-
run-away, and every she took   apron   of

kwawo nu omitombe vy-omu-kwawo[35] tyinga va-ri
other and necklaces of other   as they were

m' oru-haka r-oku-tupuka, ndino   arire tyi
in haste   of running-away, now it happened that

va-tupuka k' onganda.[36]
they ran   to kraal.

  N' omuatye umwe wa-dhembire etanda[87] e-purura[87]
And child   one   she forgot (see note) (see note)

p' ehi.[88]   Ndino 'kakurukadhe   arire   ty'
on ground. Now little-old-woman it happened that

  a-pingene   p' epurura,   n'a-tora,
she followed (and came) on *epurura*, and picked-up,

  arire ty'   a-twa-mo m' ondyatu.[39]   Nu   ing'
it happened that she put-in into bag.   And   that

omuatye umwe wa-tya: me-yaruka[40] me-ka-pura[41]
child   one she said: I return   I go to ask

epurura   randye   k' omu-twa,[42] oka-kurukadhe,
epurura   my   from Bushwoman, little-old-woman,

tyiri!⁴³ hi n' oku-ri-etha-ko.⁴⁴ Imb' ova-kwawo
truly! not-I with leaving-it-there. Those others

va-tyere: muatye! arikana,⁴⁵ omundu eingwi,⁴⁶
they said: Child! please (beware of) person that,

ngu, maku-dhu,⁴⁷ utwa ovanatye m' odhondyatu,
who, it-is-said, she puts children into bags

nu i-ko!⁴⁸ N'e wa-tyere:⁴⁹ kako! me-ka-eta
and goes away! And she said: No! I go to bring

epurura ra mama oku-kotoka k'omutwa
epurura of my-mother to return from Bushwoman

oka-kuru-kadhe. Nu imb' ovakwawo avehe
little-old-woman. And those others all

va-ire k'onganda, n' eye, a- kotoka, a- ende
they went to kraal, and she, she returning, she going

n' a- riri⁵⁰ n' oma-kono k' otyi-uru. Nu
and she weeping with hands on head. And

ty'a-ri m'ondyira kokure, arire ty'
when she was on road far-away, it happened that

a-ravaere,⁵¹ a-ithana, a-tya: Mu-tyimba,⁵²
she cried-aloud, she called, she said: Pauper,

kakurukadhe, eta nguno epurura ra mama,
little-old-woman, bring here *epurura* of my mother,

ndi wa-tora. Nu omukadhendu wa-tya:
which you picked-up. And woman she said:

Indyo, kambura. N'e-a-ende, a-me-utuka, arire
Come here, take (it). And she went, she running, and

ty' a-tumbuka popedhu, n' a-tya: Kakurukadhe,
so she approached near, and she said: Little old woman,

eta nguno epurura ra mama. N'e wa-tya rukwao:⁵³
bring here *epurura* of my mother. And she said again:

Kambura, n' arire ty'a-tumbuka, n' arire
Take (it), and so she approached, and it came to pass

ty' e-mu-tono oru-pyu k' otyi-tama, nu
that she her struck slap on cheek, and

APPENDIX I. 251

okakurukadhe   a- hakahana[54]   oku-wira-ko[55]
little old woman   she hastened   to fall-upon-her

n' a- petere[56]   m' ondyatu, n'arire ty' a- kutu
and she doubled (her) up   into bag,   and so   she tied

ondyatu   n' omuvia, n' arire ty'a- kutu ondyatu
bag   with thong, and so   she tied   bag

p'etambo,   n' a- vereka,[57]   arire   ty'
on back,   and she carried (her),   it happened   that

a- i   a- tedha   ku-kwa-i[58]   ova-natye
she went   she followed   where-there-went   children

k'onganda.   Nu   m' onganda   mwa-vadherwe[59]
to kraal.   And   in kraal   there-was-arrived,

a-mwa-tu   omu-kandi.[60]   N'e we-ere[61]
it-there-died   feast.   And she came (in the)

ongurova n' a- kare kongotwe y- onganda m' okuti.
evening and she sat behind   the kraal in the field.

Nu kombunda ova-natye ve-mu-munu,[62]   arire
And afterwards children   they-her-saw,   it happened

tyi   va-raerere   ku ihe[63]   a-ve-tya: Tate,[63]
that they cried aloud to their-father they said: Father,

omukadhendu ingwi eingwi[64] okakurukadhe ngu-
woman   this   she (is) that little-old-woman who

a-dhepa ova-natye nu ngu-a-twa-mo omu-atye wetu
she kills children and who has put in   child   our

m' ondyatu.   Nu va-purire ku ihe a-ve-tya:
into bag.   And they-asked from father, saying:

Nga-tu-mu-tyite vi ?[65]   Nu ingwi ihe wa-tyere;
We are to (to) her do what?   And this father he said:

Wererekee[66] ongurova   tyi   mamu-aruka[67]
Catch-with-guile (in) evening   when   you (pl.) begin

oku-rara.   Nu   imb(a)   ova-natye ongurova
to sleep.   And   these   children (in the) evening

tyi   ma-ve-aruk (a)   okurara,   ve-ere[68]   p'
when   they began   to sleep,   they came   to

okakurukadhe n' a-ve-tya : Mama kakurukadhe,
little-old-woman and they said : Mother, little-old-woman,

mo-vanga tyike,⁶⁹ ku-tya tu-ku-pe ? N'e
you want what that we may give you? And she

wa-tyere : namba⁷⁰ ami me-vanga tyike ? vanatye
she said : now, for my part, I want what ? children

vandye, ke-ndyi-pahere⁷¹ uri⁷² orukune (o) ru-nene ;
 my, go (for) me look-for just log-of-wood large ;

mba t'⁷³ombepera. N'owo va-ire, arire
I am dead (with) cold. And they, they went, it happened

tyi va-ka-paha oru-kune (o)ru-nene, ndu
that they went-to-seek log large, which

va-muna rukuru,⁷⁴ n'arire tyi va-tora
they saw long-ago, and it happened that they-lifted

omumbeumbeu,⁷⁵ n'arire tyi va-eta,
 all-together and it happened that they brought (it),

a-ve-tya ; kakurukadhe, twe-ku-etere⁷⁶
saying : Little-old-woman, we-to you-have-brought

orukune oru-twedhu,⁷⁷ ndu-rara n' omundu,
 log thick, which sleeps with person,

omukadhendu okakurukadhe o-tya ove,⁷⁸
 woman old as you,

n' a-yanyuka oviandonya.⁷⁹ N'arire
and she stretches (herself) out (on) back. And

tyi ve-mu-etere orukune. M' ou-tuku
so they (to) her brought log. In night

ty' a-rara, ova-natye arire tyi ve-kutura⁸⁰
when she slept, children and so they untie

ondyatu, n' arire tyi va-itha-mo omu-atye
 bag, and so they take-out-of-it child

n'ovi-na ovi-tyuma⁸¹ nu m'ondyatu m'
and things vessels and into bag into

otjipurukute⁸² arire tyi va-ongere-mo
 dry bag it happened that they collected into (it)

APPENDIX I. 253

ou-puka,⁸⁸ ngamwa,⁸⁴ 'kapuka ke-rumata akehe.⁸⁵
animals, all sorts, animal it bites everyone.

Nu ondyatu otyi-purukute, arire tyi va-kutu rukwao,
And bag dry bag, so they tied again,

n' owo a-ve-i k'onganda n' a-ve-twara omu-atye
and they went to kraal and they carried child

n' ovi-na mbi⁸⁶ va-ithire m' ondyatu, nu
and things which they had taken-out from the bag, and

ve-vi-twarere ku ihe. Ihe
they-then-brought to the father. The father

wa-dhepere omukandi, a-koho nao⁸⁷
he killed (a beast for) the feast, he cleansed with it

omu-atye. Nu kombunda 'kakurukadhe
the child. And afterwards the old woman

arire ty' a-nununga ondyatu, a-tyangovathi,⁸⁸
it happened that she felt the bag, she thought,

omu-atye om' e-ri⁸⁹ arire ty' a-kutura
the child in it she was and so she untied

ondyatu n'e wa-tire omadhenge
the bag and she was (nearly) dead (with) rage

tyinene, kutya⁹⁰ ovanatye va-ithire-mo m'ondyatu.
truly, that the children had taken-out from the bag.

Ndino oupuka arire tyi wa-sakumukire
Now the animals it happened that they crawled-out

mu-ye, n'arire tyi wa-hiti m'orutu rwe aruhe,
on her, and so they entered into body her whole,

m' otji-nyo na m' oma-yuru na m' omeho, n'arire
into mouth and into nostrils and into eyes, and so

ty'a-koka. Oputyo.⁹¹
she ended. This is all.

NOTES

[1] *Pa* locative prefix; *ri* verb 'to be.' *Pari* is the perfect tense, the one with the suffix corresponding to *-ile* is a 'Pluperfect,' or distant past. In the Present, the prefix would be *pe*, not *pa*.

[2] Herero has a somewhat peculiar way of forming compounds. Instead of saying *omu-ndu omu-kadhe* 'female person,' or using *omu-kadhe* by itself as a noun, 'woman,' the root *-ndu* is suffixed. See *ante*, p. 215, and note 23, on *oruhoroti*; also Meinhof, *Lautlehre der Bantusprachen*, p. 135. Another curious feature, to some extent analogous to the above, is the insertion of the interrogative particle *ke* between prefix and root, as *omu-ke-ti*, 'what sort of tree?' *omu-ke-ndu*, 'what sort of person?'

[3] *-kadhe* is suffixed to *omu-kuru*, which by itself means 'old (person),' in order to indicate the feminine. *-kazi* is similarly used in Zulu (as in *indoda-kazi* 'daughter,' *inkosi-kazi* 'queen': there is no independent word *um-kazi*), though less frequently. The Herero are supposed to have a mixture of Hamitic blood, or at any rate to have been in contact with Hamitic tribes (*e.g.*, the Galla or Somali) before their southward migration, and they might have borrowed from them the notion of a feminine suffix—which is quite foreign to the genius of the Bantu languages.

[4] *ngu* relative pronoun of the third person. In the Present it immediately precedes the verb-stem; *ngu-twa* 'who puts'; in the Perfect it is followed by *-a: ngu-a-twa* (or *ngu-ya-twa*; the *y* no doubt introduced to prevent the two syllables from gliding into *ngwa*) 'who put.'

[5] The singular of this noun is *omu-atye*, the *n*, which, as we know from other languages, belongs to the root, seems to have dropped out.

[6] *ondyatu* 9 is a leather bag or wallet, carried over the shoulder by people who go out to collect roots, etc.

[7] The 5th prefix is in Herero abbreviated to *e* (as in Zulu to *i*): its full form is *eri*, the pronoun *ri*. *Ejuva* is the same word as Sango *lidyuva*, Nyanja *dzuwa*, Swahili *jua*, etc.

[8] *Rira* 'become,' 'be,' (*rire* is the Historic Aorist); for its idiomatic use as an auxiliary, see below.

APPENDIX I.

⁹ *ov-engi* for *ova-ingi*, adjective agreeing with *ovanatye*. *ova-kadhona* 'girls' is, though a noun, practically equivalent to an adjective, being placed in apposition with *ovanatye*.

¹⁰ *ire*, pluperfect of the defective verb *ya* 'go.'

¹¹ The frequent use of *ku*, even where it would seem superfluous, as here before the Infinitive, seems a peculiarity of Herero.

¹² Same root as Swahili and Pokomo *dindi* 'hole' or 'pit'—more especially applied to a deep place in the bed of a river or the sea. It also appears in such place names as Lindi, Malindi, Kilindini (the harbour at the south end of Mombasa Island), etc. The Herero use *erindi* to mean what is called in South Africa a 'pan'—*i.e.*, a depression in which water collects during the rains, drying up partially or wholly after they are over.

¹³ *a-rire*, followed by *tyi* is equivalent to 'it happened that,' 'it came to pass that,' etc.,—or merely 'and so.' The pronoun *a* (instead of *u*) is prefixed to the 'Historic Aorist' and the Subjunctive.

¹⁴ *tyi* 'say,' like Zulu *ti*, here used as a conjunction (cf. Zulu *ukuti*)=that.

¹⁵ Pl. of *oru-vanda* 12; the singular is not used in this sense. The word means a kind of apron or kilt worn by little girls (under 15 or 16) and consisting of a number of hide thongs (in Cape Dutch *rimpies*), hanging from a belt. In front these reach the feet,—behind they are long enough to sweep the ground. A more ornamental kind of *okavanda* is the *otjim-bakutu* (pl. *ovimbakutu*), mentioned a little lower down, which consists entirely of *omitombe* (see next note).

¹⁶ *omitombe* 4 are strings of small disks cut from the shells of ostrich-eggs, and rounded by rubbing their edges on a stone. As the process of preparing these 'beads' is slow and tedious, they are highly valued. They are worn, either in single strings, as necklaces, or the strings are looped together to form a sort of bodice, called *omutombe* 3.

¹⁷ *ovimbakutu*, see note 15.

¹⁸ *oundyendye* 14, (imported) glass beads, usually worn in strings round the neck.

¹⁹ Pl. of *ombongora*, 9, a string of disks similar to the *omitombe* (see note 16), but made from the shells of snails or other molluscs.

APPENDIX I.

[20] 3rd pers. pl. 'emphatic aorist' of *punda* 'descend'; in this tense the final vowel is assimilated to that of the stem.

[21] An adverb composed of *ku* and *ombunda* 9 'the back'—therefore 'behind' or 'after.' In Herero, the *u* of *ku* is often elided before another vowel, instead of turning into *w*.

[22] 3rd pers. sing., pluperfect of *tara* 'look.'

[23] *oru-horoti* is a compound of *omu-ti* analogous to *omu-kadhendu*. It means 'a long stick,' and is used in apposition with *oka-ti*, so that it is practically an adjective='long.' But Brincker's Dictionary does not give *oruhoro* in any sense which would imply this.

[24] *Nu* is used to join sentences (or, in other words before a verb)—*na* nouns.

[25] *-kuao* (=*kwawo*) is given in the grammars and dictionaries as an adjective meaning 'other,' but really it is the possessive pronoun of the 3rd pers. pl. agreeing with Class 15. All three persons are used with the prefixes of Class 1 and Class 2:—*omu-kwetu* 'my (our) companion, house-mate, person of the same village, etc.,' pl. *ova-kwetu*, *omu-kwenu* 'you, etc.,' *omu-kwawo* 'his, her, their, etc.'—like Zulu *abakiti* (see p. 236 *ante*) of which, however, there is no singular form corresponding to *omu-kwetu*.

[26] Imperative plural of *ya* 'come.'

[27] *tupukee*, applied form of *tupuka*, taking the direct object (*o*) *kakurukadhe*.

[28] Diminutive of *omu-kurukadhe* (note 3). Compare the use of *kizee* in Swahili for an old woman, mostly used of a witch or other uncanny person.

[29] *Indino*, properly a demonstrative agreeing with *eyuva* 5 'day' (lit. 'sun'): 'this day,' and so 'now.'

[30] *Tyi* here used in the sense of 'when.' *Tya* is the form used as an independent verb, when the meaning is actually 'say.'

[31] *avehe* 'all,' agreeing with Cl. 2. The root is *he* which always prefixes *a-* followed by the personal or class-pronoun: *a-tu-he* 'all of us,' *a-mu-he* 'all of you,' etc.

[32] 'Historic Aorist' (Viehe), one of the tenses which assimilates its final vowel to that of the stem—cf. *pundu* (note 20).

[33] *Auhe*: *-he* 'all' agreeing with Cl. 1—singular of *avehe*.

APPENDIX I.

[84] *oruhira* 11, a goat-skin apron worn next the skin, the other articles mentioned being put on over it. The initial *r* of the next word stands for *ra*, the 11th possessive particle, agreeing with *oruhira*. This elides the *a* (instead of combining it, as in Zulu, with the initial vowel of the noun)—no doubt because the initial *u* has already been modified to *o* (as is also the case in Ganda).

[85] The possessive particle of Class 3 is *vya* (not as in most languages *ya*), preserving a hint of the original γ. *Nu* before *omitombe* seems to contravene the rule given in note 24, but may be a printer's error.

[86] *onganda* 9 is the word generally used for 'kraal,' 'village'; the word used in S.W. Africa is *werft* (Cape Dutch, though in this sense it seems to be peculiar to that district)—see Pettman, *Africanderisms*, p. 550. The Zulu *umuzi* 3 represents the word used in most Bantu languages; it is found in in Herero as *oru-dhe* 11, meaning 'principal village.' Brincker translates *onganda* by *Viehdorf* 'cattle-village,' which among the pastoral Herero would be the normal type of settlement. A village without cattle is *ondua* (which, *ex hypothesi*, appears to be a Nama village) or *otjihuro*.

[87] *etanda* and *epurura* appear to be more or less synonymous and consist of strings of iron and copper 'beads,' or hollow balls, fastened to the lower edge of the *omutombe*.

[88] *ehi* 5 is the word which appears in Swahili as *nti* 9; in Zulu, Nyanja, etc., as *pa-nsi* (it is not used by itself); just as -*he* 'all,' corresponds to Nyanja -*onse* and Zulu -*onke*. But it is something of a puzzle that Zulu should have the *ns* in *pansi*, and so is the elimination of the vowel in Herero).

[89] Herero, as we have seen, prefixes *pa*, *ku* or *mu* to a noun, and does not possess the suffixed locative of Zulu, etc. It also suffixes the pronouns -*po*, -*ko* -*mo* to the verb accompanying the noun—a usage also found in Nyanja, where the noun, moreover, frequently takes both prefix and suffix as *m'nyumba-mo* 'in the house.'

[40] The inseparable pronoun in Herero varies to an extraordinary degree. 'I' is *me*- with the Present, *e*- with the Aorist, *mba*- with the Perfect, and with the 'Jussive,' *ng'e*- or *hi*-; while it also has a distinct object-form *ndyi*-.

[41] The particle *ka* has a 'directive force' as *mekatona* 'I go (to) strike'—*i.e.*, 'I am going to strike.'

[42] *Omu-twa*, pl. *ova-twa* (cf. Zulu *umu-twa, aba-twa*) originally meant 'Bushman,' but seems to be used in a depreciatory

sense of any non-Herero, and hence with the meaning of 'slave,' 'bondsman,' etc. *Omu-tyimba*, applied further on to the same old woman, is used by the Herero of people who have no cattle, but pick up a living as they can in the Bush (and so = 'pauper'); but other tribes apply it to the Herero themselves.

⁴³ *tyiri*, invariable, is called by Brincker an 'interjection of assurance.'

⁴⁴ *edha*='leave'; *ri* refers to *epurura*, *ko*, locative pronoun (17).

⁴⁵ *arikana* an exclamation of entreaty, variously rendered according to the context. Similar expressions are found elsewhere—*e.g.*, the Yao *chonde!* It looks like the imperative of a reciprocal verb, but none such appears to be now in use.

⁴⁶ *e-ingwi* for *eye ingwi*. *Eye* is frequently contracted to *e*.

⁴⁷ *dhu* from *dha* 'come from' means, with the indefinite subject (*ku*) 'it is said,' *ma-ku-dhu* is the tense called by Brincker the 'Simple Present,' which prefixes *ma* to all its pronouns.

⁴⁸ *i* is the aorist of the defective verb *ya* 'go'; *ko* the locative pronoun, here best rendered by 'away,' but a better equivalent would be the French *en* in *s'en aller*.

⁴⁹ *e(ye)*, or *eye*, separable personal pronoun: *tyere*, pluperfect of *tya*.

⁵⁰ *a-riri*: this, like the preceding verbs is a participle, which in the simple form always assimilates the final vowel. *Rira* 'weep' (Zulu *lila*, Nyanja *lira*, Swahili *lia*, Pokomo *ia*) must not be confused with *rira* 'become.'

⁵¹ *Ravaera*, applied form of *rava* 'thrust in' (used, *e.g.*, of Moses putting his hand into his bosom, etc.). The sense of 'crying aloud' is derived, according to Brincker, from that of 'thrusting the tongue into the throat' (*stark die Zunge in die Kehle stecken*); in the applied form 'cry aloud to' some one, *ithana* (cf. Nyanja *itana*) is properly a reciprocal; Swahili has the simple form *ita*.

⁵² See note 42. *o* is elided in this word and the next, because they are in the vocative.

⁵³ *rukwao*, used as an invariable adverb, 'again,' but really an adjective agreeing with *oru-vedhe* 'time,'='another time.'

⁵⁴ Historic Aorist. The rule of vowel-assimilation is not usually applied to verbs of more than two syllables, but there are some exceptions.

APPENDIX I.

⁵⁵ *Ko* locative preposition. According to the usage of most Bantu languages, one would have expected *oku-mu-wira*.

⁵⁶ Pluperfect of *peta*, 'bend,' Swahili *peta* 'bend,' 'curve,' from which comes *pete* 'ring.'

⁵⁷ *vereka* means to carry on the back, as native women do babies: *bereka* is similarly used in Nyanja, and *beleka* (or *beleta*) in Zulu, where *im-beleko* is the prepared goat-skin used for tying the child on.

⁵⁸ Relative of the *ku-* class in the past. We must understand something like 'to the place,' or 'at the time' after *a-tedha*.

⁵⁹ *mwa-* is the locative pronoun for the past tenses, the subject of the verb being *m'onganda*. *vadherwe* is the passive of the applied form of *vadha* 'reach.'

⁶⁰ *Omu-kandi* is a feast of meat, when a bullock is slaughtered on special occasions. The feast is said to 'die' because it was just ending. *A-mwa-ṭu* seems to be a mistake for *a-mu-ṭu*, which is the Historical Aorist of *ṭa* 'die.' (This verb has a dental *t*, which distinguishes it from *ta* 'be equal with.')

⁶¹ *eye* plup. of *ya* 'come,' which takes *we* instead of *wa* for the pronoun of the 3rd pers. sing. in the past tenses. This and the aorist *ya* (instead of *i*) distinguish it from *ya* 'go away.' *Oku-ti* is really the locative (17) which in Herero is merged into the infinitive class (15)—see *ante*, p. 85. It means the open country—in fact is best translated by the Dutch *veld*.

⁶² *mu* is here the objective pronoun of the 1st class, not the locative prefix.

⁶³ *ihe* 'his, her, their father'—cf. Zulu *uyise*. 'Your father' is *iho* (Zulu *uyihlo*); 'my father' *tate* (cf. Nyanja *tate, atate*). This form is found in a good many languages, while others, like Zulu and Swahili, prefer *(u)baba*.

⁶⁴ *e=eye*: *eye ingwe* 'she (is) this ' (or 'that ') one.

⁶⁵ Subjunctive. In principal sentences (as here) this has *nga-* prefixed to it. For *tyita* 'do,' cf. Nyanja *chita*. *vi* is an invariable interrogative.

⁶⁶ Brincker translates *wereka* by ' do a thing treacherously; (*verräterisch etwas tun*).

⁶⁷ Second person plural of the Present, which prefixes *ma* to all the pronouns, though in the three persons of the singular it is contracted with them into *me, mo, ma*.

⁶⁸ See *ante*, note 61.

[69] *Tyike* 'what?' stands by itself after a verb, as here. When the question is asked, 'what is (are) he (it, they)?' — *-kwatyike* is used with the proper class-prefix: *omukwatyike, ovakwatyike, otyikwatyike*, etc.

[70] In the original *n'amba*, which, Prof. Meinhof tells me, is a mistake. 'It should be *namba* "now," which is derived from *pa*' ('at').

[71] *Pahere* (*e*) imperative plural of applied form (*pahera*) of *paha* 'seek.' *Ke* is the 'directive particle' *ka*, which modifies its vowel when followed by an object-pronoun. 'Go and seek for me a log.'

[72] *uri* an invariable (adverbial) particle, equivalent to 'just,' 'only,' 'so,' etc.

[73] For *ţu*, perfect of *ţa* 'die'; *ombepera*, a noun of the 9th class.

[74] Originally an adjective ('old') agreeing with *oru-vedhe*, cf. note 53, on *rukwao*. A fairly good supply of firewood is to be obtained from the mimosas and acacias of the Herero country (Büttner). People are always on the look-out for dead logs which will burn easily, and, if they see one, note the place so that they can return for it when wanted. These girls remembered that they had noticed one in the bush some time before.

[75] Translated by Brincker and Viehe 'zusammen,' 'gemeinsam'; it is evidently a noun of Class 3, but the original meaning is nowhere given.

[76] Applied form of *eta* (Zulu *leta*) 'bring,' which enables it to take the direct object (*-ku-* object-pronoun 2nd pers. sing.). *Twe*, instead of *twa*, because *a* always becomes *e* before the object-pronoun.

[77] Properly 'a log like a bull.'

[78] *i.e.*, 'which an old woman like you can sleep with': meaning that it is large enough to burn through the night, so that a person can sleep comfortably, without getting up to put wood on the fire.

[79] Properly a plural noun of Class 8, but it only seems to be used adverbially. *ondonya* 9 is both noun ('back') and adverb ('behind').

[80] Reversive of *kuta* 'tie.'

[81] A general word for 'vessels,' 'implements,' 'household stuff.' *Chuma*, in Yao, means 'beads,' (applied in Nyanja to property of any sort); in Swahili, 'iron'—but it is not certain that the three are the same word.

APPENDIX I.

[82] This seems to be a descriptive epithet applied to the bag and to mean anything made of hide which is hard and dry and rattles.

[83] Pl. of *oka-puka* (diminutive of *otji-puka*), applied to small animals and insects.

[84] *ngamwa*, indefinite numeral meaning 'all sorts,' 'of any kind whatever.'

[85] 'Every biting animal.' *rumata* 'bite': the simple form, *ruma* does not seem to be used in Herero. *Ke* pronoun of Cl. 13 with the present tense.

[86] Relative Pronoun of Class 8, agreeing with its antecedent *ovina*.

[87] 'with it' seems to refer to *omukandi*. No doubt some sort of ceremonial purification is intended, to free the girl from any evil influences which may have emanated from the old woman. The sentence seems to mean that the father killed an extra beast (*wa-dhepere* imperfect of the Applied Form, not Pluperfect) as part of the *omukandi*, which was not yet finished.

[88] This and some allied forms are derived from *tya* 'say' and *ndovathi* (*ndovadhi*) 'perhaps,' 'if haply,' and mean 'think,' 'be of opinion that.' . . . .

[89] Om'*eri* contracted from *omu eye u ri*. (Information kindly urnished by Professor Meinhof, and see Brincker, *Wörterbuch*, p. 83).

[90] *kutya* used synonymously with *tyi*.

[91] *Opu*, locative adverb, 'there,' 'in that place.' Combined with a pronoun, as here with *-tyo* (Cl. 7) it means 'that's all' (literally 'there (is) that')—*i.e.*, 'this is the end of the story.'

Connected Translation

There was once an old woman who used to put children into her bag (and carry them off). One day, a number of girls went to play in a pool; they took off their clothes and ornaments and went down into the water. After a time, one of them, looking out to a distance, happened to see an old woman who had a long

stick in her hand and a bag on her back. So the girl
said to her companions: 'Come, let us run away from
the little old woman yonder, who carries off children in
her bag.' When she spoke thus, all of them came out
of the pool, in order to run away, and every one picked
up the apron and the necklaces of her companion, as they
were in such haste to run away. So they ran as fast as
they could back to the village. But one child forgot
her *epurura* and left it lying on the ground; and the old
woman went up to it, picked it up, and put it into her
bag. So the girl said, 'I am going back to ask that
old Bushwoman for my *epurura*; I am not going to
leave it there, truly!' But the others said, 'Please
don't, dear!—they say that person puts children into
bags and goes away with them!' She answered, 'No,
I must get my mother's *epurura* back from that old
Bushwoman.' So all her companions went home, but
she turned back, and walked along, crying, with her
hands on her head. And while she was on the path,
she called out to the old woman, a long way off, saying,
'You horrid old pauper! bring me my mother's *epurura*,
which you have picked up.' The old woman said,
'Come here and take it.' The girl ran up to her, and
when she was quite near, said again: 'Old woman, bring
my mother's *epurura* here!' The old woman said
again, 'Take it!' and when the girl came close to her,
she slapped her on the cheek.* And then the old
woman made haste and seized her and thrust her into
the bag, and then tied up the bag with hide thongs and
fastened it on her back and carried it so, and went on in
the direction which the girls had taken to reach their
village, where a great feast had been going on and was
nearly ended. The old woman arrived there in the
evening and sat down outside the fence in the open
field. When, later on, the girls saw her, they called out

---

* It is not clear from the text, as it stands, whether it was the
old woman who slapped the girl, or *vice versa*. But the women
who related the story to Büttner insisted that the former was the
case.

to their father, saying, 'Father, the old woman out there is the one who kills children, and she has put our child into her bag.' And they asked their father, saying, 'What shall we do to her?' And their father said, 'Wait till the evening, when you are all thinking of going to sleep, and then you can entrap her.' So, in the evening, before those girls lay down to sleep, they came to the old woman (outside the kraal fence), and said, 'Mother, what would you like us to get for you?' And she said, 'For my part, my children, what I should like is that you should just find me a good big log (to burn), for I am well-nigh dead with cold.' So they went to look for a large log which they had marked down some time before, and lifted it all together and carried it back and said, 'Little old woman, we have brought you a regular whopper of a log, such that a woman can sleep all night beside it, lying comfortably on her back.' So they brought her the log (and put it on the fire).*

But in the night, when she was asleep, the girls went and untied the bag and took out the child and everything else that was in it, and they collected and put into it all kinds of biting insects and reptiles,—every creature that bites. And they tied up the bag again and went into the kraal, carrying with them the little girl and the things which they had taken out of the bag, and brought them to their father. And he killed another bullock for the feast, so as to purify his daughter with it. But, after a time, the old woman got up and felt the bag, thinking the girl was inside it (but she was not there), so she untied it and nearly died of rage, indeed, because the other girls had taken her out. So then all the animals crawled out on her and got into her mouth and nose and eyes (and stung her to death), and that was the end of her. That is all.

* It is to be supposed that the old woman had made a little fire for herself with such dry sticks as she could find, and only wanted fuel to keep it up through the night.

3. Ila*

The Tortoise and the Hare

Ba-nyama[1] bonse' ba-ka-fwe[2] nyotwa,[3]
The animals all, when they were about to die (of) thirst,

ba-amb,' ati:[4] 'A-tu-lukanke lubilo,
they spoke, saying: 'Let us run (with) swiftness,

tu-bone ati a-ka-shike[5] ku menzhi.'
(so that) we may see that he may arrive at water.'

Pele, Fulwe ngu a-ka-zhala[6] bana
But Tortoise (it is he) who produced children

banjibanji: u-la-ya-bu-zhika[7] mwiyu;[8] umwi
very many: he goes burying (them) in ground; one

mwana wa-mu-zhika, ku-mbadi ku[9] menzhi.
child he him buried, by side of water.

Inzho banyama baamb', ati: 'A-tu-tiane,[10]
So the animals they spoke, saying: 'Let us race,

tu-ka-shike ku mu-longa, tu-ka-nwe menzhi.'
when we arrive at the river, let us drink water.'

Ba-fuma, ba-lukanka, bonse baamb', ati:
They started, they ran, all they spoke, saying:

'Tu-bone[11] ati nguni[12] u-ka-tanguna[13] ku-shika.'
'Let us see that who is it he will be-first to arrive.'

Pele ba-lukanka odimwi,[14] ba-fulwe ba-la-ya-
But they ran again, tortoises go along

bu-amb'[15] ati: 'Imbelembele, o-ba-shana-
saying: 'Forward, those who are with

---

* Ila is spoken in North-Western Rhodesia, by the people commonly called the Mashukulumbwe, whose proper name is Ba-ila. They live on both banks of the Kafue, one of the northern tributaries of the Zambezi. They are closely allied (at any rate as far as speech goes) with the Batonga and Basubiya. The above story is extracted from the Rev. E. W. Smith's *Handbook of the Ila Language* (see Bibliography).

APPENDIX I.

sulwe.'[16]   Odimwi balukanka, odimwi baamb' ati:
Mr. Hare.'   Again   they ran,   again   they said:

'Imbelembele, obashanasulwe!'   Dimwi   izuba[17]
'Forward,   Hare & Co.!'   Another   sun

dia-ibila,   ba-la-ya-bu-ompolola: 'Dimwi[18]
it set,   they go along shouting: 'Another (day)

kwa-shia.[19]   Imbelembele,   obashanasulwe!
it has grown dark.   Forward,   Hare & Co.!'

Dimwi banyama bamana kufwa,[20] mwana[21] fulwe
Next day the animals finished to die, child (of) tortoise

o-wa-ku-di[22]   kumbadi   ku menzhi,   wo-ompolola[23]
he who was   beside   the water,   he shouted

ati: 'Imbelembele, obashanasulwe!'   Wezo
saying: 'Forward,   Hare & Co.!'   That

Sulwe wa-ya ku-fwa,[24] wa-bula[25] o-ku-shika ku
Hare was going to die, he was-without arriving at

menzhi.   Mwana fulwe   owakudi   kumbadi
water.   Child (of) tortoise   who was   beside

ku menzhi   wa-ba-letelela[26]   menzhi mu-kanwa:
water   he brought-for them   water in mouth:

ke-ziza[27]   ku-lapwila[28] banyama.   Ati:
let him come   to spit-out-for animals.   He said

'Ndimwe mwa-ku-zumanana, ati, "Fulwe
'It is you you were quarrelling, saying, "Tortoise,

tu-la-mu-shia[29]   lubilo."   Inzho
we shall him leave (behind) (in) swiftness."   So

mwa-ba-nji[30] ku-shika?   Mu-di ba-nichi.[31]
you have become what to arrive?   You are children.

Ndimi   mukando, nda-shika ku menzhi.
It is I (who am) a big man, I have arrived at water.

Mudi banichi.'   Ngonao[32]   wa-ba-lapwila
You are children.'   Immediately   he spit-out-for them

menzhi   a-ku-di   mu-kanwa.   Ba-bula
water   it was   in (his) mouth.   They were without

o-ku-mu-ngula: ba-usa   budio.[83]   Inzho
answering him: they were-sad only.   So

banyama   baamb' ati: 'Tu-ka-fumbe[84]   mu-kalo,
animals   they said: 'Let us dig   water-hole,

tu-ka-ku-nwa[85]   u[86]-mukalo   menzhi.'   Inzho
that we may drink in water-hole water.'   So

ba-fumba.   Basulwe   ba-kaka   kufumba,   inzho
they dug.   Hares   they refused to dig,   so

baamb' ati: 'Bu[87] mwa-kaka   kufumba,   inzho
they said: 'Since you refused to dig,   so

ta-mu-ti-mu-nwe[88]   menzhi.   Mu-la-mana
you shall not drink   water.   You shall finish

  ku-fwa   nyotwa.'   Kwa-shia,
  to die   (of) thirst.'   It grew dark,

    bakaka   kufumba,   ba-ya   ku mukalo,
they (who) refused to dig, they went to hole,

ba-kwiba.[89]   Inzho banyama bamwi baamb' ati:
they stole.   So   animals other they said:

  'A-tu-ba-zube[40]   basulwe,   tu-ba-
  'Let us hide (from) them the hares, (that) we may see

bone.'   Inzho   ba-ba-bona,   ba-ba-kwata,
them.'   So   they saw them,   they caught them,

  ba-ba-anga.   Pele   baamb' ati: 'Bu mwa-
they bound them. But   they said: 'Since you

  tu-anga,   inzho   twa-beba.   A-mu-
(have) tied us, so   we (have) repented. Let you

  tu-tole[41]   a-bwina,   mu-ka-tu-yayile[42]   ngona.'[43]
carry us   to burrow, (that) you may kill us   just there.'

NOTES

¹ *Nyama*, in most Bantu languages, is a noun of the ninth class (though, in Swahili, when meaning 'an animal,' it usually takes the concords of the first). In Ila it has the prefix *mu-* (pl. *ba-nyama* 2) and is thus included in the person-class. Other names of animals are treated in the same way, *e.g.*, *munyati* 'buffalo' (Z. *innyati* 9; Ny. *njati*) *mu sefu* 'eland,' *muzovu* 'elephant.' Some names of animals (also included in Class 1) are compounded with the prefixes *sha=*'father of' and *na=*'mother of' (Smith, p. 18). This seems to be distinct from the use of *sha-* or *shana-* as an honorific prefix, *e.g.*, *shana-sulwe*, for *sulwe* 1 'hare.' (*Sulwe*, ordinarily, has no prefix in the singular, but, being included in Cl. 1 on account of its meaning, its plural is *ba-sulwe* 2.) This is very common in African tales—*e.g.*, in Ganda 'elephant' is *enjovu* 9, but when he figures in a story he is called *Wanjovu*, and in Yao stories the names of animals have the title *Che* prefixed to them. (Cf. 'Brer Rabbit,' 'Miss Cow,' etc.)

² Future Subjunctive (Smith, p. 161). This seems, incongruously, to be used as a principal verb, but in reality it is equivalent to an adverbial clause, with 'when' understood. 'The relation of time is often expressed not by an adverb, but by moods and tenses of the verb. . . . [*e.g.*] the preterite indicative and the subjunctive.' (Smith, p. 240).

³ *Nyota* means 'thirst' in some dialects of Swahili, also in Nyamwezi, Karanga, etc. Cf. also Ganda *enyonta*, Yao *njota*, Herero *onyota*, Sutu *lenyora*.

⁴ *Ati*, properly 3rd pers. sing. of *ti* 'say,' is used regardless of number or person, in a way which comes to be equivalent to the conjunctive 'that.' For other idiomatic uses of *ti*, see Smith, p. 185.

⁵ Lit. 'that he may arrive (first) at the water,'—*i.e.*, 'who will arrive first.'

⁶ Past (Preterite) of *zhala* 'bear,' 'beget': Zulu, *zala*, Swahili *vyaa (zaa)*.

⁷ Properly the 'Immediate Future Habitual' tense (Smith, p. 156): the narrator goes back to the actual time of the incidents and treats them as if they were happening before his eyes.

⁸ Locative,=*mu ivu* 'in the ground.' Mr. Smith spells

mwivhu, but the sound—see p. 7 of his Grammar—is clearly that of 'bilabial v.'

⁹ We should have expected *kumbadi kwa menzhi*, *mbadi* 9 being placed in Cl. 17 by prefixing the locative *ku*, but see Smith, p. 223. *Mbadi* is not given in the vocabulary as a noun, but cf. Nyanja *mbali* 9 'edge, side, rim;' no doubt the same word used in Swahili as an adverb 'far,' etc.

¹⁰ *tia* 'be afraid' (cf. Swahili *tisha* 'frighten'—probably a causative of the verb usually written *cha* 'fear'), and so 'run away': *tiana* reciprocal, but apparently with the meaning 'run against' (or, 'in competition with') and not 'run away from' each other.

¹¹ Present Subjunctive, used in place of Imperative.

¹² *Nguni*, interrogative (Smith, p. 101), lit.: 'it is who?' A relative is understood after it, or rather, it is an example of a construction very common in the Bantu languages, even where relative pronouns exist: the demonstrative, or even the ordinary personal pronoun are often preferred, as though it were less trouble to make a fresh assertion than to link up the clause with the preceding one.

¹³ Second Future (Smith, p. 157)—probably distinguished from the Preterite by *tone*.—*tanguna*, evidently a derived form of *tanga* 'begin,' but the force of the termination is not very clear: it can scarcely be reversive (Smith, p. 130).

¹⁴ *Dimwi* 'another' (agreeing with *izuba* 5 'day,' or some similar noun, understood), and preceded by the instrumental preposition *o* (Smith, p. 224), so meaning 'again.'

¹⁵ Same tense as in line 4—see above, note 7.

¹⁶ *Obashanasulwe*, a kind of collective pl., including the person named and those with him—see above, p. 48, and Smith, p. 18. This, or a similar idiom seems to be universal in Bantu—*e.g.* Sumbwa: *nge Bandega*, 'ce sont des hommes de Ndega' (P. Capus); Swahili: *kina Hamisi*, etc. *Oba-* is the plural relative prefix (Smith, p. 108).

¹⁷ *Izuba* 5 'sun'—here used for 'day.' The same form of the word is found in Tonga (Zambezi), and cf. Nyoro *izoba*, Konde *ilisuba*, Ganda *enjuba*, etc. Other forms are *lyuwa*, *dzuwa*, *riua*, *jua*, *iruwa*, *eyuva*, *loba*, etc. The pronoun for Class 5 is in Ila *di*. *Dia* is the form with past tenses.

¹⁸ *Dimwi* agreeing with *izuba* understood.

¹⁹ *Kwa* 17 (*ku-* with the past tense) is the 'indefinite subject,' equivalent to 'it' or 'there' ('there was darkness').

APPENDIX I.

²⁰ Idiomatic use of *mana* 'finish' (see Smith, p. 187), meaning 'they all died together.' The sequel shows that 'died' is not to be taken literally.

²¹ *Wa* omitted after *mwana*.

²² Past tense of verb 'to be' (*di*, Smith, p. 200), preceded by relative particle *o*.

²³ *wo* for *wa* : *a* becoming *o* before the verb *ompolola* (see Smith, pp. 12-13). The tense is the 'aorist' (Smith, p. 150).

²⁴ Aorist of *ya* 'go,' followed by infinitive *ku-fwa*. *Wezo* is the demonstrative pronoun of the first class meaning 'that' (already referred to).

²⁵ *bula* 'lack,' 'be without,' sometimes followed by a noun, as *ndabula shidyo* 'I have no food,' sometimes, as here, by the infinitive preceded by a relative particle. 'He was without arriving'='he failed to arrive.'

²⁶ *letelela*, 'Double Relative' (Applied) form of *leta* : *let-ela* 'bring to,' *let-el-ela* 'bring to' a person 'for' his use.

²⁷ 3rd pers. sing. Imperative of the irregular verb *kweza* (=*ku eza* or *ku iza*) 'come'—see Smith, pp. 182, 183.

²⁸ *lapwila*, Applied ('Relative') form of *lapula* 'spit'—see Smith, p. 120. We should have expected *ku-ba-lapwila*.

²⁹ Immediate Future Tense (Smith 155).

³⁰ *ba* is the verb 'to be,' also used in the sense of 'become' (Smith, p. 184). Translate 'What has become of you that you did not arrive?'

³¹ Pl. of *mwanichi* (or *mwaniche*) 'youngster.' The ordinary word for 'child' is *mwana*.

³² =*ngon'awo* : 'substantive locative pronoun'=('the place) just there' combined with the demonstrative *awo* 16 (Smith, p. 216). Here used as an adverb of time, 'just then,' or 'immediately.'

³³ *budio* 'merely.' Smith suggests that it may be a noun of Class 14 meaning 'nothingness.' But the fourteenth prefix is '*the basis of a number of adverbs of manner*' (Smith, p. 217) and possibly -*dio* might be explained as a pronominal stem agreeing with some 5th class noun understood.

³⁴ Future Subjunctive used as Imperative.

³⁵ Another form of the Future Subjunctive—(see Smith, p. 162).

³⁶ *u* is the form assumed by the locatives *mu* and *ku* before

nouns which already begin with those prefixes—*e.g.*, *u-kuboko*, for *ku-kuboko* or (as here) *u-mukalo* for *mu-mukalo*.

⁸⁷ *Bu*, used as a conjunction and meaning 'since,' is probably a pronoun, perhaps agreeing with *busena* 14 'place,' understood.

³⁸ Negative Future (Smith, p. 171).

⁸⁹ *Kwiba=kuiba* 'steal.' Cf. Zulu (*e*)*ba*, Nyanja *ba*, Swahili *iba* (in the northern dialect *jepa*, which may preserve a trace of the lost initial consonant).

⁴⁰ 1st pers. pl. Imperative (Second Form: Smith, p. 163). *Zuba* 'hide' (intr.) as it takes a direct object of the person, must mean 'hide from;' but we should have expected the Applied Form.

⁴¹ Second Augmented Form of the Present Subjunctive, with the particle *a* prefixed (Smith, p. 163).

⁴² Future Subjunctive of *yayila*, which is the applied form of *yaya* 'kill.' The force of the Applied Form is not obvious here, as *tuyayile* would ordinarily mean 'kill . . . . for us,' and no second object is expressed—or, indeed, required by the sense.

⁴³ Locative demonstrative emphasised: 'just on that place).' (Smith, p. 91.)

Connected Translation

[This story is not very clear as it stands, but it seems to be a confusion of two different tales, both of which are widely distributed in Africa: that of the race between the Tortoise and the Hare, in which the former wins by planting out his family along the track (cf. *Uncle Remus*, 'Mr. Rabbit finds his match at last'), and one where all the animals join together to dig a well: the Hare refuses, and is not allowed to draw water, but does so by a trick, which is finally detected and frustrated by the Tortoise. This latter story is found in Jacottet's *Contes Populaires des Bassoutos* (*Le Chacal et la Source*), in Theal's *Kaffir Folk-Lore*, in the Swahili collection entitled *Kibaraka* (*Sungura na*

Mgomba and *Hadithi ya Vinyama*), in Mrs. Dewar's *Chinamwanga Stories* ('The Rabbit and all the other Animals') and elsewhere. All details of the trick by which the water was stolen and that by which the thief was captured are here omitted.]

Once upon a time, when all the animals were dying with thirst, they said to each other: 'Let us run swiftly and see who reaches the water first.' But the Tortoise, who had borne very many children, went on burying them in the ground (along the course), and one child she buried beside the water. So the animals said, 'Let us race each other, and when we reach the river, we shall drink the water.' They started, they all ran, they said, 'Let us see who will be the first to arrive.' They ran again, and the Tortoises went on saying, 'Forward! forward! Mr. Hare and his friends!' Again they ran, again they said, 'Forward! Mr. Hare and his friends!' The sun set once more, and they went on shouting, 'Once more it has become dark. Forward! Mr. Hare and his friends!' Next day the animals all died together,* and the young tortoise who was beside the water shouted, saying, 'Forward!' as before. The Hare was just about to die, without reaching the water. The young Tortoise who was beside the water brought them some water in his mouth, in order to spit it out for the animals. He said: 'It is you who were spiteful, saying, "As for the Tortoise, we have outrun him." Now what has become of you that you did not arrive? You are only children! I am a grown man—I have reached the water—but you are children!' Thereupon he spat out the water which was in his mouth. They could not answer him; they remained sad and silent. Afterwards the animals said: 'Let us dig a water-hole, and then we shall be able to drink.' So they dug. But the hares refused to dig, and so the others said: 'Since you have refused to dig, you shall not drink any water.

---

* Probably this is to be understood in the sense of being 'kilt entirely.'

You shall all of you die of thirst.' When it was dark, those who had refused to dig went to the water-hole and stole water. So the other animals said, 'Let us lie in wait for the hares, so that we may see them.' So they saw them and caught them and bound them. But they (the hares) said, 'Since you have tied us, now we repent. Carry us to our burrow, that you may kill us just there.'*

4. NYANJA

The Story of the Cock and the Swallow†

Tambala ndi namzeze		**a-na-palana**
Cock and swallow		they made-with-each-other
chi-bwenzi,[1] **ndipo namzeze**	**a-na-ti,**[2]	**'Koma**[3]
friendship, and swallow	he said,	'But
u-dze[4] **kwatu.**[5]	**Ndipo**	**tambala**
you (must) come to our (house).	And	Cock
a-na-muka, a-na-ka-peza[6] **namzeze, a-li pa nsanja.**[7]		
he went, he found swallow, he is on *nsanja*.		
Ndipo mkazi wa namzeze, a-na-pula[8]		**ma-ungu,**
And wife of swallow, she took-off		pumpkins,
ndipo namzeze a-na-lengalenga,[9]		**a-na-tenga**
and swallow he-flew-up-aloft,		he took

---

* This seems inconclusive, but no doubt the sequel is omitted as too obvious: *viz.*, that the too credulous animals did as they were asked. Brer Rabbit more subtly entreated Brer Fox *not* to 'fling me in dat briar-patch.'

† MS. collected at Blantyre, from a boy whose home was in the neighbourhood of the Murchison Falls, on the Shire River. Mr. R. S. Rattray has published a longer version of the same story (from Central Angoniland) in *Some Folk-Lore, Stories and Songs*.

APPENDIX I. 273

maungu, na-patsa[10] tambala, ndipo tambala a-na-ti,
pumpkins, and-gave (to) cock, and cock said,
 '**Udze kwatu.**'[5]   Ndipo tambala a-na-nka
'You (must) come to us.' And cock went
kwao,[6] na-uza mkazache[11] kuti,[12] 'u-ndi-ika[13] ine
home, and told his-wife saying, 'you-me-put me
mu mpika[14] wa mponda,[15] 'ndipo a-na-m-pika
into pot of gourds,' and she-him-cooked
pa moto. Ndipo namzeze a-na-dza, na-peza
on fire. And swallow he came, and found
tambala a-li mu mpika,[16] ndipo namzeze a-na-ti,
cock he is in pot, and swallow he said,
'**Pulani**[17] **mponda, ndi-funa ku-nka kwatu.**' Ndipo
'Take-off gourds, I want to go home.' And
mkazi wa tambala a-na-pula mponda, ndipo
wife of cock she took-off gourds, and
a-na-peza tambala, a-ta-fa,[18] namzeze
she found cock, he-was-already-dead, swallow
a-na-bwerera[19] kwao wo-sa-dya[20] mponda.
he-returned home not-having-eaten gourds.

NOTES

[1] *Chi-bwenzi* 7, from *bwenzi* 5 'friend' (see p. 55). *Ndipo*, properly the copula joined with the pronoun of the 16th locative) class, is very commonly used in Nyanja for 'and,' 'and so,' 'and then.' In Swahili it is more often found in its original sense of 'that is where,' 'that is how,' etc.

[2] Nyanja has the verb *ti* 'say' conjugated in all, or most, of its tenses, while keeping its original force, unlike Zulu, where it is apt to pass into adverbial, etc., senses. This is the past tense in -*na*-. See Hetherwick, *Manual*, p. 50.

[3] *Koma* 'but,' often begins a sentence in this way, where there seems to be no adversative meaning; but perhaps a kind of polite deprecation is implied.

S

⁴ *u-dze*, subjunctive (used for imperative) of *dza* 'come.'

⁵ *Kwatu* possessive pronoun of Class 15, 1st person plural. *Chez nous* is a closer parallel than any we have in English. But it should be noticed that it is always *kwatu*, never *kwanga*, even when the speaker is referring to himself only. It is the same in the second and third persons—cf. *kwao* (*chez lui*), lower down, where I have translated it simply by 'home.' Some nouns of relationship are always used with a plural possessive in the Bantu languages—cf. *udade wetu* 'my sister,' *umne wabo* 'his elder brother,' in Zulu.

⁶ For this tense see Hetherwick, *Manual*, pp. 150, 156. It here seems to indicate the interval between the act of starting from home (*muka*) and 'finding' the Swallow—as though we had to understand 'and, when he arrived, he found.' . . . *Peza*, as here used, involves a sort of bull; it is not meant that the Cock saw the Swallow sitting on the *nsanja* (see next note),—but that he did not see him: he found him not there, he being on the *nsanja*. It is very common for Africans to say, 'I saw him not there,' or the like—which, after all, is not very different from 'I found him already gone,' as we often say—illogically, perhaps, but not irrationally.

⁷ *Nsanja* is a kind of staging erected over the central fire-place in a hut, on which meat is placed to be smoke-dried, and seed-corn, beans, etc., to protect them from the attacks of mice and insects. It forms a little loft under the point of the conical roof.

⁸ *Pula* 'to take a cooking-pot off the fire,' is often used, by an extension of meaning for 'dishing-up food,' and in European households generally means 'bring in dinner.'— *Ma-ungu*, plural of *dz-ungu* 5.

⁹ He would, as a matter of fact, have come *down* from the *nsanja*, but having descended (probably at the back) under cover of the smoke, he would then fly up, as if emerging from the boiling pot.

¹⁰ 'And' in Nyanja, is *ni* or *ndi*, not, as in some other languages *na*. This *na-* is made up of *ni* and the pronoun *a*, and is often found in continuous narrative, prefixed to the second of two consecutive verbs. Cf. below, *na-uza, na-peza*, etc.

¹¹ *mkazache*. Nouns expressive of relationship are often combined with the possessive in this way: Nyanja: *amako* 'thy mother,' *amache* 'his mother' (but in some dialects *mai wake*); Swahili *mkeo* 'thy wife,' *mkewe* 'his wife,' etc. The

APPENDIX I. 275

rule does not apply uniformly, for Nyanja has *atate wako* 'thy father,' while Swahili has *babangu, babako, babake* (often further abbreviated into *bake*) as well as *mamangu*, etc. (See Hetherwick, p. 87).

[12] Literally 'to say'; equivalent to 'that,' but often used (as here) where 'that' would be superfluous in English.

[13] We should have expected *u-ndi-ike*, and possibly the MS. is wrong. *Ine* 'me' follows for emphasis : 'But, as for me, you must put me.' . . In Mr. Rattray's version, the corresponding sentence runs: '*Mawa* (to-morrow) *u-pike maungu, ndi-ka-itana* (and then I will call) *bwenzi langa, ndipo ine u-ndi-ike m' mpika momo.*' Here the position of *ine* is varied for still greater emphasis. *Momo* is a strengthened form of *mo* 'in it.'

[14] This is written without a hyphen, because the *mu* really has prepositional force. Had it still been felt as the locative prefix *(mu-mpika,* or *m'pika* 'the-inside-of-the-pot') it would have been followed by *mwa*, not *wa*, as the possessive particle.

[15] *Mponda* are a small kind of gourd, not unlike the species known to cultivation as 'custard-marrows,'—very delicate if properly cooked.

[16] Here, again, it is not meant that the Swallow saw his friend in the pot, otherwise what follows would lose all point. Of course the meaning is 'He did not find him, for he was in the pot.'

[17] In Nyanja and some other languages, such as Makua and Venda, the plural of the second person is used instead of the singular where special politeness is intended. But this idiom does not seem to be very general in Bantu.

[18] The verb *ta* 'finish' is used as an auxiliary, particle to indicate 'complete action.' See Hetherwick, p. 161.

[19] *Bwer-era*, applied form of *bwera* 'return,' appears to imply a return *from*, though only the place *to* which he returned is expressed in words.

[20] *Wo-sa-dya* for *waku-sa-dya*, literally 'of to-not-eat' is a kind of negative participle in very common use. In the Likoma dialect, where the ordinary negative serves to express the future (*si-ni-chite* 'I shall do') this participial form is almost the only one, and is used without reference to person or time : *wo-sa-chita*, pl. *o-sa-chita* 'not doing,' *wo-sa-lima* 'not cultivating,' etc., etc., see pp. 118, 169.

Connected Translation

The cock and the swallow made friendship with each other, and the swallow said, 'But you must come to my house.' And the cock went, and did not see the swallow, for he was sitting on the staging over the fireplace. And when the swallow's wife took the pumpkins off the fire, the swallow flew up (through the smoke, as if he had come out of the pot) and took of the pumpkins and gave them to the cock, who said 'you must come (in return) to my house.' And the cock went home and told his wife to put him into the pot of *mponda* gourds (which she was going to cook for the guest). So she cooked him over the fire, and when the swallow came, he did not see the cock, who was inside the pot. (After waiting for some time), the swallow said, 'Please dish up the gourds, for I want to go home.' She did so and found the cock already dead (in the pot). So the swallow went home, without having eaten any of the gourds.

5. SWAHILI

(a) *Lamu Dialect (Kiamu)*.

Stories about the People of Shela*

I. Pa-li-kuwa na[1] mtu wa Shela,[2] hu-amkuliwa[3]
   There was   a man   of Shela,   he was called
Bwana Mgumi,   a-ka-twaa[4]   kibarua[5]
   Mr. Mgumi,   and he took   a day-labourer
ku-m-tilia[6]   mai[7]   katika[8]   kasiki[9], na kasiki
to pour for him   water   into   a jar,   and jar

---

* Dictated by Muhamadi bin Abubakari (Kijuma)

hiyo[10] hu-ngia - mi-tungi[11] esherini. Ule[12]
that-one there go in jars twenty. That

kiba-rua a-ka-tia mai, hatta kasiki i-ka-yaa,[13]
labourer and he poured water, till the jar it was full,

a-ka-mwambia, 'Bwana, kasiki i-me-ziye
and he said to him, 'Master, the jar it has exceeded

ku-yaa.'[14] Ka-mwa-mbia, 'Shindilia[15] mai,
to be full. And he said to him, 'Press down the water,

twaa mti[16] huu, u-ka-shi-ndilie,'[17]
take pestle this, that you may press down.'

A-ka-m-pa mti, ule akapiga,
And he gave him the pestle, and that (man) struck,

kasiki i-ka-vundika[18] tini[19] (kasiki ile
the jar it was broken below (jar that

i-me-zikwa tiati[20] nusu), mai
it was buried (in) the ground half), the water

ya-ka-shuka; akamwambia, 'U-me-ona,
it went down; and he said to him, 'You have seen,

ongeza[21] tena basi[22] mai!' Hatta[23] mai
add again then water!' Until the water

yakashuka kwa tini,[24] ndipo a-lo-po-yua[25]
and it went down from below, that is where he knew

kasiki imevundika. Ndiye akatoa[26] habari
the jar it is broken. It is he (who) put forth the news

kibarua.
the labourer.

II. Mngwana[27] wa Shela mmoya, a-li-weka
    Gentleman of Shela one, he put away

baruti, i-ka-ngiwa[28] mai, akamwambia
gunpowder, and it was entered (by) water, and he told him,

mtumwake,[29] 'Twaa kikaango,[30] weke moto-ni,
his slave, 'Take frying-pan, put on fire,

na-taka ku-kaanga baruti yangu,
I want to roast (dry) powder my,

    i-me-ngiwa mai,   na-taka kukaanga mimi
it has been entered by water, I want to dry (it)   I

mwenyewe,[31]   wewe   hu-to-yua[32] kwa   uzuri.'[33]
myself,   you   will not know   properly.'

Mtwmwake   a-ka-twaa   kikaango,
His slave   and he took   the frying-pan,

     kaweka   motoni   kamwambia,   'Bwana,
and put (it) on the   fire   and said to him,   'Master,

tayari!'   Kenda[34]   bwana,   akatia
ready!'   And he went,   the master,   and he poured

   baruti   kikaangoni,   baruti
the powder   into the frying-pan,   the powder

i-ka-m-teketeza   uso[35] na ndevu   zake.[36]   Hini[87]
and it burnt him   the face and beard   his.   This

habari ya-tendeka Shela.
affair is done (at) Shela.

    III. Mwinda   kungu[88]   a-li-pata   kungu,
A hunter (of) bush-buck, he got (caught) a bush-buck,

    a-ka-m-funga   kisu   na ukumbuu[89]
and he tied (on) him   a knife   with (his) girdle

ka-m-wambia,   'Enda kwa Mwana[40]
and said to him,   'Go to the Mistress, (tell her)

a-ku-tinde,[41]   nso na ini   a-ni-wekee
she is to kill you,   kidneys and liver   let her put by for

mimi,   kiya,   nitwelee[42]   mkakambe.'[43]
me, when I come, that I may add (them to my) porridge.'

A-ka-mw-eta[44]   kenenda   ule,   kisa[45]
And he sent him   and went   that one,   afterwards

   a-ka-rudi,   mwinda   akenda   nyumbani
and he returned,   the hunter   and he went   to-house

kwake[46]; mke wake ka-mu-pa mkakambe mtupu,[47]
to his;   wife his   and gave him   porridge   bare,

     kamwambia,   'Nso   na   ini   li[48]   wapi?'
and he said to her, 'Kidneys and   liver   is   where?'

APPENDIX I.

Akamwambia,	'Hu-ku-eta,'
And she said to him,	'You did not send' (them),
kamwambia,	'Ni-me-m-tuma Bwa' Kungu,[49]
and he said to her,	'I have sent him, Mr. Bush-buck,

ni-me-m-funga ukumbuu na kisu';
I have tied (on) him a girdle and a knife';

kamwambia, 'Ha-ku-ya';
and she said to him, 'He has not come';

a-si-le[50] mkakambe, katoka
and he did not eat the porridge, and he went out

kenda ku-m-zengea,[51] a-si-mu-one. Basi,
and went to seek him, and did not find him. So,

hatta sasa watu wa Shela u-ki-w-amkua 'Bwa'
until now the people of Shela if you call them 'Mr.

Kungu, hu-teta.
Bush-buck,' they quarrel (with you).

NOTES

[1] *Pa* is the pronoun of Class 16 (locative), and it is quite easy to translate *pa-li-kuwa* 'there was,' but the *na* which follows seems superfluous. We must remember, however, that the pronoun represents some noun meaning 'place' (no doubt the obsolete *pantu*, which has been replaced by *pahali* or *mahali*) and that the construction is, literally, '*The place it was with*'—*i.e.*, 'it had'—cf. the French use of *avoir* in *il y avait*.

[2] Shela is a town within a half-hour's walk of Lamu, but the people consider themselves quite distinct, and the Lamu men affect to look down on them as stupid and ignorant, and tell numerous tales against them, of which the three given in the text are specimens. They resemble those of the exploits attributed to the men of Gotham, or the mutual taunts of 'Hampshire hogs' and 'Wiltshire moon-rakers.'

[3] *Amkua*, elsewhere meaning 'salute' is used at Lamu for 'call.' A Mombasa man would have said *huitwa* or *aliitwa*. The 'habitual tense' in *hu-* (see Steere, *Handbook of the*

APPENDIX I.

Swahili Language, p. 126), which has no distinction of number or person and may refer either to present or past, is more freely used in the Lamu dialect than in the more southerly ones.

[4] *Twaa* 'take,' here means 'hire,' 'engage.' It is the same word as the Zulu *twala*, which, however, means 'carry' (on the head)—a good illustration of how identical roots may diverge in meaning.

[5] *Kibarua*, literally 'little letter,' has come to mean, first, the 'ticket' given to people hired by the day and handed in when their wages are paid, and, then the person so hired.

[6] *Tilia*, applied form of *tia*, 'put,' 'pour'—Zulu *tela*.

[7] *Mai* (*mayi*), Kiamu for *maji*. See *yaa, yua, mmoya*, etc., later on.

[8] Originally *kati ka* 'the middle of' (perhaps a trace of the *ka-* class which has disappeared from Swahili). Used like a preposition in the sense of 'in,' 'on,' etc.

[9] *Kasiki*, a large earthen jar, three feet or more in height, sometimes seen at the door of a small village mosque, instead of the usual tank (*birika*), which holds the water for ablutions.

[10] *Hiyo*, demonstrative, Cl. 9; here='the aforesaid.'

[11] Plural of *m-tungi* 3 'water-jar'; the usual size holds about a gallon. *Esherini* (*ishrin, ishirini*) is Arabic, like the other words generally used for the higher numerals.

[12] *Ule*, Kiamu for *yule*, Distant Demonstrative of Class 1.

[13] *i-* pronoun, agreeing with *kasiki* 9; *-ka-*, sign of the Narrative tense (Steere, *Handbook*, p. 134). *Yaa=jaa* in Mombasa and Zanzibar Swahili: cf. Nyanja *dzala* and Zulu *zala* 'be full' (dist. from *zala* 'bring forth ').

[14] An idiom implying 'not only full but overflowing.' *Ziye*, for the more usual *zidi* (Arabic) 'be abundant,' 'exceed,' etc.— *Kamwambia;* the initial pronoun of the *ka-* tense is sometimes omitted.

[15] *Shindilia* (doubly applied form of *shinda* 'conquer,' of which the original meaning was, probably, 'beat down,')— used for pressing down grain into a basket or measure, to make it hold more.

[16] *Mti*, with dental *t* (Zanzibar *mchi*) seems to be a distinct word from *mti* 'tree,' which has the cerebral *t* and does not change in the Zanzibar dialect. The 'pestle' used for pounding grain is a pole of some heavy wood, about four or five feet long and of a thickness to be easily grasped in the

APPENDIX I.

hand. The pestle used in Nyasaland (*munchi, munsi*) is much thicker and is raised between the open hands which do not meet round it.

[17] For the subjunctive with -*ka*-, see Steere, *Handbook*, p. 141.

[18] Neuter-passive of *vunda* (Zanzibar, *vunja*). The implication is that 'it was in a state of being broken,'—' it was found to be broken '; if the man's agency had been emphasised, *i-ka-vundwa* would have been used.

[19] Zanzibar, *chini*: it is really the locative of *nti* (*nchi*) 'earth,' 'ground.' Cf. the Zulu adverb *pa-nsi*, which has survived the introduction of the locative in -*ni* and the loss of the noun -*nsi*.

[20] *Tiati* 'earth,' only found in Lamu and other northern dialects. I have been unable to arrive at its derivation.

[21] Causative of *ongea*, the intransitive verb meaning 'increase,' no doubt the applied form of *onga*, not in use.

[22] *Basi*, sometimes spelt *bassi* (but it is better to avoid double consonants in writing Bantu words), is the Hindustani *bass* ' enough ! '—constantly used in a variety of ways, *e.g.*, 'that's all ! '—' well ! '—' and so '—' so then '—etc. The position here is unusual.

[23] Arabic for ' until,' but often used for ' even,' or (in narrative) as a mere connective.

[24] See note 19. *Kwa* might be taken here as having something like an instrumental force, indicating the way by which the water disappeared.

[25] *a-lo-po-*, Kiamu form of the relative (*alipo*). *Yua* for *jua*—see note 7. *Ndipo* is the 16th pronoun combined with the copula, to form the kind of demonstrative (see Steere, *Handbook*, pp. 116-117), which means ' This is he, it, etc. '; in this instance ' this is that (place) where '—*i.e.*, ' the time when.'

[26] For the various meanings of *toa*, primarily ' put out,' ' take out,' see Madan's *Swahili-English Dictionary*, s.v.

[27] *Mngwana* ' a free man ' (not a slave) and therefore often used to denote an educated or civilised person,—or a man of good position. Also *mungwana*, and, on the southern Mrima, or among inland tribes *mulungwana*, though it seems doubtful whether a derivation from *Mulungu* could be made out. The word is not in Krapf. *Mmoya*, see note 7.

[28] *ngia*, sometimes heard as *ingia*, but in the north at any rate, the former seems to have better authority. The con-

struction illustrates the Bantu use of the passive in cases where it would be unexpected, or even impossible in a European language: cf. also *amefiwa ni mume* for 'her husband has died,' and *amekwenda kwitwa* ' he has gone to be called '—*i.e.*, ' some one has gone to call him.'

²⁹ For *mtumwa wake*. Such contractions are mostly confined to words denoting relationship, *e.g.*, *babake*, *mamake*, *mumeo*, *nduguze*, etc.

³⁰ *Kikaango* (from *kaanga*, 'roast,' 'fry') is used for a European frying-pan, but in native households denotes a shallow earthen pipkin, which serves a similar purpose.

³¹ When following a pronoun this word means 'myself,' 'yourself,' etc.: it is really a contraction of *mwenye wake* ' the owner of it ' (*i.e.*, it is to be supposed, of the identity expressed by the pronoun).

³² *Hu-to-* negative future prefix of the 2nd pers. sing., instead of *ha-u-ta-*. See Steere, *Handbook*, p. 149, where this form is only recognised as used with the Infinitive and is derived from *toa* ' take out.' Comparison with other Bantu languages suggests that it may have had a different origin.

³³ *Vizuri* is often used in the sense of 'rightly,' etc.; at Lamu, the abstract noun (*uzuri*) preceded by the instrumental *kwa*, is preferred.

³⁴ For *a-ka-enda*. The subject, by a not unusual exception, follows the predicate.

³⁵ The idiom here is more easily parallelled in French than in English: (*la poudre*) *lui brûla le visage*. See Steere, *Swahili Exercises*, p. 20: the possessive, in a similar sentence, is seldom, if ever, used in Swahili.

³⁶ *zake* agrees with the second noun only. *Ndevu* 10 is really the plural of *udevu* 11, which means ' one hair of the beard.'

³⁷ Kiamu form of the ninth pronoun (*hii*). *Tendeka*, perhaps because no agent is mentioned; otherwise one would have expected the passive. But perhaps the meaning is ' Such things are (only) *possible* to be done at Shela !'

³⁸ Usually the noun-agent formed by prefixing *m-* to the unaltered verb-root is followed (as here) by a noun as object —so that it might almost be called a participle. Occasionally, however, a noun of this kind is found standing alone, as *mgema* (not *mgemi*) ' palm-tapper.'

³⁹ ' A girdle made of a narrow cloth ' (Steere). The con-

APPENDIX I. 283

struction 'he bound his knife on him' is similar to that mentioned in note 35.

⁴⁰ *Mwana*, used for 'mistress,' 'lady,' and, with a woman's name, as the equivalent for 'Mrs.' or 'Miss'—*e.g.*, *Mwana Somoye*, *Mwana Esha*, etc. This is sometimes called the feminine of *Bwana* and is practically employed so to a certain extent, though *bibi* is more usual at Mombasa and *nana* (originally 'grandmother' at Lamu). Krapf enters this *mwana* as a different word from *mwana* 'child' (which, in Swahili, seems to be confined to the meaning 'son'). It is possible that they may be either (1) different words which by phonetic change have become identical in form, or (2) the same word which has become differentiated in meaning. But Burton's suggested derivation from the Arabic *ummanâ* 'our mother' (see Taylor, *African Aphorisms*, p. 31), seems very doubtful.

⁴¹ *Tinda*, Zanzibar *chinja* 'slaughter'—especially in the correct Moslem fashion. Probably it was the time required for this ceremony that made the hunter unwilling to stop.

⁴² *Twelea* (spelt by Krapf *toelea*) is to add the fish, chicken, or other *kitoweo* to the rice or porridge.

⁴³ Old word for 'porridge' (*sima* or *ugali*).

⁴⁴ *eta*, Kiamu for *leta*, which means 'bring' or 'send' (a *thing*) according to circumstances (*tuma* is used of sending a person), *kenenda* for *a-ka-enenda*: *enda* and *enenda* are synonymous. *Ule*, of course, is the *kungu*.

⁴⁵ Mombasa *kisha*, for *a-ki-isha*; 'when he had finished,' but now practically an adverb. Good Swahili speakers at Lamu prefer it to the Arabic *khalafu* (*halafu*).

⁴⁶ Locative concord: in Nyanja it would be *ku nyumba kwache*; the *ku*, implying motion towards, has been replaced by the locative *-ni* in Swahili.

⁴⁷ *-tupu* 'bare,' 'naked' is often used thus ('porridge and nothing more,'—whereas it is always eaten with some 'relish' —*kitoweo* or *mtuzi*). Cf. the line from a popular song:
'*Wanipa maji matupu kunisonga moyo.*'
'You have given me mere water (the barest minimum of hospitality), to twist my heart.'

⁴⁸ Pronoun agreeing with *ini* 5, the last subject. (*Nso* 10, cf. Zulu *izi-nso*.)

⁴⁹ A common shortening of *Bwana* in the Siu and neighbouring dialects.

⁵⁰ Subjunctive, because the action follows and is in a sense dependent on what goes before: he did not eat because he had been told that the buck had not come. Similarly, in next line *asimuone* 'without finding him' ('so that he did not find him'). *Ha-ku-ya* (Kiamu for *ha-ku-ja*): Negative Past which can be used either for 'did not' or 'has not.'

⁵¹ *Zeigea*, used at Lamu instead of *tafuta* 'seek.'

Connected Translation

I. There was a man of Shela who was named Bwana Mgumi, and he engaged a day-labourer to fill a large jar, holding about twenty gallons, with water. The man poured in water till the jar was full and then said, 'Master the jar is full and running over.' The master answered, 'Take this pestle and press it down'—giving him a pestle, with which he pounded the bottom of the jar (which was buried in the ground for half its height), till it cracked, and the water began to go down. So the master said, 'Do you see?—now pour in some more water!' And he did so, and it was only when the water kept running away at the bottom that he knew the jar was broken. It was through the labourer that this story got about.

II. A certain gentleman of Shela had put away some gunpowder, and (after a time, found that) the damp had got into it, so he said to his slave, 'Take a frying-pan and put it on the fire; I want to dry my powder, which has got damp; but I want to do it myself, as you will not know how to do it properly.' So the slave took the frying-pan and put it on the fire and said, 'Master, it is ready.' Then the master went and poured the powder into the pan and it (blazed up and) scorched his face and his beard. This is the sort of thing that happens at Shela.

III. A hunter caught a bush-buck and tied his knife round it with his girdle and said to it: 'Go to my wife and ask her to kill you and put by the liver and kidneys,

so that I can eat them with my porridge in the evening.'
So he let him go, and the buck disappeared. In the evening, when the hunter returned home, his wife gave him nothing but porridge for supper, so he said to her, 'Where are those kidneys and that liver.' She said to him, 'You did not bring any'; and he said, 'I sent Mr. Buck and tied a knife round him with my sash'*— but his wife said, 'He has not come.' He would not eat his porridge, but went out to look for the bush-buck and could not find him. And so, to this day, the Shela people get angry with you if you address them as *'Bwa' Kungu.'*

(b) *Kimvita (Mombasa Dialect)*

Story of the Man who did not know when he was well off.†

Alikuwako mtu mmoja maskini sana, akaketi
There was man one poor very, and he sat

siku hiyo,[1] **akasema, 'Ni-ta-kwenda kwa**
day that, and he said, 'I will go to

Mwenyiezi Muungu, ni-ka-ombe ni-pawe[2]
Almighty God, that I may pray I may be given

riziki[3] **yangu, kwani n-na**[4] **dhiki sana.'**
living my, for I have trouble greatly.'

A-ka-ondoka a-k-enda zakwe[5]**, akafika**
And he rose up and he went his (ways), and he arrived

mbali sana, akaona ziwa li-na[6] **maji mangi.**
far very, and he saw a lake it has water much.

Akaoga, kisha akenda zakwe.
And he bathed, afterwards he went his (way).

---

* As a rule, in telling this story, the narrator repeats the speech in full. In dictation, it was given more concisely.

† Dictated by Muhammad bin Maᶜalim 'l Betawi, at Mombasa.

Akenda,   akamwona⁷   simba,   ha-oni,
And he went, and he saw him a lion, he does not see,

a-na-konda⁸   na ndaa,   akamwambia,
and he was thin with hunger, and he said to him,

'Mwana Adamu, wenda wapi?'   Akamwambia,
'Child (of) Adam, you go where?' And he said-to him,

'Nenda kwa Mwenyiezi Muungu,⁹   nenda   omba¹⁰
'I go to Almighty God,   I go pray

nipawe   nami   riziki.'
I may be given I too   a living.'

Akamwambia,   'Ukenda¹¹   ni-ombea
And he (the lion) said to him, 'When you go pray for me

na mimi,   ni-funuke   mato yangu,
also me,   I may be opened (as to) eyes my,

ni-pate na chakula ni-le.'   Akamwambia,
I may get also food (that) I may eat.' And he said-to him,

'Vyema.'   Akenda   zakwe.   Akamwona
'Good.' And he went his (way). And there saw him

nyoka,   a-ka-mw-uliza,   'Wenda wapi?'
a snake,   and he asked him,   'You go where?'

Akamwambia   'Nenda kwa Muungu,   nenda
And he said to-him 'I go to God, I go (to)

omba   riziki   yangu.'   Akamwambia,
pray (for) living my.'   And he said-to him,

'Ukenda,   niombea   na mimi;   jua
'Where you go, pray-for me also me; the sun

li-na-zidi,¹²   sipati   chakula; basi, nataka
has exceeded, I do not get food; well, I wish

mvua   i-nye   tu-pate   chakula.'
rain may fall, (so that) we may get food.'

Akenda   zakwe.   A-ka-tokea¹³   mji
And he went his (way). And he appeared (at) town

mkubwa,   akamwona   surutani   mwanamke,
large,   and he saw the sultan, a woman,

APPENDIX I.

akamwambia, 'Wenda wapi?' Akamwambia
and she said to him, 'You go where?' And he said to her
'Nenda kwa Muungu, nenda omba riziki yangu.'
'I go to God, I go (to) pray (for) living my.'
Akamwambia 'Ukenda niombea na mimi,
And he said-to him 'When you go pray-for me also me,'
mimi surutani, mwanamke, raia zangu
I (am) a sultan, a woman, subjects me
ha-wa-ni-sikizi, na mji ha-w-ishi[14] vita. Basi,
do not obey me, and town does not finish war. Well,
nataka ya-ondoke haya.'[15] Akenda
I wish they may go-away, these (matters).' And he went
zakwe.
his way.

Akafika, akamwambia Mwenyiezi
And he arrived, and he said-to Almighty
Muungu, 'Mimi, n-na-ku-ja, na-ona dhiki sana
God, 'As for me, I have come, I see trouble much
kwa umaskini, nnakuja omba
through poverty, I have come (to) pray
u-ni-wasii[16] kwa riziki.' Akamwambia,
you (to) me assign for (my) living.' And he said to him,
'Riziki[17] zako sasa nyingi sana,
'(means of) living thy now many very,
zamwayika.' Akamwambia, 'Ni-li-po-ku-ja
they are being wasted.' He said to him, 'When I came
huku, na-li-mw-ona mwanamke, a-me-ni-ambia,
hither, I saw a woman, she said to me,
"na mimi, niombea kwa Mwenyiezimgu, mimi
"and me (too), pray for me to Almighty God, I
ni mfalme, raia zangu hawanisikizi, na
am a queen, subjects my do not obey me, and
mji wetu hawishi vita."' Akamwambia,
town our does not end war."' And he said to him,

'Mwambie, "wewe ni mwanamke, pata mume
'Tell her, "you are a woman, get a husband
a-ku-oe,[18] ya-ta-ondoka,
that he may marry you, they will go-away,
yote hayo."' Akamwambia: 'Kisha
all these (things)."' And he said to him: 'Afterwards
n-na-ona nyoka, ameniambia, jua ni lingi,
I saw a snake, he has told me, the sun is much,
hawapati chakula, ataka mvua.'
they do not get food, he wants rain.'
Akamwambia, 'Na-tue[19] johari
And he said-to him, 'Let him put down the jewel
iliyo kitwani, i-ta-shuka mvua nyingi
which is in (his) head, it will come-down rain much
sana.' Akamwambia, 'Kisha na-li-ona simba
very.' And he said-to him, 'Then I saw a lion
ha-oni, akanambia, "niombea kwa
he does not see, and he said-to me, "Pray for me to
Mwenyiezimgu nipate mato yangu,
Almighty God that I may get eyes, my,
kisha nipate chakula."'
(and) then (that) I may get food."'
Akamwambia, 'Mwambie apake mate
He said to him, 'Tell him he is to smear spittle
yakwe matoni, yatafunuka mato, na
his on his eyes, they will be opened, the eyes, and

a-taka-cho-ona[20] mbele na-le, ndio
that which he sees before (him) let him eat, that-is
riziki yakwe.' Akamwambia, 'Hewallah!'
living his.' And he said-to him, '*Hewallah!*'[21]

akenda zakwe. Akamwambia yule surutani
and he went his (way). And he said-to her that queen

kama a-li-vyo-ambiwa.[22] Mwanamke
like (that) which he had been told. The woman

APPENDIX I.

akamwambia, 'N-oa[28] wewe, utapata mali
said-to him, 'Marry me you, you shall get property

mangi; kisha[24] u-ta-ku-wa mfalme wewe.'
much; (and) then you shall be king you.'

Yule akasema, 'Sitaki mali wala
That-one and he said, 'I do not want property nor

sitaki ufalme, mali mimi nayo mangi
I do not want kingdom, property I with it much

sana, na-pawa, ni Muungu.'[25]
very, I am being given (it), it-is God.'

Akenda zakwe. Akamwona nyoka,
And he went his (way). And he saw him the snake,

akamwambia kana[26] alivyoambiwa.
and he said to him like (that) which he had been told.

Nyoka akamwambia, 'Twaa wewe hii
The snake said to him, 'Take yourself this

johari.' Yule maskini akasema, 'Si-i-taki,
jewel.' That poor man he said, 'I do not want it,

mimi, mimi mali yangu ni mangi
for my part, I property my is much

sana, ni-li-o-pawa, sitaki tena.'
very, which I was given (it), I do not want again.'

Akenda zakwe. Akamwona simba,
And he went his (ways). And he saw him the lion,

akamwambia, 'Mwenyiezimgu akwambia,
and said to him, 'God Almighty says to you,

"Paka mate yako, mato yako ya-ta-funuka.
"Smear spittle your, eyes your will be opened.

Chakula chako u-taka-cho-ona mbele."'
Food your (is) that which you will see in front (of you)."'

Akapaka mato yakwe, yakafunuka.
And he smeared eyes his, and they were opened.

Aka-mwona yeye anasimama,[27]
And he saw him him (where) he stood,

T

akapeleka	mkono[28]	akamshika,	akasema,
and he stretched out	paw	and seized him,	and said,

'Nitapata	wapi	chakula	chengine, mimi?'	Yule
'I shall get	where	food	other, I?'	That

mwana Adamu	aka-sema,	'Mimi	na-ku-ombea,
son (of) Adam,	he said,	'As for me,	I pray for you,

yanafunuka	mato yako,	sasa	wataka
they have been opened	eyes your,	now	you want

nila?'	Akamwambia,	'Sijui,
eat me?'	And he said to him,	I do not know (but),

mimi,	nitakula,	nitimize	maneno
as for me,	I will eat you,	that I may fulfil	words

yako.'	Akamla.	Hadithi	inafika
your.'	And he ate him.	The story	it has arrived

hapa.[29]
here.

NOTES

[1] *Hiyo* is the demonstrative implying 'that previously referred to'— here meaning the day to which the story relates.

[2] *Pawa*, Kimvita passive of *pa* (Lamu *powa*, Zanzibar *pewa*) *Omba* is used for 'pray' in the sense of making a definite request (also used for 'beg') -*ku-sali* means to repeat the ritual prayers.

[3] From the Arabic *raxaqa* 'provide,' (hence *er-Razzaq*, one of the names of God);—it is used for 'subsistence,' 'daily bread,' 'rations,' etc.

[4] For *nina*: the contraction of this pronoun is specially common at Mombasa. Cf. Stigand, pp. 29-30.

[5] -*akwe* for -*ake*, the Kimvita form of the possessive 3rd pers. sing. Stigand unaccountably says (p. 29), 'this is not often heard.' The expression *enda zako* (*zake, etc.*) has *njia* (*ndia*) (pl.) understood after it, and corresponds exactly to the Scottish provincial 'go your *ways*.'

[6] *li* is the pronoun agreeing with *ziwa* 5 (Nyanja *dziwe* 5,

Ila *i-zhiba* 5). Zulu and Ganda have the same word with the prefix of Class 7: *isi-ziba, eki-diba*. *Mangi*, Kimvita—more southern dialects *mengi*.

⁷ The construction leaves it uncertain whether the lion saw the man or *vice versa;* the insertion of the objective pronoun would favour the former view, as this usually indicates that some definite person or thing is meant (performing to a certain extent the office of the definite article), while, on the other hand, it is obvious that, if the lion was blind he could not see any one. However, *ona* is often used for 'meet' or 'find,' as well as 'see,' and this rendering seems to suit the context best.

⁸ *A-na-ḳonda*, not, as in the Zanzibar dialect, a present, but a perfect, cf. *li-na-zidi* later on.

⁹ *Kwa* only used in this sense before nouns denoting persons, like the French *chez*. Really the possessive particle of the locative *ku-* class (17) with a noun understood; (*nyumbani=ku-nyumba*) *kwa*. The instrumental *kwa* (as in *kukata kwa kisu*), though the same in origin, is, in usage quite distinct. *Mwenyeezi*, compounded of *mwenye* 'owner' and *ezi*, (*enzi*, Arabic *'izz*), 'power,' 'authority,' is never used unless followed by *Muungu* (*Mungu, Mngu* or *Mgu* as below). The name *Allah* is not often used by Swahili Moslems, except when speaking Arabic; it seems to be confined to expressions like *Hewallah !*—which is now nothing more than a form of assent, and *Allah Allah !* originally an adjuration—'for God's sake,' —but generally used to mean 'be sure you don't forget,' 'be quick, whatever you do,' etc.

¹⁰ *Nenda omba*. The infinitive following a finite verb (especially after *enda, ja* and *isha*) often drops the *ku*, thus constituting a seeming exception to the rule that the verb-stem is never found without a prefix, except in the Imperative.

¹¹ Both *-ka-* and *-ki-* are frequently contracted before *enda*. Here the sense requires *-ki-*.

¹² This looks like the present in *-na-*, but that tense is not used at Mombasa, where the *-na-* tense has a perfect force —*i.e.,* it implies an action which has taken place in the past, but whose effects are still continuing. Cf. *anakonda* (note 8), which means 'he became thin and is (or was at the time when the events occurred) thin.' Cf. also *nnakuja*, lower down. The perfect in *-me-*, however, is also used at Mombasa.

¹³ *tokea*, applied form of *toka*, 'come out,' properly means to 'come out to or for some one'—*i.e.,* appear to him (it is therefore used of ghosts, etc.) and always implies a spectator or

spectators. Here the meaning is 'he came in sight of (the inhabitants of) a town.'

[14] *Hawishi* for *ha-u-ishi*: *u* agreeing with the subject *mji* 3. *Isha*, is here used actively.

[15] *Haya* demonstrative 6 agreeing with *mambo* understood.

[16] More usually *wasia* (from the Arabic *wasi*)—properly, 'make a will,' 'give testamentary directions,' and thence 'appoint,' 'assign.' Some word like *vitu* or *mali* is understood after it.

[17] *riziki* is here treated as a plural. *Mwaya* (also *mwaga* 'spill,' 'empty.' The neuter-passive, *mwayika*, is best rendered by 'are going to waste,' or 'are lying unused.'

[18] *oa* 'marry' (only used of the man, *olewa* is the word applied to the woman and *oza*, 'give in marriage' is said of the parents or guardian), is the same word as the Zulu *lobola*, and illustrates the degree of attrition stems may undergo in Swahili through the loss of medial consonants.

[19] *tua* 'set down,' as a load off the head, also (Madan)'settle down,' 'rest,' etc.; hence the applied form *tulia* 'be calm,' 'be quiet.' Cf. Zulu *tula* 'be silent,' *etula* 'take off' (as a hat, or a pot off the fire), which are probably the same word, the *e* having been introduced to differentiate the latter. (Of the fairly numerous Zulu verbs in *e* some have lost an initial consonant and are in process of shedding the vowel, as *emba*, or *mba* 'dig,' in others the *e* seems to be an accretion (as above).—*Na tue*, less usual than *katue* (Steere, *Handbook*, p. 140).—The jewel in the snake's head seems to be taken for granted as if possessed by all snakes, but it may be less summarily treated in the original story.

[20] For the construction of the Objective Relative, see Steere, *Handbook*, p. 119. *A-* is the pronoun of the 3rd person agreeing with the subject (*simba*), *-taka-* the sign of the future, *-cho-* the relative pronoun, object, agreeing with *kitu* understood. We should, however, have expected the object-pronoun to be inserted as well as the relative: *a-taka-cho-ki-ona*. For *nale*, see last note.

[21] See above, note 9.

[22] The full form would be *vitu alivyoviambiwa* 'the things which he had been told them,' but the pronouns of the 8th class are often used without reference to a subject—cf. the adverbial use of *vizuri*.

[23] It is more usual to substitute the Subjunctive for the Imperative when there is an object-pronoun (*e.g.*, *mpe* 'give him'), but we also find *nipa* 'give me.'

²⁴ *Kisha*, in this case, 'moreover,' 'besides'—not 'afterwards.'

²⁵ If a connective particle is expressed after the Passive (there is sometimes none) it is oftener *ni* than *na* which would be the natural word to use, according to European ideas. The literal rendering of the *ni* construction is—*e.g.*, in this passage: 'I am being given—it is God (who gives).'

²⁶ *Kana*, equivalent to *kama*, but not so common.

²⁷ *anasimama*, Perfect in *-na-*: so, too, *yanafunuka* and *inafika*, lower down.

²⁸ *mkono*, properly used of human beings, but also of quadrupeds when the paw is—as here—used like a hand.

²⁹ Meaning, 'The story having arrived at this point, it ends here.'

Connected Translation

There was once a very poor man, who, on a certain day, said to himself, 'I will go to (the house of) Almighty God and pray to him to give me enough to subsist on, for (as it is) I am in great distress. So he rose up and went his way, and when he had reached a place a long distance off, he saw a lake containing much water. He bathed and then went his way. As he went, there met him a lion who was blind and very thin with hunger and said to him 'Son of Adam, where are you going?' So he said, 'I am going to the abode of God, to pray that I may be given enough to live on.' And the lion said, 'When you go, pray for me also that I may have my eyes opened and get food to eat.' The man replied, 'Very well' and went his way. Then he saw a snake who asked him, 'Where are you going?' and he said, 'I am going to God to pray for sustenance'; and the snake said, 'When you go, pray for me also; there has been such a drought that I cannot find anything to eat, so I want the rain to come that we may get food.' The man went on till he reached a large town, where the Sultan, who was a woman, saw him and said to him 'Where are you going?' [He answered as before.] She said, 'When you go, make a request for me also. Though I am the Sultan, I am a woman, and my subjects do not obey me, so that the quarrelling and fighting in my town never cease. My prayer is that this state of things may come to an end.' So he went on.

And he arrived and said to the Almighty, 'I have come, because I am in great trouble through poverty—I have come to beg you to assign me sufficient means of living.' And He said to him, 'You have abundance to live on now, but it is being wasted.' The man then said, 'On the way here I saw a woman who said to me, "Pray for me also to the Almighty: I am a queen, but my subjects do not obey me and war never ends in our town."' He said 'Tell her; "You are a woman, you had better get married, then all these troubles will cease."' The man then said, 'After that, I saw a snake who told me that, because of the drought, his people cannot get food—he would like it to rain.' The Lord answered, 'If he lays aside the jewel which is in his head, the rain will fall abundantly.' The man went on, 'After that I saw a lion who was blind and who asked me to pray that he might recover his sight and also be provided with food.' The Lord said, 'Tell him to smear his eyes with his spittle, and they will be opened, and then let him eat whatever he sees before him,—that is (assigned him for) his subsistence.' So the man said '*Hewallah!*' and went his way. When he came to the queen, he gave her the message with which he had been charged, and she said, 'Marry me yourself, you will acquire much wealth, and you shall be king.' But the man answered, 'I do not want your wealth, nor do I want the kingdom, I for my part have very much wealth of my own, which is being given me by God.' So he went on. When he came to the snake, he likewise gave him his message, and the snake offered him the jewel out of his head, which the man refused, saying 'I have just had a large property given me, I do not want any more.' Then he went on and came to the lion, and delivered the message as it was given him. The lion did as directed and recovered his sight, and, seeing the man standing before him, stretched out his paw and seized him, saying, 'Where shall I get any other food than this?' The man said to him, 'Why, I prayed for you, and your eyes have been opened, and now are you going to eat me?' And the lion said, 'I don't know about that, but I have to eat you in order to carry out your directions.' So he ate him. And the story ends here.

6. GANDA*

The Story of Ndyakubi and Ndalakubi

Awo[1] **o-lwa-tuka**[2] **omu-saja**
Well then, which arrived (there was a) man

eri-nya-lye[3] **Ndya-kubi,**[4] **ne-ba-ta**[5]
name his Ndya-kubi, and they made

omu-kago ni Ndalakubi. Awo Ndalakubi
blood-brotherhood with Ndalakubi. So Ndalakubi

n-a-gamba Ndyakubi, nti,[6] **'O-ja-nga'**
and he said (to) Ndyakubi, saying, 'Come'

n-o-n-daba';[8] **awo Ndyakubi n-a-genda**
and me see'; so Ndyakubi and he went

n-a-tuka ewa[9] **Ndalakubi. Ndalakubi**
and he arrived at (the house of) Ndalakubi. Ndalakubi

n-a-gamba mu-kazi-we,[10] **nti, 'Genda**
and he said (to) wife his, saying, 'Go (that)

o-fumbire[11] **omu-genyi emere.'**[12] **Awo omu-kazi**
you may cook for guest plantains.' So wife

---

* From *Engero za Baganda*, p. 38. A slightly different version is given in *Manuel de laugue Luganda*, p. 237.

n-a-genda a-fumba[18] emere n-e-gya[14]
and she went she cooked plantains and they were done
n-a-gi-reta,[15] omugenyi n-a-lya
and she them brought (to) guest and he ate
na-ta-kuta.[16] Nagamba Ndalakubi
and he was not satisfied. And he said (to) Ndalakubi
nti, 'Muna-nge[17] sikuse.'[18] Ndalakubi
saying, 'Friend my I am not satisfied.' Ndalakubi
nagamba omukazi nti 'Genda ofumbe
and he said (to) wife saying 'Go that you may cook
emere, omugenyi ta-kuse, ofumbe
plantains, guest is not satisfied, (see) that you cook
nyingi.' Awo omukazi nagenda afumba
many.' So wife and she went she cooks
emi-wumbo[19] gy-emere e-tano, na-gyo[20]
bundles of plantains five, and those
n-a-gi-reta Ndyakubi, n-a-lya
and she brought them (to) Ndyakubi, and he ate
n-a-gi-mala-wo,[21] era[22] natakuta.
and when he had finished them still he was not satisfied.
Nagamba Ndalakubi, nti, 'Munange,
And he spoke (to) Ndalakubi, saying, 'My friend,
sikuse.' Ndalakubi nagamba
I am not satisfied.' Ndalakubi and he spoke (to)
omukazi nti, 'Genda ewa munange
wife saying, 'Go to (the house of) my friend
gundi,[23] o-n-sabire-yo[24] emere, nze[25]
so and so, that you may beg for me there plantains, I
e-mpwede-ko.[26] Omukazi nagenda asaba
they are finished for me. Wife and she went she begs
emere, nagireta, nafumba
plantains, and she brought them and she cooked
emiwumbo kikumi,[27] nagireta; Ndyakubi
bundles 100, and she brought them; Ndyakubi

APPENDIX I.

nalya emere	nagimalawo
and he ate plantains	and when he had finished them
natakuta. Nagamba,	Ndalakubi
he was not satisfied. And he spoke,	Ndalakubi
nti, 'Munange, sikuse.'	Ndalakubi
saying, 'My friend, I am not satisfied."	Ndalakubi
n-a-damu,[28] nti 'Emere	empwedeko.'
and he answered, saying 'Plantains	are finished for me.'
Ndyakubi nagamba nti,	'Kale[29]
Ndyakubi and he spoke saying,	'All right,
ka-n-gende enjala, munywanyi[30]	wange,
let me go (with) hunger, dearest friend	my,
n-fire ku kubo[31]	enjala.'
that I may die on road (with)	hunger.'
Na-da-yo ewu-we.	Na
And he returned there to his (own house.)	And
Ndalakubi ya-laba[32] a-genze,[33] naye	nagenda
Ndalakubi he saw he has gone, he too	and he went
oku-mu-kyalira, natuka	ewa
to visit him, and he arrived	at (the house of)
Ndyakubi. Ndyakubi nagamba	omukazi
Ndyakubi. Ndyakubi and he spoke (to)	wife
nti, 'Genda ofumbe	emere
saying, 'Go that you may cook	plantains
y-omugenyi.' Omukazi	nagenda
of guest.' Wife	and she went
nagifumba,	negya
and she cooked them,	and they were done,
nagireta; Ndalakubi	n-a-lya-ko[34]
and she brought them; Ndalakubi	and he ate of them
katono. Awo obude[35]	te-bwa-lwa
a little. So time of day	it did not delay
ne-bu-ziba. Ndalakuki	nagamba
and it is stopped up. Ndalakubi	and he spoke

Ndyakubi nti, 'Nasula wa?'[86]
(to Ndyakubi saying, 'I shall pass the night where?'
Ndyakubi nagamba nti, 'Na-ku-segulira[87]
Ndyakubi and he spoke saying, 'I will remove for you
ku-kitanda[88] **kwange kw-o-no-sula.'**
from bedstead my where you will pass the night.'
Ndalakubi nagamba nti, 'Si-gya-wo.'[89]
Ndalakubi and he spoke saying, 'I do not get-in there.'
Ndyakubi nawangulawo empagi,
Ndyakubi and he pulled out there a post,
Ndalakubi nagenda yebaka.[40] **Nendyakubi**
Ndalakubi and he went he slept. Ndyakubi too
neyebaka. Yali yebase, Ndalakubi
and he slept. He was he is asleep, Ndalakubi
na-mu ita, nti, 'Munange,
and he called him, saying, 'My friend,
we-n-suze[41] **si-gya-wo ebi-gere,**
where I have put up I do not get in (as to) my feet,
bi ri, bweru.' Ndyakubi nagamba
they are outside.' Ndyakubi and he spoke (to)
mukaziwe nti, 'Genda ewa gundi,
his wife saying, 'Go to (the house of) so and so,
a-m-pole[42] **emuli.'**[43] **Omukazi nagenda**
that he may lend me reeds.' Wife and she went
na-zi-reta. Ndyakubi na-kokera[44]
and she brought them. Ndyakubi and he pushed out
enyumba ekiro ekyo. Ndalakubi nagenda
house night that. Ndalakubi and he went
yebaka, bwe-yebaka[45] **ebi-gere bya-gukira**
he sleeps, when he slept feet they projected
bweru. Naita Ndyakubi nti,
outside. And he called Ndyakubi saying,
'Munange, bwe-wa-ja ewange wa-lya
'My friend, when you came to my (house) you ate

emere nyingi, laba nze kakano, ebigere biri,
plantains many, see me now, feet are
bweru, ebi-solo bi-ja ku-n-dya bigere.'
outside, animals they are going to eat me the feet.'
Ndyakubi nagamba nti, 'Si-ri-ko[46]
Ndyakubi and he said saying, 'I have not
we-na-gya muli zimpwedeko,
where I shall take out reeds they are finished for me,
nemiti si-ri-na.' Ndalakubi nagamba
and poles I have not.' Ndalakubi and he spoke
nti, 'Bwe-wa-ja ewange ba-ku-fumbira
saying 'When you came to my (house) they cooked for you
emere nyingi, nolya nogana
plantains many, and you ate and you refused
okukuta emere, ne-zi-gwa-ko
to be satisfied (with) plantains, and they were finished
n-o-ng'amba nti, 'Munywanyi wange,
and you spoke to me saying, 'Dearest friend my,
kang'ende enjala' nange kale! leka
let me go (with) hunger' and I—well! let (be)—
ebisolo bindire[47] ebweru, munywanyi
animals they may eat me outside, dearest friend
wange.' Ndyakubi nagamba nti,
my.' Ndyakubi and he spoke saying,

'Munange, wefunye,[48] leka kulanama,[49]
'My friend, draw up (your legs), cease to stretch out,

nange bwe-na-ja-nga[50] ewuwo na-lya-nga-ko
and I whenever I come to your (house) I will eat

katono, m-onerede.'[51] Ndalakubi nagamba
a little I have repented.' Ndalakubi and he spoke

nti, 'To-kola-nga[52] bwotyo, nze
saying, 'Never do like that, I

bwe-na-kw-etondera[53] nti, "Emere
when I admitted to you saying, "Plantains

empwedeko,"	wa-yomba	buyombi,[54]
are finished for me,"	you quarrelled	a quarrelling,
nange no[55]	**leka nefunye,**	**nawe**
and I—just	let me draw up (my legs),	and you
bwojanga	**ewange,**	**emere**
whenever you come	to my (house)	plantains
o-gi-rya-nga	**bulungi.'**[56]	
you shall eat them	decently.'	

NOTES

[1] *Awo* is here a mere connective, equivalent to 'and so,' or the like. It seems to be a distinct word from the locative *awo*.

[2] The subject of *olwatuka* is *olu-naku* 11 'day' understood: (on) the day which arrived' being equivalent to 'once upon a time.'

[3] *-lye*, possessive 5: in Ganda the possessives of the 2nd and 3rd persons singular are usually suffixed to the noun.

[4] *Ndyakubi* means 'I eat badly,' (the *l* of *lya* becoming *d* after *n*) and *Ndalakubi* (from *lala*) 'I sleep badly.' *Lala* does not seem to be used in this sense now, having been replaced by *ebaka*.

[5] This is the 'narrative tense' (Pilkington, p. 18) of the verb *'ta*, which properly means 'kill,' but is used idiomatically. *Oku'ta omukago* appears to be the technical term for 'making blood-brotherhood.' See Roscoe, *The Baganda*, p. 19. The 3rd person plural is here (as often) used impersonally, like the French *on*.

[6] *nti* seems to be the only trace left in Luganda of the verb *ti* 'say,' unless the adverb *otyo* is connected with it, as suggested in *Elements of Luganda Grammar*, p. 206.

[7] The Imperative with -*nga* suffixed is called in *Elements* (p. 68) the 'Far Future Imperative,' but it is doubtful whether it can be restricted to distant time. With a Negative Imperative, -*nga* has the force of 'never.'

[8] 2nd person singular, narrative tense of *laba* 'see,' for *na-u-n-laba*. *Na+u* contracts into *no*, and *l* becomes *d* after -*n*-, which is the object-pronoun of the first person.

APPENDIX I.

[9] *Ewa* is the locative particle, corresponding to *pa* and *kwa* in other Bantu languages and equivalent to the French *chez*. *Kwa* does not seem to be thus used in Ganda, though we do find it as the possessive particle of the r5th class: *okufa kwa kabaka* 'the death of the king.' *Ewa* is a double locative: *wa=pa*, while *e* is a separate prefix meaning 'at' or 'to' (see *Elements*, p. 97) and possibly connected with the Zulu locative prefix (*ante*, p. 83). It is often found with suffixed possessive—*ewa-nge*, *ewu-wo*, etc.

[10] *-we* suffixed possessive, 3rd person. *Gamba* is the vero found in Swahili as *amba* (generally used in the applied form *ambia* 'say to,' 'tell'). From it we get *eki-gambo* 7 'word,' cf. Yao *magambo* 6 'discussion.'

[11] 2nd person singular subjunctive of the applied form of *fumba* 'cook.' Contrary to what we find in Zulu, Swahili, Nyanja, etc., it is accented *fúmbire*. This difference in accentuation and an apparent preference for short vowels make the sound of spoken Ganda very puzzling to one accustomed, *e.g.* to Swahili or Nyanja.

[12] *emere*, 9, properly 'steamed and mashed plantains,' but used for 'food' in general, this being the staple dish of the Baganda. (See Roscoe, pp. 435-6).

[13] 3rd person singular, present tense (used for past).

[14] *gya* 'be cooked,' 'be done,' etc; Nyanja *psya* (*pya*), Herero *pya*, etc., originally, had the sense of 'burn,' like the Zulu *tsha*. It must be distinguished from two other verbs both of which occur further on in this extract: *gya* 'take out' and *gya* 'get into' (a space).

[15] *reta*=Zulu (and other languages) *leta*, Herero *eta*, etc. (*r* and *l* are to a certain extent interchangeable in Ganda, the former being heard before *a*, *o* and *u*, and the latter before *e* and *i*). *-gi-* is the object-pronoun of cl., 9 the subject-pronoun being *e-* or *y-*. It is very rare to find, except in Class 1, the object-pronoun differing from the subject; its position seems to have preserved the initial consonant, which has been worn away at the beginning of a word.

[16] The *k* in *kuta* 'be satisfied' is the 'exploded' or 'long' consonant (see *Elements*, pp. 14, 15) indicated in C.M.S. books by a prefixed apostrophe (*'kuta*), and in those of the French Fathers by doubling the consonant (*natakkuta*): the former method seems preferable. The sound is really a combination of a consonant with the glottal stop, which is very common in Hamitic languages (*e.g.* Galla). These 'exploded' consonants are not marked in the text from which our extract is taken and it has not been thought necessary

to distinguish them here. *Natakuta* is negative narrative tense.

[17] *muna* means 'one of' and is therefore never used without a possessive pronoun or a noun following: *muna-fe* 'one of us,' *muna-Budu* 'a man of Budu.' Properly it should not be used with a singular pronoun, but it has acquired the sense of 'friend,' 'companion,' etc.

[18] *si-kuse*, Negative Perfect of *kuta*, 2nd person *tu-kuse*, 3rd *ta-kuse*. *ta* is the negative particle corresponding with the Swahili *hā*.

[19] *omu-wumbo* 3 (from *wumba* 'wrap up for cooking in a leaf') is a bundle of plantains, which are always prepared in this way. In the *Manuel de Langue Luganda*, it is translated '*marmites*,' but this is evidently a mistake—*gyemere* for *gya emere*—note *gya* 4, agreeing with *emiwumbo*.

[20] (*e*)-*gyo*, demonstrative, agreeing with *emi-wumbo*: the -*gi*- in the next word has the same agreement, and is consequently 4 not 9.

[21] Narrative tense, followed by the locative relative -*wo* (here='when,' like -*po* in Swahili). *mala* 'finish,' with its derived forms *malira*, *maliza*, is found in Swahili (though here almost ousted by *isha*), Nyanja, Yao, etc.

[22] *era* seems to be used either as an adverb or as a conjunction. It may also mean 'and,' 'besides.'

[23] *gundi*, used like *goa* in Pokomo and *fulani* (Arabic) in Swahili, to designate some one whom one cannot or will not name.

[24] 2nd person singular subjunctive of *sabira*, applied form of *saba* 'ask':—*o*- (before a vowel *w*-) subject-pronoun, 2nd person singular; -*n*-, object-pronoun, 1st person singular; *yo*- locative suffix, equivalent to 'in that place' (*Elements*, p. 70): the whole word meaning 'where you may request food for me.'

[25] *nze*, separable pronoun, 1st person singular—here used for emphasis='as for me.'

[26] Perfect (*wede*) of *gwa* 'come to an end,' agreeing with *emere* 9 and followed by the locative pronoun -*ko*. The -*mp*- represents the object-pronoun of the first person, this being the form assumed by *n* before *w*. The construction suggests a common Irish idiom, *e.g.*, 'He's lost it on me' (Jane Barlow, *Irish Idylls*.)

[27] Note the difference between *ekumi* and *kikumi*. *Lukumi* is 1,000 and *kakumi* 10,000.

APPENDIX I.

²⁸ *da* ' return ' seems in *da-mu* ' answer ' to be compounded with *mu* in a way not quite easy to explain, but probably growing out of the usage by which *va-mu* (*e.g.*) means ' get out from inside.' (*Elements*, p. 71).

²⁹ *kale*, interjection of ' exhortation,' here equivalent to ' Oh! very well!' or the like. *kang'ende* subjunctive, preceded by *ka*, which is generally added to the 1st person singular and plural (*Elements*, p. 69). Note *ng'ende*, not *ngende*—*n* and *g* combining into *ng'*.

³⁰ *munywanyi* a term of endearment, sometimes equivalent to ' light of my eyes,' ' darling,' etc.

³¹ (*e*) *kubo* 5 is ' a path trodden down,' possibly connected with *kuba* ' beat.'

³² *ya-laba*, 3rd person singular (note the difference in the pronoun) of the ' Far Past ' Tense (*Elements*, p. 27).

³³ *-genze*, perfect of *genda*.

³⁴ This is the ' Partitive ' use of *-ko* (like French *en*)—see *Elements*, p. 70.

³⁵ *obude* 14, constantly used in indications of time. *Obude buziba* is, literally ' the time of day becomes stopped ' (as a bottle with a cork: the *Manuel de Langue Luganda* renders, ' *le moment se bouche* ' *te-bwa-lwa*), Negative [Far Past, agreeing with *obude*. The whole phrase means ' it was not long before it got dark.'

³⁶ *wa*, adverb, indicative of ' place generally,' used interrogatively for ' where ? ' (*Elements*, pp. 46, 51). It is the locative pronoun *pa*, a primitive *p* becoming *w* in Ganda.

³⁷ *Segulira* should properly be the applied form of a reversive verb derived from *sega*, which, however, does not occur in the vocabularies in any meaning that would be appropriate. *Seguka*, intr. is ' move one's position.' *Na-ku-segulira* here means, not ' I will make room for you ' on my bed, but ' I will give up my bed to you.'

³⁸ *Ku-kitanda* 17, treated as one word and therefore followed by the possessive *kwange*. *Kwonosula* = *ku-o-no-sula*: 2nd. pers. sing. of the Near Future, preceded by *ku* = on (which). Note the distinction between *sula* ' pass the night ' and *ebaka*, used of actual sleep.

³⁹ This is *gya* ' get into a space '—see Note 14 above.

⁴⁰ *ebaka*, properly a reflexive verb, *e* being the reflexive pronoun (Zuli *zi*, Swahili *ji*, Nyamwezi *i*, etc.). But many such verbs have acquired distinct meanings of their own. (*Elements*, p. 117.) As it begins with a vowel, the Past is *y-ebaka*, for *ya-ebaka*.

[41] *suze*, perfect of *sula*; *we-* adverb corresponding to the ocative *wa* 16 (*Elements*, p. 96), as in *wano we-n-tambula*, 'here where I walk.'

[42] For *a-n-wole*, from *wola* 'lend.' The nasal n preserves the *p* sound elsewhere lost in Ganda and is itself modified by the influence of the *p* into *m*.

[43] *emuli* 10 plural of *olu-muli* 11. Reeds are used in thatching a house, the thatch reaching down to the ground.

[44] Ndyakubi, having previously pulled out one of the supports in order to give his friend more room, now makes an extension to the thatch with the borrowed reeds. Huts being round, the foot of the bedstead (placed so that, in a square room it would be parallel with the wall), would necessarily come in contact with the thatch.

[45] *bwe*, relative='when' agrees with *obude* 14 understood.

[46] *na* understood after *ri*, as often in the negative. *Gya* 'take out,' as from a store.

[47] For *bi-n-lire*, applied form of *lya*.

[48] *efunya*, reflexive of *funya* 'clench' (the fist), 'fold' etc.—used here of drawing up the knees. *Wefunye=o-efunye*, 2nd person singular of the Subjunctive.

[49] *lanama*, by its form and sense is evidently a stative, but no verb *lana* appears to be in use.

[50] The suffix-*nga* may denote either present, past or future action, so long as it is repeated or habitual. (*Elements*, p. 91.) Here it is equivalent to 'whenever I come.'

[51] For *n-bonerede*, perfect of *bonera*, 'repent'; *b*, after changing *n* to *m*, disappears.

[52] Negative Imperative: *-nga* suffixed to this mood implies a general prohibition (*Elements*, p. 35); *-otyo* is an adverb meaning 'just so' and *bw* (*e*) 'how,' depends on some implied 14th class noun meaning 'state' etc. (*Elements*, pp. 94-106.)

[53] *etonda* 'confess a fault and be sorry for it' (Blackledge); *etond-era* 'confess to (any one)' here used of the regretful admission that his provisions are exhausted.

[54] That is 'merely quarrel,' 'do nothing but quarrel';—for this peculiar use of the 14th prefix, see *Elements*, p. 107.

[55] *no* is an 'intensive interjection'; *leka*, 'let,' "allow,' often used before the subjunctive, like our 'let' though its primary meaning seems to be 'leave' ('let alone.') Some languages have it with the meaning 'stop' (intr.)

[56] Abstract noun, (from *-lungi* 'good') used as an adverb (Pilkington, p. 69.)

Connected Translation

Once upon a time there was a man whose name was Ndyakubi, and he made brotherhood with Ndalakubi. And Ndalakubi said to him, 'Come and see me (some day.)' So Ndyakubi went, and arrived at Ndalakubi's house, and the latter said to his wife, 'Go and cook food for the guest.' So the wife went and cooked food, and, when it was done, she brought it, and the guest ate, but he was not satisfied, and he said to Ndalakubi, 'My friend, I have not had enough.' Ndalakubi said to his wife 'Go (again) and cook a great deal of food, for our guest is still hungry.' She went and cooked five bundles of food and brought them also to Ndyakubi, and he ate it, and when he had finished he still had not had enough and said to Ndalakubi, 'My friend, I am not satisfied.' Ndalakubi said to his wife, 'Go to my friend so and so and ask him for some plaintains, for mine are all finished.' The wife went and asked for plaintains and brought them and cooked a hundred bundles. Ndyakubi ate the food and when he had finished it, he was still unsatisfied and said . . . [as before.] Ndalakubi answered, 'I have no food left,' so Ndyakubi said, 'Never mind, I will go away hungry, my dear friend, and die by the roadside (if I must).' So he returned home. Ndalakubi saw that he had gone, and (some time afterwards), he, too went to pay a visit to him, and when he arrived at Ndyakubi's house, the latter said to his wife 'Go and cook food for the guest.' His wife went and cooked it and brought it when it was done, and Ndalakubi ate a little of it. Soon after this it grew dark. Ndalakubi said to Ndyakubi, 'Where am I to sleep?' Ndyakubi answered, 'I will give you my bedstead so that you can sleep.' Ndalakubi said 'There will not be room for me,' so Ndyakubi pulled out one of the posts of the house, and Ndalakubi went and lay down to sleep. Ndyakubi also slept. When he was asleep,

Ndalakubi called him and said, 'My friend, in the place you have given me to sleep in, there is no room for my feet, they are outside.' Ndyakubi said to his wife, 'Go to so and so and borrow some reeds,' and the woman went and brought them, and Ndyakubi made an extension to the house that night. Ndalakubi went and slept, but when he was asleep (he thrust) his feet (through the thatch and awoke and found that they) were projecting outside. So he called out to Ndyakubi, 'My friend, when you came to my house you ate large quantities of plantains—now, see how my feet are outside, and the wild animals will come and eat them.' Ndyakubi said, 'There is no place where I can get any more reeds they are all done and I have no poles.' Ndalakubi said, 'When you came to my house, they cooked for you an enormous amount of food, and you ate, and yet you kept on saying you had not had enough, and when the food was all finished, you said to me, " My beloved friend! let me go away hungry!"—and so I say, " Never mind, dearest friend—let the wild beasts eat me outside your house!"' So Ndyakubi said, 'Oh! my friend, just draw up your legs and don't stretch them out; and I, too, next time I come to your house, I will only eat a little; I am truly sorry for my behaviour.' Ndalakubi answered, 'Never act again as you did when I told you, very much to my regret, that there was no more food in the house, and you did nothing but quarrel with me. Well, let me just draw up my knees (till the morning), and when you come to my house again, remember to eat like a decent human being.'

A free version of this tale is to be found in Roscoe, *The Baganda*, p. 482. The point of it lies in the mutual obligations of blood-brothers, on which Ndyakubi presumes beyond all permission.

APPENDIX II: BIBLIOGRAPHY

This Bibliography makes no attempt at completeness, being intended merely as a guide to the books available for the study of the more important Bantu Languages. Continental works not easily accessible have only, as a rule, been indicated where no English ones appeared to exist.

Languages marked * are those into which the whole Bible has been translated; those marked † possess complete versions of the New Testament. These versions are of unequal linguistic value, but as a rule are welcome aids to the student. (Most of them, though not all, are published by the British and Foreign Bible Society.) Many others, besides those marked, have translations of separate parts of the Scriptures, and school reading-books, etc., which will often be found useful.

Books marked * are to be found in the library of the African Society (open to members) at 64, Victoria Street, S.W.

I. GENERAL

*Anthropos. Revue Internationale d'Ethnologie et de Linguistique, Salzburg (Zaunrith).

From 1906 onwards. Separate items under Congo (Kiyombe, Kanyoka), Fang, Fipa.

W. H. J. Bleek. Comparative Grammar of the South African Languages. Part I. (Phonology), 1862.

Part II. The Concord. Section I. The Noun. 1869. (No more published.) London (Trübner and Co.)

C. G. Büttner. Zeitschrift für Afrikanische Sprachen. Berlin (A. Ascher and Co.), 1887-90.

Contains many valuable contributions, some of which are entered as separate items in the Bibliography. The periodical was discontinued on Dr. Büttner's death in 1890.

*R. N. Cust. A Sketch of the Modern Languages of Africa, 2 vols. London (Trübner and Co.), 1883.

Journal of the African Society. (Quarterly.) London (Macmillan and Co.) From 1902 onwards. Contains some valuable linguistic articles.

J. T. Last. Polyglotta Africana Orientalis. London (S.P.C.K.), 1885.

Contains vocabularies of over fifty East African Languages (including a few non-Bantu). They are not very full, but form useful starting points for languages not already studied.

*C. Meinhof. Die moderne Sprachforschung in Africa. 1910, Berlin: Berlin Evangelical Missionary Society (Georgenkirchstrasse).

*—— An Introduction to the Study of African Languages. (Translated by A. Werner.) London and Toronto (Dent), 1915.

Being the English edition of the preceding.

*—— Grundriss einer Lautlehre der Bantusprachen (Second edition). Berlin (Dietrich Reimer) (Ernst Vohsen), 1910.

*—— Grundzüge einer vergleichenden Grammatik der Bantusprachen. Same publisher. Berlin, 1906.

—— Das Dahlsche Gesetz. *Zeitschrift der deutschen morgenländischen Gesellschaft* Bd. LVII., p. 302.

An exposition of the important law of Dissimilation referred to on p. 229.

C. Meinhof. Linguistische Studien in Ostafrika. Berlin, 1904-8. Mitteilungen des Sem. für orient. Sprachen. Bd. VII-XI.

Phonetic Studies of Swahili, Shambala, Nyamwezi, Sukuma, Digo, 'Nika,' Pokomo, Bondei, Zigula, Mbugu, Dzalamɔ, Makua, Yao.

*Mitteilungen des Seminars für orientalische Sprachen an der königlichen Friedrich-Wilhelms-Universität zu Berlin, etc. Berlin (W. Spemann, afterwards G. Reimer), 1898, etc.

These 'Transactions' appear annually in three sections, of which the third is devoted to Africa, under the title of *Afrikanische Studien*. Some of the more important items are entered separately, under the several languages. Referred to as Mitt. B. Sem. Or. The series of handbooks (*Lehrbücher des Seminars für orientalische Sprachen*) issued by the same institution contains a number of valuable works, entered under the separate languages.

Another series of which several volumes will be found entered under various languages is the *Archiv für das Studium deutscher Kolonialsprachen* (same publisher), 1895.

*B. Struck. Collections towards a Bibliography of the Bantu Languages of British E. Africa. Journal of the African Society, London, 1907.

J. Torrend, S. J. A Comparative Grammar of the South African Bantu Languages, comprising those of Zanzibar, Mozambique, the Zambezi, etc., etc. London (Kegan Paul, Trench, Trübner and Co., Ltd.), 1891.

*Zeitschrift für afrikanische und oceanische Sprachen. Berlin (Dietrich Reimer), 1895-1903.

Edited by A. Seidel; 5 vols. square royal 8vo., appeared between January, 1895 and January, 1900. Publication was then suspended, but resumed (in a smaller *format*) in

1902, and ceased with the first issue for 1903. Some important contributions are entered under special languages, *e.g.*, Sumbwa, Tabwa. 4 vols. in African Society's Library.

Zeitschrift für Kolonialsprachen. (Quarterly.) Berlin (D. Reimer) and Hamburg (Boysen). From 1910 onwards.

II. Special Languages

Aduma (Duma). Spoken along the Ogowe River in the northern part of French Congo.

R. P. Dahin. Vocabulaire Adouma-Français. Part I., French-Aduma, pp. 72. Part II., Aduma-French, pp. 72. Kempten (Bavaria), (Jos. Kösel), 1895.

Angola. See Mbundu.

Bangala. See under Congo Languages.

Bangi. See under Congo Languages.

**Bemba.* Between the Lualaba and Lake Nyasa.

*W. G. Robertson. An Introductory Handbook to the Language of the Bemba People. London (L.M.S.), 1904.

*Father Schoeffer. Grammar as spoken in North-east Rhodesia. Edited by J. H. West Sheane. Arranged with Preface by (the late) A. C. Madan. Oxford (Clarendon Press), 1907.

Benga. (Corisco Bay, West Africa.)

*J. L. Mackey. Grammar of the Benga Bantu Language, revised by R. H. Nassau. New York (American Tract Society), 1892.

The original edition of Mackey's Grammar was published at New York (Mission House, 23, Centre Street), in 1855.

C. Meinhof. Das Zeitwort in der Benga-Sprache. Berlin, 1890. Zeitschrift für Afr. Sprachen, Vol. III., pp. 265-284. Benga und Duala, ib. II., pp. 190-208.

Bondei. Spoken inland from Tanga in East Africa.

G. Dale. Bondei Exercises. Holy Cross, Magila, 1892.

*H. W. Woodward. Collections for a Handbook of the Bondei Language. London (S.P.C.K.), 1882.

――― Stories in the Bondei Language with some Enigmas and Proverbs. Written by Native Students and edited by the Rev. H. W. Woodward. (S.P.C.K.)

Bube. (Fernando Po.)

John Clarke. Introduction to the Fernandian Tongue. Berwick-on-Tweed (Daniel Cameron), 1848.

R. P. Joaquin Juanola. Primer Paso a la Lengua Bubé, pp. 190. This seems to be the most complete grammar hitherto published. Madrid (A. Pérez Dubrull).

*Sir H. H. Johnston. George Grenfell and the Congo, Vol. II., Appendix I., p. 882. London (Hutchinson and Co.), 1908.

This work contains specimen vocabularies of a great many other West African Languages, and a discussion of the various Bantu migrations. The greatest amount of space is devoted to a comparison of numerals.

Bunda. See Mbundu.

Chaga. (Čaga, Dšagga, Djaga, etc.) The Wachaga live on Kilimanjaro.

*J. Raum. Versuch einer Grammatik der Dschagga-Sprache (Moschi-Dialekt). Archiv. für d. Stud. deutscher Kolonialsprachen, Vol. XI. Berlin (Georg Reimer), 1909.

H. A. Fokken. Das Kisiha. Mitteil. des Sem. für orient. Sprachen. Jahrg. VIII., Abt. 3. Berlin, pp. 44-93, 1905.

Siha is a dialect of Chaga.

Chasu (also called Pare).

*E. Kotz. Grammatik des Chasu in Deutsch, Ostafrika. Berlin (G. Reimer), 1909. Archiv für das Studium deutscher Kolonialsprachen, Vol. X.

Spoken in the mountains south of Kilimanjaro.

Chinamwanga. See Namwanga.

Chinyanja. See Nyanja.

Chiswina and *Chizwina.* See Karanga.

Chwana (Sechwana, Secwana).

It is practically identical with Sutu (Sotho, Sesuto), and works relating to both are entered under this heading.

James Archbell. A Grammar of the Bechuana Language. Graham's Town (Meurant and Godlonton), 1837.

J. Brown. L.M.S. Secwana Dictionary. Frome (Butler and Tanner), 1895.

E. Casalis. Études sur la Langue Séchuana. Paris (Imprimerie Royale), 1841.

This is really Sutu. The book is interesting as being one of the earliest on the subject, and the Introduction gives a valuable account of the establishment of the French Mission in Basutoland and its relations with Moshesh.

*W. Crisp. Notes towards a Secwana Grammar, 1900, reprinted 1905. (S.P.C.K.)

A useful book, though not very well arranged. The dialect is that of the Barolong.

K. Endemann. Versuch einer Grammatik des Sotho. Berlin (Wilhelm Hertz), 1876.

*———— Wörterbuch der Sotho-Sprache, Vol. VII. of Abhandlungen des Hamburgischen Kolonialinstituts. Hamburg (L. Friedrichsen and Co.), 1911.

These are really Chwana rather than Sutu, which is noticed as a dialect under the name of 'Süd-Sotho.'

APPENDIX II. 313

E. Jacottet. Practical Method to learn Sesuto. Morija (Sesuto Book Depot), 1906.

───── Elementary Sketch of Sesuto Grammar, 1893. Published with Mabille's *Vocabulary*, which see.

E. Jacottet. Treasury of Basuto Lore, Vol. I. (Sesuto Book Depot), Morija, Basutoland, 1908. London (Kegan Paul).

A valuable collection of Native Tales. Subsequent volumes were intended to contain historical traditions, songs, accounts of customs, etc., but no more have yet been issued.

D. Jones and S. T. Plaatje. Sechuana Reader. University of London Press (Hodder and Stoughton), 1916.

F. H. Kruger. Steps to Learn the Sesuto Language (Fourth edition). Morija (Sesuto Book Depot), 1905.

A. Mabille. Sesuto-English and English-Sesuto Vocabulary. (Preceded by Jacottet's *Grammar*, which see.) (P. E. Mission Press), Morija, 1893.

A. Mabille and H. Dieterlen. Sesuto-English Dictionary. Revised and considerably enlarged. (Sesuto Book Depot), Morija.

*S. T. Plaatje. Sechuana Proverbs with Literal Translation. London (Kegan Paul), 1916.

Puisano ea se-Sotho le se-English. Phrase-Book. Sesuto-English. Morija (Sesuto Book Depot), 1908.

A. J. Wookey, L.M.S. Secwana Grammar, with Exercises. Frome (Butler and Tanner), 1905.

Congo (languages of). The languages included under this heading are:

†*Bangi*, (Bobangi, Kibangi, Kiyanzi). On both banks of the Congo, from the confluence of the Sankuru to that of the Lulongo.

Kanyoka, between Lulua and Upper Sankuru.

Kele, below Stanley Falls.[1]

*Kongo, (Congo, Fiote.)

†*Lolo*, (Mongo, Lunkundu)—on the Equator, within the great northern bend of the Congo.

Lulua, on one of the Kasai tributaries.

Ngala, (Bangala, Lingala). Middle Congo, between the confluences of the Mubangi and the Mongala.

Ng'ombe, west of the Ba-ngala.

Poto, at and near Bopoto (Upoto), at the top of the Congo bend.

Soko, near the mouth of the Aruhwimi.

Teke, north of Stanley Pool (also called Ifumu).

Yombe, (Kiombe) in the Mayombe country, North of the Lower Congo, and inland from the Ba-vili.

An excellent bibliography of all publications dealing with the Congo languages up to 1906 (the work of Professor Starr), was issued by the University of Chicago[2] in 1908.

J. Barfield. Concords of the Congo Language, as spoken at Palaballa. (East London Mission Institute), Harley House, Bow, 1884.

W. Holman Bentley. Dictionary and Grammar of the Kongo Language. London (Trübner and Co.), 1887.

——— Appendix to the Dictionary, etc. (Same publishers), 1895.

De Boeck. Grammaire et Vocabulaire du Lingala ou Langue du Haut Congo, 1904

---

[1] Not to be confused with Di-kele, the language of a different tribe of Ba-kele, living near the Gabun estuary.

[2] Department of Anthropology, Bulletin V.

Fra Giacinto Brusciotto di Vetralla. Regulae quaedam pro difficillimi Congensium idiomatis faciliori captu ad grammaticæ normam redactæ. Romæ, 1659.

*Brusciotto di Vetralla. Grammar of the Congo Language, as spoken 200 years ago, translated from the Latin, and edited, with a preface, by H. Grattan Guinness. London (Hodder and Stoughton), 1882.

*R. P. J. Calloch. Vocabulaire Francais-Ifumu (Batéké), précédé d'éléments de Grammaire, 1911.

R. P. Cambier. Essai sur la langue Congolaise. Brussels (Imprimerie Polleunis and Ceuterick), 1891 (Boko dialect of Ngala).

*H. Craven and J. Barfield. English-Congo and Congo-English Dictionary. London (Harley House), Bow, 1883.

A. Courboin. ' Bangala,' Langue Commerciale du Haut-Congo, Élements, Manuel de Conversation, Lexique. Paris (A. Challand), 1908.

R. P. A. Declercq de la Congrégation du C. I. de Marie, Missionnaire au Congo belge. Eléments de la langue Kanioka (Kanyoka.) Vanves près. Paris (Imprimerie Franciscaine Missionnaire), 1900.

——— Vocabulaire Français - Kanioka. (Same publishers), 1901.

——— Vocabulaire Kanioka - Français, (Same publishers), 1901.

——— Grammaire du Kiyombe. *Anthropos*, Vol. II., pp. 449-466, 761-794. 1907.

R. P. A. Declercq. Grammaire de la Langue des Bena Lulua. Brussels (Polleunis and Ceuterick), 1897.

——— Légendes des Bena Kanioka (Text, with interlined French translation). *Anthropos*, Vol. IV., pp. 71-86, 449-456, 1909.

*L. M. Hailes. Kilolo-English Vocabulary. (East

London Institute for Home and Foreign Missions), Harley House, Bow, 1891.

H. H. Johnston. The River Congo. (Sampson Low), 1884, Second ed., 1895.

Contains vocabularies of Kongo, Teke, Buma and Bangi (Yanzi).

J. and F. T. McKittrick. Guide to the Lunkundu Language. (A dialect of Lolo.) (East London Institute for Home and Foreign Missions), 1897.

*A. T. Ruskin. Proverbs and Similes of the Bamongo (Mongo is a dialect of Lolo.) (East London Institute for Home and Foreign Missions), 1897.

────── Outlines of the Grammar of the Lomongo Language.

A. Sims. Vocabulary English-Kibangi (Bangi). London (East London Institute) : Boston (American Baptist Mission Union), 1886.

A. Sims. Vocabulary English-Kiteke and Kiteke-English (Teke), 1886.

*W. H. Stapleton. Comparative Handbook of Congo Languages, being a Comparative Grammar of the eight principal languages, with appendices on six other Dialects (Baptist Mission Press), Yakusu, Stanley Falls, 1903.

The eight languages included in this book are: Kongo, Bangi, Lolo, Ngala, Poto, Ng'ombe, Soko, Kele.

The six noticed in the Appendix are: Teke, Sakani (a dialect of Lolo), Lomongo (Mongo, also a dialect of Lolo), Boko (a dialect of Ngala), Lulua, and Mpombo, which is not Bantu.

*W. H. Stapleton. Suggestions for a Grammar of Bangala (the Lingua Franca of the Upper Congo), with 2,000 words and many useful phrases. Yakusu (Baptist Missionary Society), 1903.

R. P. Ussel. Petite Grammaire de la Langue Fiote, Dialecte du Loango, pp. 85. Loango (Mission Press), 1888.

(This is spoken by the Ba-vili, whose country is somewhat to the north of the Congo estuary. The author is a missionary of the Congrégation du St. Esprit.)

R. P. Alexandre Visseq. Dictionnaire Fiot (French-Kongo), 1889.

—— Dictionnaire Fiot (dialecte Sorongo), 1890.

—— Dictionnaire Fiot (dialecte du Kakongo), 1890.

—— Grammaire (Sorongo dialect spoken at St. Antonio). Paris (Mission of the Congregation of the Holy Ghost), 30 Rue Lhomond, 1889.

J. Whitehead. Grammar and Dictionary of the Bobangi Language. London (Kegan Paul, Trench, Trübner and Co.), 1899.

*Duala.

Th. Christaller. Handbuch der Duala-Sprache. Grammar and exercises; story with literal interlined translation; dialogues; vocabulary. Basle, 1892.

C. Meinhof. Die Sprache der Duala in Kamerun, Vol. III. of *Deutsche Kolonialsprachen*, 1912.

W. Lederbogen. Duala-Märchen. Mitt. B. Sem. Or. IV, V, VI, Abt. 3, 1901-3.

A large collection of tales, with German translation in parallel columns.

A. Saker. Grammatical Elements of the Dualla Language, with vocabulary. Cameroons (Mission Press), 1853.

A. Seidel. Leitfaden zur Erlernung der Dualla-Sprache (with readings and vocabulary). Berlin (Carl Heymann), 1892.

—— Die Duala-Sprache in Kamerun. Systematisches Wörterverzeichnis und Einführung in die Grammatik. Julius Groos' Verlag. Heidelberg, Paris, London, Rome, Petersburg, 1904.

Duma. See Aduma.

Dzalamo (Zaramo, Zalamo). East Coast, South of Zanzibar.

A. Worms. Grundzüge der Grammatik des Ki-Zaramo in Deutsch-Ost-Afrika. Zeitschr. für afr. u. ocean. Sprachen III, p. 289, 1897.

C. Meinhof. Linguistische Studien in Ostafrika, No. XII., Mitt. B. Sem. Or. X., Abt. 3, pp. 90-110, 1907.

Ediya, see *Bube*.

Fan (Fang, Fanwe, Pahouin, Pamwe, etc.). West Equatorial Africa, North of the Ogowe.

*Rev. H. M. Adams. Fañwe Primer and Vocabulary. Compiled by the Rev. R. H. Nassau, M.D., Gaboon and Corisco Mission [from the MSS. of the Rev. H. M. Adams.] New York (printed by E. G. Jenkins), 1881.

V. Largeau. Encyclopédie Pahouine, 1901.

Includes Grammar and French-Fan Dictionary, containing many valuable anthropological notes and also texts with translation.

R. P. L. Lejeune. Dictionnaire français-fang. Paris (Favre and Teillard), 1892. With a Grammatical Sketch.

*A. Osorio Zabala. Vocabulary of the Fan Language (Fan-Spanish.) London (S.P.C.K.), 1887.

A number of stories, with French translation were published by P. Trilles in *Anthropos*. Vol. IV., pp. 945-971, Vol. V., pp. 163-180.

Fernandian (*See* Bube).

Fiote (Kongo. *See* under Congo).

Fipa (East side of S. part of L. Tanganyika).

B. Struck. Die Fipa-Sprache (Deutsch-Ostafrika). *Anthropos*, Vol. VI., 1911, pp. 951-993. Grammatical Sketch.

*——— Vocabulary of the Fipa Language. Journal of the African Society, October, 1908 (Vol. VIII.).

Ganda (Luganda).

*G. R. Blackledge. Luganda-English and English-Luganda Vocabulary (S.P.C.K.), 1904.

*H. Wright Duta. Engero za Baganda (Proverbs in the Luganda Language.) (S.P.C.K.), 1902.

*Elements of Luganda Grammar (Exercises and Vocabulary.) By a Missionary of the Church Missionary Society in Uganda. (S.P.C.K.), 1902.

*C. W. Hattersley and H. W. Duta (eds.). Luganda Phrases and Idioms. (S.P.C.K.), 1904.

*Sir H. H. Johnston. The Uganda Protectorate, 2 vols. London (Hutchinson), 1904.

Vol. II. contains vocabularies of a number of languages besides Ganda.

Apolo Kagwa. Engero zabaGanda (Folk-stories). Mengo (C.M.S. Press), 1901.

*Ekitabo kyo Bakabaka beBuganda (Book of the Kings of Uganda). London (Headley Brothers), printed, n.d. [1900 ?]

*G. L. Pilkington. Handbook of Luganda. London (S.P.C.K.), 1892 (last edition, 1911).

White Fathers. Manuel de Langue Luganda, par L.L. et C. D. des Pères Blancs (Grammar and Tales). Einsiedeln, Switzerland (Benziger and Co.), 1894.

Giryama.

W. E. Taylor. Grammar of the Giryama Language (out of print).

—— Giryama Vocabulary and Collections (Grammatical notes, and two tales, with translation). London (S.P.C.K.), 1891.

Gisu (Masaba). Spoken on and near Mount Elgon.

*Rev. J. B. Purvis. A Manual of Lumasaba Grammar (S.P.C.K.), 1897.

†*Gogo.* Ugogo (the country of the Wagogo) is about half-way between Zanzibar and Tabora and is traversed by the Dar-es-Salaam railway.

G. J. Clark (C.M.S.) Vocabulary of the Chigogo Language. London (Gilbert and Rivington), 1877, pp. 58.

Zimbazi ze Zifumbo, Nhandaguzi ne Zisimo ze Cigogo (Gogo Reading Book—Native Proverbs, Riddles and Fables). London (S.P.C.K.), 1901.

Collected and written out by Andereya and Nhonya. C.M.S. native teachers at Mpwapwa. Preface in English, signed J. E. B[everley].

Gwamba. A dialect of Thonga, spoken in N. E. Transvaal.

P. Berthoud. Grammatical Note on the Gwamba Language [1885]. Journal of the Royal Asiatic Society, Vol. XVI., Part I.

P. Berthoud. Leçons de Si-Gwamba. (Imp. J. Chappins), Lausanne. 46 pp., lithographed, 1883.

Hehe. About 300 miles north of Lake Nyasa and to the south of the Gogo country.

C. Velten. Die Sprache der Wahehe. Mitt. B. Sem. Or. Vol. II. Vol. III. contains a Hehe-German and German-Hehe Vocabulary, by P. Cassian Spiss, O.S.B.

†*Herero.*

P. Brincker. Wörterbuch und kurzgefasste Grammatik der Otji-Herero Sprache. Leipzig (T. O. Weigel), 1886.

The Appendix contains some tales, with literal and free translation into German. Some additional tales, collected by Büttner, are published in Ztschr. für afr. Sprachen.

P. H. Brincker. Deutscher Wortführer für die Bantu-Dialekte, Otji-Herero, Oshindonga, und Oshi-Kuanjama in S. W. Afrika. Elberfeld (R. L. Friderichs & Co.), 1897.

A very full German-Herero, etc., dictionary, in four columns.

C. Hugo Hahn. Grundzüge einer Grammatik des Herero, pp. X+197. Berlin (W. Hertz); London (Williams and Norgate), 1857.

F. W. Kolbe (L.M.S.) English-Herero Dictionary, with an Introduction to the Study of Herero and Bantu in general. Cape Town (Juta), pp. LV. + 569, 1883.

*C. Meinhof. Die Sprache der Herero in Deutsch Südwest-Afrika (Deutsche Kolonialsprachen, Bd. I.). Berlin (Dietrich Reimer), 1909.

*A. Seidel. Praktische Grammatik der Haupt-sprachen Deutsch Südwestafrikas (Nama, Otji-Herero, Oshindonga), Vienna, Leipzig (Hartleben), 1892.

G. Viehe. Grammatik des Otjiherero (with Vocabulary). Vol. XVI. of Lehrbücher des Seminars für orientalische Sprachen.
Stuttgart, Berlin (W. Spemann), 1897.

Ifumu (Teke). *See* under Congo.
†*Ila* (Seshukulumbwe).

*E. W. Smith. Handbook of the Ila Language. Oxford (University Press), 1907.

Isubu. Bimbia Peninsula, Cameroons, north of the Duala.

C. Meinhof. Das Verbum in der Isubu-Sprache. Zeitschrift für Afr. Sprachen. Vol. III., pp. 206-234, Berlin, 1889-90.

Joseph Merrick. A Dictionary of the Isubu Tongue. (No publisher's name given in the British Museum copy), 1854. Part I. Isubu-English, only completed as far as I.

——— A Grammar of the Isubu Tongue. Unfinished.
This is out of print and no doubt rare. The British Museum copy (Press mark 12907 bb. 22) is bound up in a volume of 'Philological Tracts.'
Kafir. *See* Xosa.

Kaguru (Kimegi). One of the dialects of Usagara, lying east of Ugogo.

J. T. Last. Grammar of the Kaguru Language. London (S.P.C.K.), 1886.

Kamba. Spoken in Ukambani, E. Africa—the district in which Nairobi is situated.

E. Brutzer. Handbuch der Kamba-Sprache. Berlin, 1906. Mitt. B. Abt. Sem. Or. IX., 3, pp. 1-100.

*H. Hinde. Vocabularies of the Kamba and Kikuyu Languages. (Cambridge University Press), 1904.

*J. T. Last. Grammar of the Kamba Language, pp. 40. London (S.P.C.K.), 1885.

*A. D. Shaw. Vocabulary of Four East African Languages. *See under Swahili.*

C. G. Büttner, Deutsch-Kikamba Wörterbuch. Ztschr. f. afr. Spr. Vol. I., pp. 81-123, 1888.

Kami. Spoken in the Ukami country, of which Mrogoro, on the Dar-es-Salaam railway, is the centre.

A. Seidel, in Ztschr-für afr. u. oc. Spr. II., 1, p. 20. (Grammatical sketch and short vocabulary).

C. Velten. Die Sprache der Wakami in Deutsch-Ostafrika. Mitt. B. Sem. Or. III., Abt. 3, pp. 1-56, 1899. Grammatical Sketch and Vocabulary.

A few words and phrases are to be found in Last's *Polyglotta Africana Orientalis*, pp. 69-72.

Kanyoka. *See* under 'Congo.'

†*Karanga*(Chino, Chiswina, Chizwina, Mashona, Shuna).

E. Biehler (S.J.) English-Chiswina Dictionary, with Outline Grammar. Roermond (J. J. Romer and Sons), 1906.

——— Four Methods of Teaching English to the Maswina. Roermond (same publishers), 1906.

——— Testamente. (BibleStories). Roermond (same publishers), 1906.

Rev. H. Buck. A Dictionary with Notes on the Grammar of the Mashona Language, commonly called Chiswina (Compiled at St. Augustine's Mission, Penhalonga.) (S.P.C.K.), 1911.

W. A. Elliott. Dictionary of the Tebele and Shuna Languages, 1897.

The second edition of this book (1911) which omits the 'Shuna' edition is entered under 'Zulu.'

Louw, Mrs. C. S. A Manual of the Chikaranga Language (Grammar, Exercises, Useful Phrases and Vocabulary), p. 397. Bulawayo (Philpot & Collins), 1915.

Rev. A. M. Hartmann (S. J.). Outline of a Grammar of the Mashona Language. Cape Town, 1893.

Kele (Lokele). *See* under 'Congo.'

Kele (Dikele). Spoken near the Gabun Estuary.

Missionaries of the A.B.C.F.M. A Grammar of the Ba-kele Language. New York, 1854.

Kikuyu.

*A. R. Barlow. Tentative Studies in Kikuyu Grammar and Idiom. Edinburgh (Blackwood), 1914.

Rev. Father A. Hemery. English-Kikuyu Handbook. Zanzibar-Nairobi (Roman Catholic Mission), 1903.

*A. W. McGregor (C.M.S.) English-Kikuyu Vocabulary. (S.P.C.K.), 1904.

—— A Grammar of the Kikuyu Language. London (Clay and Sons, printed), 1905.

H. Hinde. Vocabulary (*See Kamba*).

Kinga.

*R. Wolff. Grammatik der Kinga-Sprache (Deutsch-Ostafrika, Nyassagebiet), nebst Texten u. Wörterverzeichniss. Berlin, 1905. Archiv für das Studium deutscher Kolonialsprachen, Vol. 3.

Kiniassa. See Nyanja.

Kiyanzi (=Bangi, Kibangi). *See* under 'Congo.'

Konde. North end of Lake Nyasa.

C. Schumann. Grundriss einer Grammatik der Kondesprache. Berlin, 1899.

Kongo (*See* under 'Congo.')

Kwanyama. Spoken by a branch of the people called Ovambo, in S. W. Africa.

P. H. Brincker. Lehrbuch des Oshikuanjama in Verbindung mit Oshindonga. (Stuttgart) Berlin, 1891.

———— Deutscher Wortführer für . . . Otji-herero, Oshi-ndonga, u. Oshi-kuanjama. (*See* also under Herero.)

*H. Tönjes. Lehrbuch der Ovambo-Sprache Osikuanjama. Lehrb. d. Sem. f. or. Spr., Vol. 24.

*—— Wörterbuch der Ovambo-Sprache. Ib., Vol. 25. Berlin (G. Reimer), 1910.

Lala-Lamba. Spoken to the south of Lake Bangweolo.

*A. C. Madan. Lala-Lamba Handbook. Oxford (Clarendon Press), 1908.

*—— Lala-Lamba-Wisa-English, and English-Lala-Lamba-Wisa Dictionary. Oxford (Clarendon Press), 1913.

Lenge. Also called Chopi and Tswa. Spoken in Portuguese S. E. Africa, between Inhambane and the Limpopo.

*Bp. Smyth and J. Matthews. A Vocabulary with a short Grammar of Xilenge. London (S.P.C.K.), 1902, 1912.

Lenje. North-Western Rhodesia; allied to Ila, which adjoins it on the west, and Tonga, spoken to the north.

*A. C. Madan. Lenje Handbook. (Oxford University Press), 1908.

Lolo. *See* under 'Congo.'

Lomongo (Mongo) = Lolo. *See* under 'Congo.'

Luba.

W. M. Morrison. Grammar of the Buluba-Lulua Language, and Dictionary. Privately printed, 1907.

'The Buluba and the Lulua people . . . together occupy a large area . . . extending, roughly speaking, from the junction of the Lulua and Kasai rivers in a general south-easterly direction into Garenganze, where the language is called Ciluba' [Chiluba—elsewhere Bu-luba]. (Preface).

P. A. Declercq. Grammaire de la Langue Luba, with Vocabulary, pp. 504. Louvain (Istas), 1903.

—— Grammaire pratique de la Langue Luba. Brussels (Polleunis and Ceuterick), 1911.

Lulua. See under 'Congo.'

Lunda. An important language spoken on the watershed between the Congo and Zambesi, near the sources of the Kasai, and to the south of the Luba country.

H. A. Dias de Carvalho. Methodo Pratico para fallar a lingua de Lunda. Lisbon (Imprensa Naçional), 1890.

Luyi (Rotse). Spoken by the people of Barotseland (Lewanika's country on the Upper Zambezi.)

E. Jacottet. Etudes sur les langues du Haut-Zambèze. 1re Partie. Grammaire Soubiya et Louyi, 1896. 3me Partie. Textes Louyi, Contes, Légendes. Superstitions et Vocabulaires. Paris (Ernest Leroux), 1901.

Machame. A dialect of Chaga spoken by about 16,000 people living on the western side of Kilimanjaro.

*Julius Augustiny. Kurzer Abriss des Madschamedialekts. Berlin, 1914. Archiv. für d. Stud. deutscher Kolonialsprachen. Vol. 16.

Makonde. Spoken in the country north of the Rovuma. (E. Africa), about as far as Lindi.

E. Steere. Collections for a Handbook of the Makonde Language. (U.M.C.A.), Zanzibar, 1876.

Makua. In Mozambique

*Chauncy Maples. Collections for a Handbook of the Makua Language. London (S.P.C.K.), 1879.
Archdeacon Woodward is preparing a new and revised edition of this little work.

D. J. Rankin. Arabian Tales, translated from Swahili to Makua. (Tugulu dialect), London, 1887.

Mang'anja. See Nyanja.

Masaba. See Gisu.

Matumbi.

B. Krumm. Grundriss einer Grammatik des Kimatumbi, 1912. Mitt. B. Sem. Or. XV., Abt. 3, pp. 1-63.
Spoken by the inhabitants of the Matumbi hills, inland from Kilwa. Vocabulary, ib. XVI. Abt. 3, pp. 1-57.

Mbundu (Bunda, Kimbundu, Umbundu, Angola.)
Spoken in Portuguese W. Africa, south of the Congo.

B. M. de Cannecattim. Diccionario da Lingua Bunda ou Angolense. Lisbon (Impressão Regia.), 1804.
Three parallel columns: Portuguese, Latin, Mbundu.

——— Collecção de Observaçoes grammaticaes sobre a Lingua Bunda ou Angolense, 1805.
Appended to this is a brief Dictionary in four columns. Portuguese, Latin, Mbundu, Kongo. Second edition, 1859.

*H. Chatelain. Kimbundu Grammar (Grammatica elementar do Kimbundu ou lengua de Angola.) (Port. and English), Geneva, 1889.

——— Grundzüge der Kimbundu-Sprache, 1890.
Published in *Ztschr. für afr. Sprachen*, avowedly as an abstract of the preceding, though the author says he has introduced some new points.

*——— Folk-tales of Angola. Boston, New York, 1894.
Published by the American Folk-Lore Society. Mbundu text, with English translation on opposite page.

W. H. Sanders, W. E. Fay and others. Vocabulary of the Umbundu Language, comprising, Umbundu-English and English-Umbundu. Boston (Beacon Press), A.B.C.F.M., 1885.

Contains 3,000 words of the dialect spoken inland in Benguela.

W. M. Stover. Observations upon the Grammatical Structure and use of the Umbundu. Boston, 1885.

Mongo (= Lolo). *See* under 'Congo.'

Mpongwe. *See* Pongwe.

Namwanga. Spoken by the Winamwanga, N. W. of Lake Nyasa.

E. H. Dewar. Chinamwanga Stories (with English translation.) (Livingstonia Mission Press), 1900.

†*Ndonga*. The language of one of the tribes known collectively as Ovambo, in the northern part of 'Damaraland.'

*P. H. Brincker. Lehrbuch des Oshikuanjama in Verbindung mit Oshindonga. Lehrbücher des Seminars für orient. Sprachen, Vol. VIII. Berlin, 1891. *See* also Kwanyama.

P. H. Brincker. Deutscher Wortführer für die Bantudialekte . . . Oshindonga, etc. *See* under Herero and Kwanyama.

*A. Seidel. Grammatik des Oshindonga, etc. Also entered under *Herero*.

Ngombe. *See* under 'Congo.'

Nika (more correctly Nyika).

There is no language properly called by this name, which is applied to the Rabai, Giryama, Duruma, Digo and five smaller tribes.

*J. L. Krapf and J. Rebmann. A Nika-English Dictionary. Edited by T. H. Sparshott. London, 1887.

The words in this book are chiefly Rabai.

A. D. Shaw. *See* Vocabulary of four E. African Languages *v.* Swahili.

†*Nyamwezi*. Spoken over a large area to the south of Lake Victoria. Sukuma and Sumbwa are dialects of it.

*E. Steere. Collections for a Handbook of the Nyamwezi Language. London (S.P.C.K.), *n.d.*

R. Stern. Eine Kinyamwesi Grammatik, Berlin, 1906. Mitt. B. Sem. Or. IX. 3, pp. 129-258.

*C. Velten. Grammatik des Kinyamŭesi (with Vocabulary). Göttingen. (Vandenhoeck and Ruprecht), 1901.

Nyanja (Chinyanja, Mang'anja, Nyasa, Chinyasa).

Is also virtually identical with Sena, and very similar to Nyungwe (Tete).

*Rev. H. C. R. Barnes. Nyanja-English Vocabulary. London (S.P.C.K.), 1902.

This is an enlarged edition of Miss Woodward's Vocabulary of 1892, 1895, q.v.

V. J. Courtois, S.J. Eléments de Grammaire Tetense (Lingua Chi-Nyungüe). Coimbra (University Press), 1900.

G. Henry. A Grammar of Chinyanja. Aberdeen, (G. and W. Fraser), 1891. Second edition, 1904.

A. Hetherwick. A Practical Manual of the Nyanja Language. London (S.P.C.K.), second edition, 1912.

R. Laws. English-Nyanja Dictionary. Edinburgh (James Thin), 1894.

*R. S. Rattray. Some Folklore, Stories and Songs, with English translation and notes. London (S.P.C.K.), 1907.

*J. Rebmann. Dictionary of the Kiniassa Language. Edited by L. Krapf. St. Chrischona, near Basle, 1877.

(Ki-nyasa=Chi-nyanja. The Anyanja are called Anyasa by the Yaos and Swahili. Rebmann obtained his materials from released slaves in East Africa.)

*Rev. D. C. Scott. Cyclopædic Dictionary of the Mang'anja Language. Edinburgh (Foreign Missions of Church of Scotland), 1892.

*M. E. Woodward. English-Chinyanja and Chinyanja-English Vocabulary, 1892, reprinted 1895 (S.P.C.K.)

Another edition, revised and enlarged by the Rev. H. Barnes, appeared in 1913.

*—— Exercise-book (S.P.C.K.), 1898, 1909.

Nyika. See Nika.

*Nyoro (Uganda Protectorate).

*H. E. Maddox. Elementary Lunyoro Grammar, with Lunyoro-English Vocabulary. London (S.P.C.K.), 1902.

Nyungwe (Tete). Spoken in the country about Tete on the Zambezi. Very similar to, if not identical with Nyanja.

V. J. Courtois. Diccionario Cafre-Tetense-Portuguez, 1900.

—— Diccionario Portuguez-Cafre-Tetense, 1900.

—— Elementes de Grammatica, 1909.

A. v. d. Mohl, S. J. Grammatik der Bantusprache von Tete. Mitt. B. Sem. Or. VII. Abt. 3, pp. 32-85, 1904. Vol. VIII. 3 (1905), contains a collection of tales with German translation.

Pahouin. See Fan.

Pogoro. Spoken in E. Africa, somewhat east of the north end of Lake Nyasa, and north of the Rovuma.

*J. Hendle (O.S.B.). Die Sprache der Wapogoro. Berlin (G. Reimer), 1907. Archiv für deutsche Kolonialsprachen, Vol. VI.

†*Pokomo.* Tana River, British East Africa.

*C. Meinhof. Linguistische Studien in Ostafrika. No. VII. Mitt. B. Sem. Or. Jahrg. XIV., Abt. 3. Berlin, 1911.

Pokomo-Grammatik mit Uebungsstücken. (The work of one or more of the Neukirchen missionaries, but no author's name appears.) Neukirchen, Missionsbuchhandlung (Stursberg und Cie), 1908.

*F. Würtz. Wörterbuch des Ki-tikuu und des Kipokomo. Published in Zeitschrift für afrikanische und oceanische Sprachen, Vol. I., p. 193.
This is a German-Tikuu and Pokomo Dictionary. (Tikuu is a Swahili dialect. *See* under Swahili).

—— Grammatik des Pokomo, ib. Vol. II., pp. 62, 168.

Vol. 1. of the same periodical contains some Pokomo songs, and Vol. II. some traditions (all with German translation).

Some grammatical notes (1889), and a Pokomo-German vocabulary had previously been published by F. Würtz in Büttner's Zeitschrift für Afrikanische Sprachen.

Pongwe (Mpongwe). Spoken in the country adjoining the Gabun estuary, French Congo.

J. R. Wilson (a late Missionary). Heads of the Mpongwe Grammar, containing most of the principles needed by a learner. New York (Mission House, 23, Centre Street), 1879.

R. P. Le Berre. Grammaire de la Langue Pongouée. Paris (Maisonneuve et Cie), 1873.

Missionaires de la Congrégation de Saint Esprit. Dictionnaire Français-Pongué, 1877-81. Dictionnaire Pongué-Français, 1881. Paris (Maisonneuve et Cie).

Missionaries of the A.B.C.F.M. Gaboon Mission. A Grammar of the Mpongwe Language, with Vocabularies. New York (Snowden and Prall), 1847.

Poto. *See* under 'Congo.'

†*Ronga* (Shironga). A branch of the Thonga language, spoken in the neighbourhood of Delagoa Bay.

H. A. Junod. Grammaire (with Ronga-French-English-Portuguese Vocabulary and Dialogues). Lausanne (Bridel), 1896.

—— Nouveaux Contes Ronga. Neuchatel Imprimerie (Paul Attinger), 1898. *See also* Thonga.

Rotse. *See* Luyi.

Ruanda. N. end of L. Tanganyika.

*P. Eugène Hurel. Manuel de Langue Kinyaruanda. Mitt. B. Sem. Or. XIV., Abt. 3, pp. 1-159, 1911.

Rundi. Between Tanganyika and Lake Kivu, on the north. Very similar to Ruanda.

R. P. J. M. van der Burgt, des Pères Blancs. Dictionnaire Français-Kirundi. Bois le Duc, 1900-1903.

* —— Eléments d'une Grammaire Kirundi. Mitt. B. Sem. Or. V., Abt. 3.

R. P. F. Menard, des Pères Blancs. Dictionnaire Français-Kirundi et Kirundi-Français. Paris (Guilmoto), 1909.

—— Grammaire Kirundi. Same publisher, 1908.

Sena (Lower Zambezi, virtually identical with Nyanja).

*W. G. Anderson. Introductory Grammar of the Sena Language (S.P.C.K.), 1897.

J. Torrend, S.J. Grammatica do Chisena. Grammar of the Language of the Lower Zambezi. Chipanga, Zambezia. (Mission Press), 1900.

In parallel columns, Portuguese and English.

Senga (Middle Zambezi).

*A. C. Madan. Senga Handbook. Oxford (Clarendon Press), 1905.

†*Shambala.* Usambara, East Africa, inland from Tanga.

P. E. Hörner. Kleiner Leitfaden zur Erlernung des Kischambala. Mariannhill (Natal), 1900.

*K. Roehl. Versuch einer systematischen Grammatik der Schambalasprache. Hamburg, 1911.

Frau Rösler and F. Gleiss. Schambala-Grammatik und Wörterbuch. Berlin, 1912. Vol. XIII. of Archiv für das Studium deutscher Kolonialsprachen.

E. Steere. Collections for Handbook of the Shambala Language, 1867. Revised by Archdeacon Woodward. (U.M.C.A.) Msalabani, 1905.

Shangaan. See Thonga.

Shuna. See Mashona.

Siha (Kisiha). See Chaga.

Soko. See under "Congo."

Subiya (Upper Zambezi).

E. Jacottet. Grammaires Soubiya et Louyi, 1896.
―――― Textes Soubiya, 1899. See also Luyi.

Sukuma. (On the south-eastern side of the Victoria Nyanza. A dialect of Nyamwezi.)

*Capt. Herrmann. Kissukuma, die Sprache der Wassukuma. Mitt. B. Sem. Or. I., Abt. 3, pp. 146-198, 1898. Gram. Sketch, with Vocabulary and Texts.

A. Seidel. Das Kisukuma. Grammatische Skizze (with Vocabulary), 1894.

Sumbwa. Spoken in a district of the N.W. part of Unyamwezi, between Usukuma and Uha, south of Lake Victoria, but separated from it by Uzinja.

*A. Capus (of the White Fathers). Grammaire de Shisumbwa (Ztschr. für afr. u. oc. Spr. Vol., IV., pp. 1-123), 1898.

The preceding volume of the same periodical contains (pp. 358-381) ten stories and some songs and proverbs, with literal French translation.

―――― Dictionnaire Shisumbwa-Français, pp. 147. Saint-Cloud (Impr. Belin Frères), 1901.

Swahili.

H. W. M. Beech. Studies in Ki-Swahili London (Kegan Paul, Trench, Trübner & Co.), 1918.

E. Brutel. Vocabulaire Français-Kiswahili et Kiswahili-Français, 2 ed. Brussels, 1913.

Mrs. F. Burt. Grammar and Vocabulary (Mombasa dialect). (S.P.C.K.), 1910.

C. G. Büttner. Wörterbuch der Suaheli-Sprache. 2 pts. Stuttgart (Berlin), 1890.

—— Suaheli-Schriftstücke in arabischer Schrift. Vol. X. of Lehrbücher des Seminars für orientalische Sprachen. (W. Spemann), Stuttgart and Berlin, 1892.

—— Anthologie aus der Suaheli-Litteratur. (E. Felber), Berlin, 1894. Texts (prose and poetry) with translation into German.

Habari za Wakilindi. Pt. I., *n.d.* Pt. II. 1904. Pt. III., 1907. (U.M.C.A.), Msalabani. Traditions of the Washambala written in Swahili by Abdallah bin Hemed bin Ali Liajjem.

R. P. A. Hemery de la Congrégation du St. Esprit et du Saint-Cœur de Marie. Vocabulaire Français-Swahili-Teita. Zanzibar (Mission Catholique). Paris (30 Rue Lhomond), 1901.

W. K[isbey]. Notes and Corrections of Swahili. I.-IV. Zanzibar (U.M.C.A.), 1898-1899.

Kibaraka. Zanzibar. (Univ. Mission Press), 1896. Stories written or dictated by natives.

J. L. Krapf. Outlines of the Elements of the Kisuaheli Language, with special reference to the Kinika Dialect. Tübingen (Friedr. Fues), 1850.

—— A Dictionary of the Suahili Language, with Introduction, containing an outline of a Suahili Grammar. London (Trübner & Co.), 1882.

*A. C. Madan. English-Swahili Dictionary. Oxford (University Press), 1894. Second edition, 1902.

* —— Swahili-English Dictionary. Oxford (University Press), 1903.

APPENDIX II.

*A. C. Madan. Swahili Grammar. Oxford (University Press), 1905.

C. Meinhof. Die Sprache der Suaheli. Berlin (Dietrich Reimer (Ernst Vohsen)), 1910. Deutsche Kolonialsprachen Bd. 2.

W. Planert. Die syntaktischen Verhältnisse des Suaheli. Berlin (W. Süsserott), 1907.

Ch. Sacleux. Dictionnaire Français-Swahili. Zanzibar (Mission des P. P. du St. Esprit.) Paris (30 Rue Lhomond), 1891.

—— Grammaire des Dialectes Swahilis. Paris (Procure des Pères du S. Esprit), 1909.
This book obtained the Prix Volney from the Institut de France.

*A. Downes Shaw. Pocket Vocabulary of Four E. African Languages. (Ki-Swahili, Ki-Nyika, Ki-Taita and Ki-Kamba; with vocabulary of Kibwyo dialect). London (S.P.C.K.), [1885].

*E. Steere. A Handbook of the Swahili Language, as spoken at Zanzibar. London (S.P.C.K.) First edition, 1871; second edition, 1875; third edition revised and enlarged by A. C. Madan, 1884; fourth edition, 1913.

—— Swahili Exercises. (S.P.C.K.), 1894-1908.

—— Swahili Tales, 1889. Reprinted, 1906 and 1917. (S.P.C.K.), London.

—— Practical Guide to Use of the Arabic Alphabet in writing Swahili, 1892. (Out of print.)

Capt. C. H. Stigand. Grammar of Dialects in the Kiswahili Language (with Introduction by the Rev. W. E. Taylor). Cambridge (University Press), 1915.

W. E. Taylor. Groundwork of the Swahili Language Tabulated. London (S.P.C.K.), 1898.

W. E. Taylor. African Aphorisms, or Saws from Swahililand. London (S.P.C.K.), 1891.

Swahili Proverbs, translated and annotated. Some Rabai and Giryama proverbs are appended.

C. Velten. Suaheli-Wörterbuch (Part I. Swahili-German). Berlin. Published by the Author, 1910.

——— Praktische Grammatik der Suaheli-Sprache. Berlin (W. Baensch), 1905.

——— Praktische Anleitung zur Erlernung der Schrift der Suaheli. Göttingen (Vandenhoeck und Ruprecht), 1901-1910.

A useful guide to the reading and writing of Swahili in the Arabic character.

——— *Safari za Wasuaheli.* Göttingen, 1901.

Narratives of journeys into the Interior (and in two cases to Europe), written or dictated by natives.

* ——— *Desturi za Wasuaheli.* Göttingen, 1903.

A very full account of native customs, written by natives, in Swahili.

——— Märchen und Erzählungen. Stuttgart (Spemann), Berlin, 1898. Vol. 18 of Lehrb. d. Sem. für orient. Sprachen.

——— Prosa und Poesie der Suaheli. Berlin (Published by the Author), 1907.

Contains tales, proverbs, dialogues, poems (*mashairi*) and popular songs.

Tabwa. Spoken in the Marungu country, between Tanganyika and the Lualaba.

*G. De Beerst. Essai de Grammaire Tabwa. Berlin, 1896. Published in Ztschr. f. afr. u. oc. Spr. Vol. II., Nos. 3 and 4.

Taita (less correctly, Teita). Spoken in the Taita Hills, 120 miles N.W. of Mombasa.

*J. A. Wray. Elementary Introduction to the Taita Language. London (S.P.C.K.), 1894.

A Taita Vocabulary is included in A. D. Shaw, *Pocket*

Vocabulary. *See* under Swahili. Also in Hémery, Voc. Français-Swahili-Teita. *See* under Swahili.

Tebele. *See* under Zulu.

Teke. *See* under Congo.

*Thonga. Spoken over a large area between St. Lucia Bay and the Sabi River and including among its branches Ronga, Hlanganu, Gwamba (now isolated in the Transvaal), Jonga, etc. Not to be confused with Tonga, q.v.

*C. W. Chatelain and H. A. Junod. Pocket Dictionary Thonga-(Shangaan)-English and English-Thonga. Preceded by an Elementary Grammar. Lausanne (Georges Bidel et Cie), 1904.

Shangaan (properly Hlanganu) is the name by which the Delagoa Bay natives in general are known at the Johannesburg mines. This book, while not 'limiting itself to any particular dialect' of the Thonga language, applies more especially to that spoken in the Spelonken and Leydsdorp district of E. Transvaal.

Tonga (Zambezi). The Tonga (Gitonga) of Inhambane, identical with Lenge (q.v.) or Chopi, is distinct from this. So is the Tonga found on the W. side of L. Nyasa.

J. R. Fell (of the Baila-Batonga Mission). A Tonga Grammar. London (S.P.C.K.), 1918.

A. W. Griffin. Chitonga Vocabulary of the Zambezi Valley. Oxford (University Press).

This Tonga language has been very fully studied by Father Torrend, who gives some annotated texts in the Appendix of his Comparative Grammar. The people are also called (by the Bechwana) Batoka.

Tugulu. *See* Makua.

Tumbuka. Spoken W. of Lake Nyasa.

W. A. Elmslie. Notes on the Tumbuka Language. Aberdeen (G. and W. Fraser), 'Belmont' Works, 1891.

W. A. Elmslie. Table of Concords and Paradigms of Verb. Aberdeen (Fraser), 'Belmont' Works, 1891.

Venda. Spoken in N. Transvaal, within the bend of the Limpopo. Sometimes spelt Wenda; the people are variously called Vavenda, Bavenda, Wawenda, etc.

C. Meinhof. Das Tšivenda. Leipzig, 1901. Reprinted from Z.D.M.G.

Th. and P. Schwellnus. Die Verba des Tšivenda. Mitt. B. Sem. Or. VII. Abt. 3, pp. 12-31. Berlin, 1904.

Vili. Spoken on the Luango (Loango) coast, north of the Congo. *See also* "Congo."

P. C. Marichelle. Dictionnaire Vili-Français, 1902.

―――― Méthode Pratique pour l'Etude du Dialecte Vili, 1907.

Xilenge (Shilenge, or Chopi). *See* Lenge.

Xosa ('Kafir'). Spoken in the eastern part of the Cape Province, and closely allied to (though not quite identical with) Zulu.

W. Appleyard. The Kafir Language, comprising a Sketch of its History . . . Remarks upon its Nature and a Grammar, pp. 390. King William's Town, London. (J. Mason), 1850. (Printed for the Wesleyan Missionary Society.)

J. Ayliff. A Vocabulary of the Kafir Language. London (Wesleyan Mission House), 1846.

W. B. Boyce. A Grammar of the Kaffir Language. London (Wesleyan Missionary Society and J. Mason). First edition, 1834; second edition (augmented and improved), 1844; third edition, (augmented and improved with Exercises), 1863. The Exercises were added to the third edition by W. J. Davis.

C. J. Crawshaw. A first Kafir Course, pp. 133. Lovedale, Cape Town (Juta). Third edition, 1897;

fourth edition, 1901; fifth edition, 1903. Grammar, Exercises and Vocabularies. (These are appended to each exercise, but can be easily consulted by means of an index at the end.)

Wm. J. Davis. A Dictionary of the Kaffir Language; including the Xosa and Zulu Dialects. Part I., Kaffir-English. London (Wesleyan Mission House), 1872.

―――― An English and Kaffir Dictionary, principally of the Xosa-Kaffir, but including also many words of the Zulu-Kaffir Dialect. London (Wesleyan Missionary Society), 1877.

I. Bud-Mbelle, Interpreter to the High Court of Griqualand. Kaffir Scholar's Companion. (Lovedale Missionary Press), 1903

Contains lists of words, idioms, proverbial expressions, and a variety of miscellaneous information not always easy to find elsewhere.

A. Kropf. A Kaffir-English Dictionary, pp. iv., 486. (Lovedale Mission Press), 1899.

J. McLaren. A Concise Kaffir-English Dictionary. London (Longmans, Green & Co.), 1915.

―――― A Grammar of the Kaffir Language. London (Longmans, Green & Co.), 1906.

C. Meinhof. Hottentottische Laute und Lehnworte im Kafir. (Z.D.M.G.), 1905.

Discusses the question of how far Xosa borrows sounds and words from the Hottentot language, and in particular, the origin of the clicks.

W. B. Rubusana. Zenk'inkomo Magwalandini. Second edition. Frome and London (Butler and Tanner), 1911.

Traditions and songs of the Xosa, Gcaleka, Tembu and other tribes, collected by a native minister of the Congregational Church.

J. Stewart. Outlines of Xosa Grammar, with practical exercises. (Lovedale Mission Press), South Africa, 1901.

J. Stewart. Kaffir Phrase Book and Vocabulary. Third edition. (Lovedale Mission Press), 1901.

* The late Dr. Stewart is well-known as the founder and first Principal of the Lovedale Institution.

J. Torrend. Outline of a Xosa Kafir Grammar, with a few dialogues and a Kaffir Tale. Grahamstown (T. and G. Sheffield), 1887.

†*Yao* (Chiyao, Kihiau). Spoken in the mountains S. E. of Lake Nyasa, and in the Shire Highlands.

*A. Hetherwick. Introductory Handbook and Vocàbulary. (S.P.C.K.) Second edition, 1902.

Contains both Yao-English and English-Yao Vocabulary.

A. F. Pott. Über die Kihiausprache. (Z.D.M.G.), Vl., pp. 331-348.

*E. Steere. Collections for a Handbook of the Yao Language. London, 1871.

Yaunde (a branch of Fan).

P. Hermann Nekes. Praktische Grammatik der Jaunde-Sprache. Vol. XXVI. of Lehrbücher des Seminars für or. Sprachen. Berlin, 1911.

Yombe. See under ' Congo.'

Zaramo (Zalamo). See Dzalamo.

Zigula. East Africa, near Luvu River, on the mainland opposite Zanzibar.

*W. H. Kisbey. Zigula-English and English-Zigula Dictionary. London (S.P.C.K.), 1906.

* ——— Zigula Exercises. London (S.P.C.K.), 1906.

Rev. W. G. Webster (ed.) Zigula Tales. London (S.P.C.K.), 1912.

Twenty-three stories, written down by natives.

H. W. Woodward. Collections for a Handbook of the Zigula Language. (U.M.C.A.), Msalabani, 1902.

Ziba (Lusiba). Spoken in Kiziba and some other districts adjoining Lake Victoria on the S.W. It is not very happily named, as the people speaking it appear to be called Batundu. It is closely related to Nyoro.

*Capt. Herrmann (formerly of Bukoba). Lusiba, die Sprache der Länder Kisiba, Bugabu, etc., 1904. Mitt. B. Sem. Or. VII., Abt. 3, pp. 150-200.

**Zulu.*

A. T. Bryant. A Zulu-English Dictionary, with Notes on Pronunciation, a revised Orthography, etc. (Mariannhill Mission Press), Pinetown, Natal, 1905.

An important work, somewhat spoilt by its speculative etymologies which are not based on any sound principle. The introduction, too, though containing a great deal of useful information, is of very unequal value, especially the historical part, which is not free from *parti pris*.

H. Callaway. Nursery Tales, Traditions and Histories of the Zulus. (Zulu Text, Translation and Notes). Springvale, Natal. London (Trübner & Co.), 1868.

——— Religious System of the Amazulu. (Zulu Text, with Translations and Notes. (Printed, Springvale), Natal. London, 1870.

J. W. Colenso (Bishop of Natal). First Steps in Zulu-Kaffir. Pietermaritzburg (Vause & Slatter), fourth edition, 1903.

* ——— Zulu-English Dictionary, fourth edition. Pietermaritzburg (Vause & Slatter); 1905.

——— Three Native accounts of a Visit to, Umpande, King of the Zulus. With Translation, Vocabulary and Notes. Third edition. Pietermaritzburg and Durban (Vause, Slatter & Co.), 1901.

——— Izindab'ezinhle, etc. New Testament (reprinted, 1897 for Miss Colenso), London. (Dent).

J. W. Colenso. Pilgrim's Progress. Inncwadi ka' Bunyane okutiwa Ukuhamba Kwesihambi. Pietermaritzburg and Durban (Vause, Slatter & Co.), 1901.

J. L. Döhne (Missionary to the American Board, C.F.M.). A Zulu-Kafir Dictionary. Cape Town, 1857.

*W. A. Elliott. Notes for a Sindebele Dictionary and Grammar, with illustrative sentences. (Sindebele Publishing Co.), Bristol, 1911.

Sindebele (Tebele) is the dialect of Zulu spoken by the Matabele in Rhodesia.

Lewis Grout. The Isizulu; a grammar of the Zulu Language, with historical introduction. Pietermaritzburg, Durban, London (Trübner & Co.), 1859.

James Perrin. English-Zulu Dictionary. Pietermaritzburg (P. Davis & Sons), new edition, 1901.

Rev. C. Roberts. The Zulu-Kafir Language simplified for Beginners. London (Kegan Paul). Third edition, 1909.

————— An English-Zulu Dictionary with the Principles of Pronunciation and Classification fully explained. London (Kegan Paul, Trench, Trübner & Co.), 1911.

————— A Zulu Manual or Vade Mecum. London (Kegan Paul), 1900.

A companion volume to the two preceding works, containing grammatical notes and illustrations of special idioms,—medical, zoological and botanical vocabularies, etc.

P. A. Stuart. Zulu Grammar, with 400 Useful Phrases, 1907.

INDEX

Abstract nouns, 62.
Adjective roots, 120.
Adjectives, 118, 122.
— — few real in Bantu, 118.
— concord of, 124, 128.
— derived from verbs, 120.
— nouns made to do the work of, 119.
— Nyanja, 125.
— verbs derived from, 130, 154.
— verbs used for, 119.
— which take shortened prefixes, 126.
— Zulu, 126.
Adverbial demonstratives, 99, 114.
Adverbs, 184.
— invariable, 186.
— locative, 185.
Agglutinative languages, 12.
Alliterative concord, 14, 20.
Angola and Loango languages, 5.
Animals, names of, 47, 58.
Applied verbs, 148.
Arbousset, 7.
Article, 49, 72.
Assimilation, 226.
— Incomplete, 227.
Augmentative class, 56, 66-68.
Auxiliaries, 174.

Bantu, 9.
— family, characteristic features of, 14.
— languages, number of known, 2.
— languages, principal features of, 2.
— languages, sounds of, 17.
— name, 3.
— verb, 143.
Barlow, 229.
Bentley, 116.

Bleek, 3, 8, 9, 13, 49, 86, 219.
Boyce's Xosa Grammar, 7.
Brusciotto, Giacinto, 6, 13, 31, 32,
Burton, 31. [35, 72.

Casalis, 7.
Causative verbs, 148.
Cerebral t and d, 222.
"Chiswina," 42.
Chwana, 4, 16, 47, 48, 52, 95.
— participle, 118.
— relative particle, 105.
— verbal nouns, 208
Class, augmentative, 56, 68.
— diminutive, Duala, 62.
— lu, 59.
— meaning attached to each,
— three, concords of, 50. [43.
Classes, hints of several other, 68.
Clicks in Zulu and Xosa, 219.
Colenso, Bishop, 170, 192, 202.
Compound tenses, 173.
Compounds, Herero, 213.
— Ila, 217.
— Nyanja, 216.
— Zulu.
Concord of adjectives, 124, 128.
Concords of Class 3, 50.
Congo, Kingdom of, 31, 43.
Conjunctions, 183.
Continuative mood, 167-8.
Copula, 49.
— combined with personal pronouns, 112.
— old demonstrative root, 111.
— sometimes prefixed to
Cust, 6. [adjectives, 114.

Dahl's Law, 228-9.
De Gregorio, 8.
Degrees of Comparison, 131.
Demonstrative, adverbial, 99.
— pronouns, 97, 98

343

Demonstrative, γa, 48.
Demonstratives, adverbial, 99, 114.
Denominative verbs, 212.
Dental t and d, 222.
Derived Forms, 144, 146, 156, 192.
Diminutive class, Duala, 62.
— in -ana, 212.
— in ka-, 60.
— plural prefix, Nyanja, [62.
Diminutives, 56.
Dinuzulu, 19.
Dissimilation, 226, 228.
Do Couto, P. Antonio, 6.
Double Agreement, 97.
Duala diminutive class, 62.
— language, 89.

Ewald, 8.

False Analogy, 226.
Fruits, names of, 52.
Fulfulde language, 44.
Future Tense, 172.

Ganda, 16, 25, 26, 66, 68, 295.
— relative particle, 105.
— verb ' to be,' 116.
Gisu, 42, 48, 49, 53, 66.
Grammatical gender, 10, 11.
Grimm's Law, 218.

Hamitic languages, 14.
Herero, 42, 45, 225, 248.
— compounds, 213.
— relative particle, 106.
— verb ' to be,' 116.
Hetherwick, Dr., 187, 202.
Hottentot language, 9.
Hottentots, 4, 10.
Human beings, names denoting, [46.
Ila, 264,
— compounds, 217.
Imperative mood, 159.
Incomplete assimilation, 227.
Indicative present tense, 171.
Infinitive mood, 159.
Inflected families of language, 10,
Initial vowel, 48.
— absent in the vocative, 49.

' Inseparable Pronoun,' 88.
Intensive verbs, 149.
' Interjectional roots,' 186.
International Phonetic Associa-
Intonation, 15, 16.   [tion, 18.
Invariable adverbs, 186.
— particle, 110.
Irregular verbs, 177.
Isolating languages, 12.

Johnston, Sir Harry, 9.
Jones, D., 19.
Junod, 186, 197.

' Kafir ' (Xosa), 4.
Ki-class, action of a verb, 55.
— collective sense, 55.
— instrumental force, 55.
— 'likeness, fashion, manner,'
Kikuyu, 225, 229.   [55.
Kimvita (Mombasa Dialect), 285.
Kinga, 68.
Kongo, 34, 42, 81, 89.
— relative pronoun, 107.
— verb ' to be,' 116.
Krapf, 7, 31.

Lamu Dialect (Kiamu), 276.
Laterals, 220.
Law of Vowel-Harmony, 228.
Lepsius, 8, 14, 19,
Lévy-Bruhl, 187, 188.
Lichtenstein, 4, 6, 9.
Liquids, words denoting, 52.
Locative adverbs, 185.
— class, 76-85, 211.
— prefixes, 66.
Locatives, in mu-, 51.
— suffixed, 82.
Luganda, see Ganda.

Marsden, William, 5.
' Mashona,' 42.
Materials, names of, 62.
Mbundu language, 6.
Meinhof, 8, 16, 19, 35, 37, 45, 48, 195, 203, 214, 219, 226, 230, 231.
Moffat's translation of the Bible into Sechwana, 7.
Monosyllabic verbs, 143, 177.

INDEX

Mood, Continuative, 167,
— Imperative, 159.
— Infinitive, 159.
— Negative, 160.
— Relative, 168.
— Subjunctive, 160.
Moods, 156-169.
Mozambique language, 5.
Müller, 8.

Negative mood, 160.
Neuter-Passive verbs, 147.
Noël-Armfield, 223.
Noun agent, 200.
— indicating result of an
Nouns, abstract, 62. [action, 205.
— made to do work of adjectives, 119.
— verbal, 200-211.
Numbers, Ordinal, 140.
Numerals, 133.
— distinct words for 'hundred' and 'thousand,' 137,
— table of, 135, 138. [140.
Nyanja, 16, 17, 42, 44, 46, 48, 62, 63, 98, 225, 272.
— adjectives, 125,
— compounds, 216.
— no true relative
— verb ' to be,' 116.

Object-Pronoun, 89.
'Onomatopœtic vocables,' 186.
Ordinal numbers, 140.

Pacconio, P. Francisco, 6.
Particle, invariable, 110.
— relative, 101.
Participles, 105-6, 118, 169.
Passive verbs, 147.
Past tense, 172.
Perfect in -ile 154, 158, 166.
Perfect tense, 173.
Phonetics, General, 230.
Pitch, 16.
Place, word for 79.
Pokomo language, 80.
Possessive, 70-75.
— particle, 74.
— pronouns, 74, 92, 93.

Pott, 8.
Prefix, eleventh, *lu-*, 59.
— fifteenth, *ku-*, 65,
— fifth, *li-*, 51.
— ninth, *in-* or *n-*, 56.
— *ti-* in Nyanja, 62.
— *ogu-*, 66.
— sixth, in Gisu, *hama-*, 53.
— tenth, 57
— *tu-*, attached to thirteenth
— twelfth, 60. [class, 61.
Prefixes, locative, 66, 77.
— not identical with Pronoun, 86.
Prepositional verbs, see *Applied*
Prepositions, 72, 84, 182. [*Verbs*.
— Pronominal forms suffixed to, 91.
Principiation of nouns, 13, 32, 33.
Pronouns, 86, 182.
— Demonstrative, 97, 98.
— Inseparable, 88.
— Longer forms of, 91.
— Object, 89.
— Possessive, 92, 93.
— Prepositional form of, 91, 92, 93.
— Reflexive, 91.
— Relative, 99.
— Separable or Substantive, 92, 94.

Rebmann, 31.
Reciprocal verbs, 151.
Reflexive Pronoun, 89-91.
Relative construction, Zulu, 119.
— ,, Chwana, 105.
— ,, Ganda, 105.
— ,, Herero, 106,
— ,, Ronga, 106.
— ,, Swahili, 101.
— ,, Zulu, 104.
— form of Locative Class,
— mood, 168. [211.
— particle, 101 *et seqq*.
— pronoun, 99, 108.
Repetitive verbs, 153.
Reversive verbs, 150.
Rhodesia, Southern, main speech
Ronga language, 54. [of, 42.

Z

Scott, Revs. D. C. and W. A., Semi-Bantu, 2. [196, 203.
Separable, or independent, pronouns, 92, 94.
Smith, E. W., 194, 195.
'Sound-pictures,' 186.
Stapleton, 186, 189.
Stative verbs, 152.
Steere, Bishop, 18.
Stress (accent), 15.
Subjunctive mood, 160.
Substantive pronouns, 94.
Sudan languages, 11, 14, 75.
Suffixes, 199, 204.
Swahili language, 7, 15, 16, 18, 28, 42, 44, 47, 67, 101, 119, 225, 276.
— verb 'to be,' 116.

Tense, 157.
— Compound, 173.
— Future, 172, 173.
— Indicative Present, 171.
— Past, 172.
— Perfect, 173.
Thonga, 17.
Torrend, 186.
Transposition, 226, 230.
Trees, names of, 51.
Tribes, names of, 50.
Tuckey's expedition to the Congo, [5.
'Uncle Remus,' 10, 47.

Van der Kemp, Dr., 7.
Velten, 192.
Venda language, 17, 54, 68.
Verb, Bantu, 143.
— stems beginning with a
— *ti*, use of, 176. [vowel, 145.
— 'to be,' 109, 110.
— ,, Ganda, 116.
— ,, Herero, 116.
— ,, Kongo, 116.
— ,, Nyanja, 116.
— ,, Swahili, 116.
— 'to have,' 109.

Verbal nouns, 201, 202, 205, 208.
Verbs, Adjectives derived from, 120
— Applied, 148.
— Auxiliary, 174.
— Causative, 148.
— Compounded forms, 155.
— Denominative, 212.
— derived forms, 144, 146, 156.
— derived from adjectives, 130.
— formed from adjective-
— Intensive, 149. [stems, 154.
— Irregular, 177.
— Monosyllabic, 143, 177.
— primitive, 179.
— Neuter-Passive, 147.
— Passive, 147.
— Perfect in -*ile*, 154, 158, 166.
— Reciprocal, 151.
— Repetitive, 153.
— Reversive, 150.
— Stative, 152.
— used for adjectives, 119.
— which do not end in *a*
'Vocal Images,' 189.
Vocative, 70.
'Voices,' 146.
Von der Gabelentz, 8.

Westermann, 187, 188.
'Whistling *s*,' 54.
Whitehead, 186, 190.
Whitney, W. D., 219.
Woodward, Archdeacon, 81.

Xosa, clicks in, 219.
— language, 4, 7, 16.

Yao, 166, 167, 225.

Zulu, 15, 16, 20, 44-48, 232.
— adjectives, 126.
— clicks in, 17, 19, 219.
— compounds, 216.
— prepositions, 84.
— relative construction, 119.
— ,, particle, 104.